T0344946

LEADING THE SUSTAINABLE BUSINESS TRANSFORMATION

EDITOR   EDITOR

Julia Binder & Knut Haanaes

LEADING THE SUSTAINABLE BUSINESS TRANSFORMATION

A PLAYBOOK FROM IMD

WILEY

Registered Offices
John Wiley & Sons, Inc., 111 River Street, Hoboken, NJ 07030, USA
John Wiley & Sons Ltd, The Atrium, Southern Gate, Chichester, West Sussex, PO19 8SQ, UK

For details of our global editorial offices, customer services, and more information about Wiley products visit us at www.wiley.com.

Library of Congress Cataloging-in-Publication Data is Available:

ISBN 9781394314072 (Cloth)
ISBN 9781394314089 (ePDF)
ISBN 9781394314096 (ePub)

Cover Design: Wiley
Cover Images: (circles) © vaeenma/Getty Images, (Earth) © aryos/Getty Images

Set in 11/14pts Avenir LT Std by Straive, Chennai, India

SKY10089601_103024

Contents

Foreword

Michel Demaré and David Bach

At IMD, we are led by our purpose: challenging what is and inspiring what can be, we develop leaders and organizations that contribute to a more prosperous, sustainable, and inclusive world. Inherent in that purpose statement is the belief that prosperity, sustainability, and inclusiveness not only are not at odds with one another, but that they must go together. The task for this generation of leaders is ensuring that we don't build future prosperity at the expense of people and the planet. Supporting leaders and organizations on this pivotal journey is what IMD is committed to.

Our school was founded in the aftermath of World War II by leaders who believed that business is the engine of positive change in the world and that by spanning borders and engaging diverse communities, international business in particular contributes to peace and prosperity. Over the past eight decades, life in most corners of the world has gotten dramatically better. We have witnessed astonishing declines in infant mortality, significant lifespan extensions, a dramatic drop in the number of violent deaths, and a much lower percentage of humans living in abject poverty. Business has been central to many of these achievements. Yet in the process, we have mortgaged our future by endangering our climate and presiding over the fastest biodiversity loss in scientifically examined history.

It need not be so. Business is pragmatic. It is solution oriented. With the right tools, leadership mindset, and supportive policy environment, we can bring economic growth into balance with societal and environmental needs. At IMD, through our daily access to global enterprises and their leaders, we are uniquely positioned to identify what works and what is holding us back. We are a vibrant meeting place for thought leaders and management practitioners, enabling us to deepen conversations and find answers to the most complex challenges. In the process, we have shifted our efforts from the "why" of sustainability to the "how."

Over the last five years, we have embedded sustainability across our institutional activities and transformed our MBA program to ensure that the leaders of tomorrow have the skills and mindset to drive positive change. We have launched a number of "Sustainability Accelerators," a suite of executive programs aimed at equipping the leaders of today with the tools that work, and supported dozens of blue-chip clients on their own sustainability journeys. In the process, we have listened, observed, studied, examined, tested, and started the cycle all over again as we've conducted comprehensive research with industry leaders.

The result is this Playbook. Based on the contributions of over 45 IMD faculty members and experts across all areas of sustainability, its aim is to support leaders looking to catalyze meaningful change by showcasing the opportunities that sustainability offers and pinpointing the organizational capabilities necessary to seize them.

We hope it will serve as a trusted companion to both challenge and inspire you as you navigate the complexities of sustainability to make a positive difference in the world.

Michel Demaré
IMD Chairman of the Foundation &
Supervisory Boards, IMD Chair of the
Board at AstraZeneca Plc

David Bach
IMD President
Nestlé Professor of Strategy
and Political Economy

Preface

Julia Binder and Knut Haanaes

In the ever-evolving landscape of global business, sustainability has emerged as the defining challenge of our time. Whether a business is an international conglomerate or a local startup, established for decades or just beginning its journey, its role in fostering a sustainable future is critical. The challenge transcends borders, industries, and organizational sizes, demanding that every aspect of an organization engages deeply with the principles and practices of sustainability.

This book is a collective endeavor by faculty at the International Institute for Management Development (IMD), in Lausanne, Switzerland. They bring together diverse expertise and viewpoints to create a comprehensive guide on how sustainability affects organizational functions. From strategy and innovation to operations and leadership, our aim is to provide a holistic, one-stop resource that helps business leaders navigate the complexities of sustainable transformation. Each chapter reflects the unique insights of our faculty, woven together to offer a unified perspective on this multifaceted challenge.

As the editors of this book, we – Julia Binder and Knut Haanaes – have driven this meaningful project with the goal of showcasing the rich knowledge and insights at IMD. We sought to bring together the deep expertise of colleagues to equip business leaders with the knowledge and actionable tools they need to lead in this new era of sustainability.

Our own respective journeys toward sustainability have been shaped by our diverse experiences. Julia Binder's academic path has been instrumental in shaping her thought leadership at the intersection of innovation and sustainability. After achieving her PhD from the Technical University of Munich, she advanced her research at École Polytechnique Fédérale de Lausanne, where she also set up the sustainability initiative Tech4Impact. Her academic work has consistently been at the forefront of sustainable innovation, with a particular focus on circularity.

Meanwhile, Knut Haanaes brings deep expertise in strategy, honed through years at BCG (formerly the Boston Consulting Group) and the World Economic Forum. At BCG, he founded and led the first global sustainability practice, with the goal to balance the dual imperatives of exploiting existing strengths and exploring new opportunities. His extensive experience in these areas has profoundly influenced his approach to sustainable business transformation, making him a key contributor to IMD's leadership in this field.

Though our paths began in different arenas, they have converged at IMD, where our shared commitment to sustainability, alongside our esteemed colleagues, has become the foundation of our work. This collaboration makes the book unique – not the product of a single viewpoint, but rather the culmination of a diverse range of perspectives, each contributing to a comprehensive understanding of how sustainability can be integrated into business. While we work from rigorous academic research, we are profoundly inspired by the business leaders who have trusted us to accompany them on their transformation journeys. At IMD, we believe that the magic happens at the intersection of academic research and real-world business challenges. This vantage point provides us with an unparalleled perspective on the complexities of sustainability – a perspective we are eager to share with you through this book.

Our goal is to offer action-oriented, practical support to business leaders ready to move beyond understanding why sustainability is essential to tackling the critical question of how to achieve it. We recognize that there are many pathways to succeed in this endeavor. This book emphasizes the elements that can empower organizations to drive transformative change. It serves as a guide, providing insights and tools to help you navigate the complexities of sustainable business transformation.

Much has been written on the topic of sustainability. Our contribution to the ongoing conversation lies in our holistic integration of the head, heart, and hands of sustainability. By "head," we refer to the strategic underpinnings guiding organizations to make informed, sustainable decisions. "Heart" encompasses the leadership qualities necessary to inspire and drive emotional commitment to sustainability throughout an organization. Lastly, "hands" represent the actionable practices that turn vision into reality, allowing companies to implement and scale sustainable solutions effectively. This three-pronged approach merges intellectual rigor with emotional resonance and practical execution, providing a distinct perspective essential for driving deep and lasting changes in sustainability practices.

Bringing together dozens of IMD faculty members across almost as many chapters was no small feat. It required a tremendous amount of dedication, collaboration, and passion. We are deeply grateful to all our colleagues who went above and beyond to make this book a reality. Their contributions reflect our shared commitment to creating a positive impact in the world.

Finally, we wish to express our deepest gratitude to you, our readers. As business leaders, you catalyze the profound changes needed to shape a more sustainable future. Your dedication and commitment are pivotal; without them, our goals remain unattainable. We understand that your journey is challenging, fraught with complex decisions and significant challenges. We hope this book serves as a resource in your endeavors – a "sparring partner" with whom you can engage deeply, challenge ideas, and refine strategies. The insights and experiences detailed within these pages aim to inspire and empower you to drive sustainable transformations and contribute a lasting, positive impact on society.

We want to thank all our wonderful IMD faculty colleagues for their kind contributions, as well as Delia Fischer for our close collaboration. The book could not have happened without you.

PART I

Framing
the Conversation

Julia Binder and Knut Haanaes

In late 2020, as the world began to emerge from the worst of the COVID-19 pandemic, Wärtsilä, a Finnish corporation specializing in power systems, made a bold decision. Despite being a well-established company with a strong track record in manufacturing and servicing on-land and marine power systems, the company faced a significant challenge. Since peaking in 2017, both its operating margin and stock price had fallen by half, largely due to its reliance on fossil-fuel technologies at a time when the world was shifting toward carbon neutrality. Sales were likely to stagnate or even decline as global warming pushed industries to move away from carbon-intensive sources.

In response, the board made a strategic move by hiring a new CEO, Håkan Agnevall, from outside the company. Agnevall had successfully led Volvo's bus division through a sustainability transformation, making it a world leader in electric-powered transportation. He proposed a similar approach at Wärtsilä, aiming to turn the threat of decarbonization into an opportunity.

Agnevall knew that the transformation would be a long-term endeavor. Customers in Wärtsilä's sectors, on-land generation and marine propulsion, were conservative and cautious – after all, their investments were meant to last for decades. And with ocean-going freighters still lacking a reliable carbon-neutral fuel, the path forward was uncertain. But rather than waiting for technology and customer preferences to catch up, Wärtsilä took proactive steps.

The company developed decarbonization as a service, aligning with its existing strategic shift towards services, already nearly half of its business. Furthermore, despite the financial constraints imposed by the pandemic, Wärtsilä invested €250 million in establishing the Sustainable Technology Hub, a research institute dedicated to advancing sustainability through collaboration with industry partners.

In November 2021, just ten months after taking the helm, Agnevall unveiled Wärtsilä's new strategy, positioning sustainability as the company's primary purpose. The strategy set out clear values, principles, and actionable targets, with the aim of making Wärtsilä a global leader in decarbonizing the marine and energy markets. While the company's stock price remained volatile and its operating margins were slow to recover, Agnevall and his team were convinced they were on the right path for the long term.

A TWOFOLD APPROACH: STRATEGY AND LEADERSHIP

The journey toward sustainability is neither simple nor straightforward. It requires a twofold approach that balances strategic vision with effective leadership – a combination of the head, which represents the logic and rationale of transformation, and the heart and hands, which embody the leadership and action needed to implement change. In many ways, this balance is the core theme of this book. To achieve true sustainability, organizations must integrate strategy with leadership, ensuring that plans are not just formulated but executed with conviction and agility.

Sustainability, at its essence, is about creating business models that are resilient, adaptable, and capable of enduring over the long haul. It's not merely about compliance or risk management – it's about fundamentally rethinking how businesses operate in a world facing profound environmental, social, and economic challenges. This shift from viewing sustainability as a risk to embracing it as an opportunity is crucial. Companies like Wärtsilä are showing that sustainability can drive innovation, open up new markets, and create long-term value.

The urgency of this shift cannot be overstated. The signals for change are all around us; climate change, resource scarcity, and social inequalities are reshaping the global landscape. Businesses can no longer afford to ignore these trends. They must act now not just to protect their bottom lines but to ensure their future viability. This is why sustainability is a global imperative, transcending borders and industries. No company, regardless of its size or location, can afford to stand still.

THE INFINITY LOOP: THE DYNAMIC INTERACTION OF STRATEGY AND LEADERSHIP

Sustainability isn't a one-time project where you develop a strategy, implement it, and move on. It's an ongoing process that requires a continuous interaction between strategic planning and leadership – a dynamic relationship that can be visualized as an infinity loop. This loop represents the constant flow between strategy and leadership, where each element reinforces and enhances the other.

On one side of the loop is strategy. Have you ever wondered how to craft a sustainability strategy that truly aligns with your company's long-term vision? It's more than just setting goals; it's about envisioning a future where your business not only survives but thrives in a rapidly changing world. This requires breaking away from the limitations of the present and imagining new possibilities. Tools like future-back thinking and scenario planning aren't just theoretical exercises; they're essential for building a strategy that's resilient and forward-looking.

Consider how this strategic approach could come to life in your organization. For example, companies like Siemens have embedded sustainability into their core strategy, not simply to mitigate risks but to lead in the global transition toward a sustainable economy. By investing in energy-efficient technologies and smart infrastructure, Siemens is positioning itself at the forefront of the energy revolution, shaping the future rather than just reacting to it.

But even the best strategy can falter without effective leadership. This is where the other side of the infinity loop comes into play. Leadership isn't just about implementing a strategy – it's about inspiring and mobilizing your organization to make that strategy a reality. Have you ever seen a great plan fall short because it didn't get the buy-in it needed? Leadership is the key to ensuring that your strategy isn't just a document but a driving force that energizes your entire organization.

Effective leadership involves creating a culture where sustainability is more than a buzzword – it becomes a shared value that influences every decision and action. Imagine an organization where every employee, from the boardroom to the front lines, understands their role in achieving sustainability goals. This level of engagement doesn't happen by accident; it's the result of leaders who are committed to fostering a sense of ownership and accountability at every level.

The infinity loop illustrates that sustainability is not a static goal but a dynamic journey. As you implement your strategy, you'll encounter new challenges and opportunities that require you to adapt and refine your approach. Are you prepared to pivot when necessary? This is where agile leadership becomes crucial, enabling you to make quick strategic adjustments while keeping your long-term objectives in focus.

The continuous interaction between strategy and leadership creates a powerful feedback loop. As your organization moves forward, you'll gather insights and data that allow you to assess what's working and what isn't. This feedback helps you tweak your strategy, ensuring it remains effective in a constantly evolving environment. Leadership, in turn, adapts to these changes, guiding the organization through the complexities of sustainability with clarity and purpose.

So, as you think about sustainability in your organization, consider how well your strategy and leadership are working together. Are they in sync, each reinforcing the other? By embracing this infinity loop of strategy and leadership, you create a dynamic process that drives real, lasting change, making sustainability not just a goal but the very essence of your business.

The Wärtsilä example, as presented earlier, illustrates an important reality: the transformation toward sustainability is not a linear process with clear-cut phases. Instead, it's an ongoing, iterative journey – an infinity loop where strategy and leadership continuously reinforce one another. Focusing on strategy can lead to missed opportunities for engagement, while concentrating on leadership may lack the strategic foundation needed for lasting change.

This infinity loop reflects the dynamic nature of sustainability, where adjustments in strategy prompt shifts in leadership and vice versa. It's not just about setting goals; it's about creating an environment where strategy and leadership are in constant dialogue, driving continuous improvement.

To succeed in this journey, leaders must develop a strategy that is not only aligned with the company's purpose but also adaptable to changing circumstances. This strategy must be communicated effectively, supported by robust reporting and a commitment to long-term goals. However, strategy alone isn't enough. Leaders must also ensure that sustainability is embedded in the company's culture, making it a shared responsibility across all levels.

Moreover, leaders need to engage with external stakeholders – regulators, NGOs, and the broader community – integrating their insights and needs into the strategy. This holistic approach ensures that the company's sustainability efforts are not only internally cohesive but also externally validated.

In this book, we offer a practical guide to navigating this complex landscape. The ideas and strategies presented here are designed to help you lead your organization toward a sustainable future – one where business success is intertwined with the well-being of society and the planet. The challenge of sustainability is immense, but with the right approach, it's an opportunity to create lasting value for all.

Chapter 1

Defining Sustainability

Julia Binder and Knut Haanaes

In today's complex and fast-paced business environment, sustainability has evolved from a buzzword into an essential element of long-term success. Yet the concept is often misunderstood or oversimplified. Some critics question the necessity of sustainability, pointing to the challenges of sustainability investing or the slow pace of global decarbonization as evidence that the idea is overhyped. But when we talk about sustainability, we're not merely discussing a moral obligation or a compliance issue. Sustainability is about ensuring that your business can survive and thrive in the long term. It's about building resilience in the face of uncertainty and positioning your company to capitalize on the opportunities of tomorrow.

As a leader, have you ever grappled with the tension between delivering short-term results and preparing your company for the future? Sustainability offers a framework for balancing these often competing demands. It's not about abandoning profitability or growth but about reimagining these concepts in a way that aligns immediate business needs with long-term viability. Sustainability is about making decisions today that will allow your business to continue thriving in an increasingly volatile world.

THE ESSENCE OF SUSTAINABILITY

At its core, sustainability is about creating business models that are resilient, adaptable, and capable of enduring over the long haul. It's not about quick fixes or symbolic gestures; it's about implementing practical, long-term solutions that integrate economic viability with environmental stewardship and social responsibility. In other words, sustainability is about aligning your business strategy with the broader trends shaping our world – trends like climate change, resource scarcity, and social inequality. By doing so, you ensure that your business remains relevant and successful in the years to come.

But what does this look like in practice? To truly grasp sustainability, let's delve into three major challenges – and opportunities – that businesses face today: climate change, resource shortages, and social unrest.

1. *Climate Change: A Business Imperative.* Climate change is no longer a distant threat; it is a present reality that

is already reshaping industries and economies around the world. The earth's atmosphere has been warming steadily since the Industrial Revolution, with scientists projecting a temperature increase of 1.5–2°C by 2040. This rise, largely driven by human activities such as burning fossil fuels, poses significant risks to both markets and societies. The potential impacts are vast, ranging from disrupted supply chains due to extreme weather events to heightened regulatory pressures as governments seek to mitigate the worst effects of climate change.

As a business leader, have you considered how climate change might impact your company? Are your operations vulnerable to disruptions caused by unstable weather patterns? Companies that proactively decarbonize and invest in renewable energy are not only reducing their environmental impact but also positioning themselves as leaders in a low-carbon economy. Take Schneider Electric. This global leader in energy management and automation has embedded sustainability into its core business strategy. Schneider Electric has committed to achieving carbon neutrality in its operations by 2025 and net-zero emissions by 2030. This commitment not only addresses the risks associated with climate change but also positions the company as a pioneer in the energy transition, offering solutions that help other businesses become sustainable.

By taking these proactive steps, companies like Schneider Electric are not just avoiding risk – they are creating new opportunities for growth. For instance, Schneider Electric's focus on sustainability has enabled it to capture a significant share of the market for energy-efficient solutions. Sustainability can be a driver of innovation and competitive advantage.

2. *Resource Shortages: Turning Scarcity into Opportunity.* The world's natural resources are under increasing strain as global populations grow and lifestyles become more resource intensive. Freshwater supplies are dwindling, arable land is being lost to desertification and urbanization, and biodiversity is declining at an alarming rate. These trends pose significant challenges for businesses that rely on these resources to produce their goods and services. But they also present opportunities for companies that are willing to innovate and adapt.

   Have you ever thought about how your business might be affected if key resources became scarce or prohibitively expensive? For example, industries that rely heavily on water-intensive processes, such as agriculture or manufacturing, will need to find ways to use water more efficiently or develop alternatives to traditional methods. Companies that fail to adapt to these changing conditions may find themselves at a competitive disadvantage.

   On the other hand, companies that embrace sustainability can turn these challenges into opportunities. Consider Patagonia, the outdoor clothing company known for its strong commitment to environmental sustainability. The firm has implemented various initiatives to reduce its resource consumption, such as using recycled materials in its products and encouraging customers to repair and reuse their gear rather than buying new items. These efforts not only reduce Patagonia's environmental footprint but also strengthen its brand by appealing to consumers who value sustainability. As a result, Patagonia has built a loyal customer base and achieved significant growth, proving that sustainability and profitability can go hand in hand.

3. *Social Unrest: Building Trust and Social Capital.* The benefits of capitalism have not been evenly distributed, leading to growing inequality and social unrest in many

parts of the world. This erosion of trust in institutions, including businesses, poses a significant challenge for companies that rely on stable social environments to operate effectively. Companies that engage in exploitative practices – whether through poor labor conditions, unfair pricing, or lack of transparency – are deepening this mistrust and risking their social license to operate.

Have you ever considered how your company is perceived by the communities it affects? What steps can you take to build a more inclusive and socially responsible business model? Businesses that actively work to build trust and contribute to social stability are better positioned to thrive in the long term. This might involve improving labor practices, engaging with communities more meaningfully, or ensuring that the benefits of economic growth are shared equitably.

A powerful example of this is Ben & Jerry's, the ice cream company known for its strong social mission. From its inception, Ben & Jerry's has been committed to using its business to promote social justice, whether by supporting fair trade practices, advocating for environmental sustainability, or standing up for human rights. This commitment has not only helped Ben & Jerry's build a strong brand but also fostered a deep connection with its customers, who see the company as a force for good in the world. As a result, Ben & Jerry's was able to achieve impressive growth while staying true to its values.

ESG VERSUS SUSTAINABILITY: UNDERSTANDING THE DIFFERENCE

In recent years, the terms ESG (environmental, social, and governance) and sustainability have often been used interchangeably, but they are not the same. Understanding the distinction between the two is crucial for business leaders who want to make informed decisions about their company's future.

ESG refers to investment criteria. Investors evaluate a company's risk profile and financial performance based on environmental, social, and governance factors. ESG is a framework focused on identifying and managing the financial risks associated with these factors. ESG criteria might include:

- Issues like carbon emissions, water use, waste management, and biodiversity (environmental).
- Factors such as labor practices, human rights, community engagement, and customer privacy (social).
- Corporate governance structures, board diversity, executive compensation, and transparency (governance).

ESG is fundamentally an "outside-in" approach, where the goal is to assess how external environmental, social, and governance issues could affect a company's financial performance. It's about protecting the company's value by minimizing risks that could arise from these factors. In this sense, ESG is very much aligned with traditional financial management practices – it's about risk mitigation and ensuring that the company remains a sound investment.

Sustainability, by contrast, takes an "inside-out" approach. It focuses on the effect that a company has on the environment and society. While ESG is concerned with how external factors might affect a company's financial health, sustainability is about how the company's operations affect the world. This people- and planet-centric approach goes beyond risk management to consider the broad implications of business decisions. True sustainability aims not only to minimize harm but to create positive impact – whether through reducing environmental footprints, enhancing social equity, or driving economic inclusivity.

Sustainability is also about redefining value creation. Instead of focusing on financial returns, sustainable businesses consider the social and environmental value they create. This might involve paying fair wages throughout the supply chain, investing in renewable energy even if it's more expensive in the short term, or developing products that promote health and well-being.

For a business leader, it's important to recognize that while ESG considerations are essential, they should not be the end goal. ESG provides a framework for identifying risks and ensuring that a company remains resilient in the face of external pressures. But focusing on ESG can lead to a "tickbox" mentality, emphasizing compliance rather than truly transforming the business for long-term sustainability.

True sustainability requires going beyond risk management to actively seek out opportunities for positive impact. This might mean decisions that are costly in the short term but that contribute to a more sustainable and inclusive future. Investing in sustainable materials or committing to zero waste, for example, might involve upfront costs, but these investments can pay off in the long run by building a stronger, more resilient brand.

THE BALANCING ACT

Navigating the path to sustainability requires a delicate balancing act, one that demands a nuanced approach to decisions. Sustainability often involves trade-offs, where environmental, social, and economic goals come into conflict.

As a leader, have you ever found yourself at a crossroads, where pursuing a sustainable initiative seemed to jeopardize short-term profitability or operational efficiency? This is the crux of the balancing act that sustainability demands.

To successfully balance these competing interests, leaders must think strategically across different time horizons. The concept of managing across three horizons is particularly useful in this context:

Horizon 1: The Present Business. This horizon represents your company's current operations – the products, services, and business models that generate today's cash flow. These activities may not yet be fully sustainable, but they are the foundation of your company's financial health. The challenge here is to maintain and optimize these operations while gradually integrating sustainable practices. For example, many automotive companies continue to produce internal combustion engine vehicles, even as they invest in electric vehicles. This dual approach allows them to fund the transition to a more sustainable future while continuing to meet current market demands.

Horizon 2: The Entrepreneurial Transition. This horizon involves the exploratory work needed to transition your business toward sustainability. It's about innovation, experimentation, and learning. In this phase, companies must invest in new technologies, business models, and processes that may not yield immediate returns but are essential for long-term success. For example, oil and gas companies investing in renewable energy projects are operating in Horizon 2. These initiatives might not yet be profitable, but they represent a critical step in the journey toward a sustainable future. The key challenge in Horizon 2 is managing the inherent uncertainty and risk associated with new ventures while ensuring that these efforts align with the company's overall strategic goals.

Horizon 3: The Sustainable Future. The third horizon represents the long-term vision for your company – a future where sustainability is fully integrated into your business model and your company thrives in a new, sustainable economy. This horizon is where the investments and innovations of Horizon 2 come to fruition. For example, companies like Tesla, which started with a bold vision of a zero-emissions future, are now reaping the rewards of their early investments. The challenge in Horizon 3 is to maintain focus and commitment over the long term, even when the path forward is not always clear.

Balancing these three horizons is crucial for leaders looking to navigate the transition to sustainability without sacrificing current performance. It requires a delicate dance between exploiting current assets and exploring new opportunities. For instance, as car manufacturers develop electric vehicles (Horizon 2), they continue to rely on the profits from their traditional internal combustion engine vehicles (Horizon 1) to fund these innovations. Eventually, the goal is to transition fully to Horizon 3, where the company's operations are entirely sustainable.

This balancing act is not just about managing resources; it's also about managing expectations – both within the company and with external stakeholders. Shareholders may demand short-term returns, while employees and customers increasingly expect companies to act responsibly and sustainably. Leaders must navigate these competing demands, ensuring that short-term decisions do not undermine long-term goals.

The challenge of balancing these horizons becomes even more pronounced in industries facing significant disruption. Consider the energy sector, where companies like

BP and Shell are investing in renewable energy projects while still heavily reliant on oil and gas revenues. These companies must carefully manage the tension between their legacy operations and the need to transition to sustainable energy sources. This requires not only strategic foresight but also the ability to communicate the company's long-term vision effectively to stakeholders, ensuring continued support during the transition period.

The long-term payoff of a proactive sustainability strategy is not just about financial returns. It's about building a business that is resilient, adaptable, and capable of thriving in a rapidly changing world. Companies that lead on sustainability are better positioned to attract and retain top talent, build strong relationships with customers and suppliers, and navigate the uncertainties of the future.

Furthermore, as investors prioritize sustainability, companies with strong sustainability credentials are more likely to attract capital and enjoy a lower cost of capital. This trend is reflected in the growing interest in green bonds, sustainability-linked loans, and ESG-focused investment funds. In the long run, sustainability pays.

Chapter 2

Why Now?

Julia Binder and Knut Haanaes

"The bigger risk today is not to jump on the train of transformation, which is of course a risk for any venture, but to be left on the platform. Because you will lose out not only on the economic benefits, from a taxation point of view, but also from a brand point of view, from recruitment of people, and in looking at yourself in the mirror."

—Jesper Brodin

These words from Jesper Brodin, CEO of the Ingka Group (IKEA) at the 2023 World Economic Forum, point to the driving reason for companies to embrace sustainability. Even with the recent backlash against ESG investment,

CEOs are faced with unprecedented pressure to address environmental and social concerns now.

Brodin started with the economic benefits of sustainability but emphasized the larger, structural reason. It's increasingly clear that governments alone cannot effectively address the three sustainability crises described in the previous chapter: climate change, declining freshwater and other resources, and rising inequality. Companies can't sit back and merely comply with the regulations set by local authorities, because those regulations will never be enough to prompt the innovation and development we need for a truly sustainable economy and society.

Along with government guidance, we need businesses to move aggressively, to transform their own operations and those of their value chain. Businesses possess unique agility, expertise, and resources to spearhead innovation and experimentation, fostering a diverse array of potential solutions. While governments provide essential oversight and support, the dynamic nature of business enables quicker adaptation and implementation, ultimately accelerating the pace of transformation.

In the past, many business leaders could operate much like the generic merchants in Adam Smith's *Wealth of Nations*. They could pursue their own personal and corporate ends, while resting assured that an "invisible hand" would promote the public good out of the workings of their and their rivals' companies. All they had to do was comply with the law. That approach worked brilliantly for generations, but the complexities of the twenty-first century have revealed its limitations. What succeeds in the short run can now pose substantial risks not just for a company but also for society as a whole.

THE RISING CHALLENGE

Worries about sustainability are not new. Back in the 1960s, scientists began sounding alarm bells about the detrimental effects of pollutants, emissions, waste, and climate change. While initial fears about resource depletion were misguided, and governments were able to reduce most noncarbon pollution, some of those concerns – especially climate change – have persisted. (See Figure 2.1, A Timeline of Sustainability Concerns.)

In the 1970s, those concerns sparked a call for "corporate social responsibility" (CSR), advocating for companies to purposefully contribute to societal needs. But this call gave rise to a regrettable trend of superficial, disconnected CSR initiatives – mere tokens aimed at showcasing a company's commitment without integrating social responsibility into its core strategy. The worries intensified in the 2010s, especially around those three worrisome areas of climate change, freshwater scarcity, and income inequality. Events such as COP conferences, Fridays for Future, and the "Occupy" movement underscored the unsustainability of business as usual. We can understand the changes in five shifts:

- *From Seeing Future Challenges to Addressing a Current Crisis.* Climate, water, and inequality have gone from vague concerns to be addressed in the future to areas that demand immediate attention. The once abstract concepts have materialized into catastrophes that affect our daily lives. With the recent surge in extreme weather events, water-driven conflicts, and antidemocratic populism, the three crises have taken on urgency.
- *From Narrow Awareness to Broad Anxiety.* In the 1970s, concerns about the environment and society were primarily confined to academia and think tanks. What had

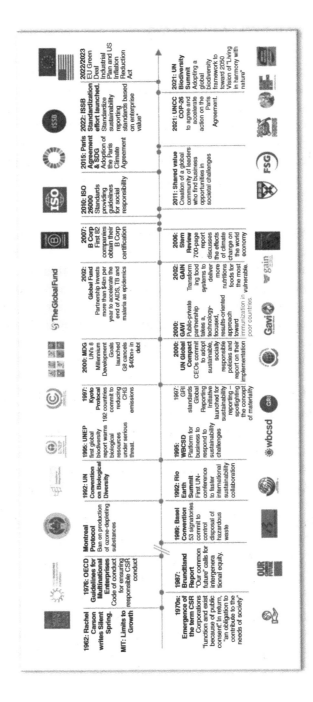

Figure 2.1 A Timeline of Sustainability Concerns.

been scientific discussion has now become general knowledge, which has helped to bring widespread awareness in civil society. This heightened awareness has also brought about a noticeable shift in people's emotional connection to these crises, with growing anxiety, particularly among the youth.

- *From Government Responsibility to Business Imperative*: The 1992 Rio Earth Summit presumed that governments held the main responsibility for taking action, with companies expected to adapt to regulatory changes. But that approach has failed to stem the crises. Fast forward to today, and the broad society expects businesses to step up and take a central role in addressing the crises. Regulation and subsidies aren't enough. Companies are no longer bystanders, but pivotal players that need to actively reduce their deleterious impact and craft sustainable solutions. Companies such as Paragonia and Vaude are actually lobbying governments to intensify regulations on sustainability in order to help them plan for major investments. And many young people say that corporate brands are better positioned than governments to solve social problems.

- *From Voluntary Communication to Mandatory Disclosure and Reporting*. Just a decade ago, few companies reported on the environmental or social impact of their activities. CSR reports were discretionary, often written by marketing or communications staffs. No more: increasingly, governments are passing laws to make companies take responsibility and disclose the environmental impact of their activities, including emissions, waste, water usage, and harmful chemical use. The European Union, for example, now addresses not just what a company does but the impacts of its entire value chain. Separate laws mandate disclosure on social issues such as compensation ratios and racial composition. With this knowledge, companies can do much more to improve their secondary impact on the world.

- *From Solo Efforts to Team Sports.* Finally, we see increased interest in collaboration among companies and between the public and private sectors. The crises we face require coordinated efforts along value chains and systemic transformations in specific sectors. These alliances can drive deep-seated and lasting change by combining expertise, resources, and influence. As these partnerships strengthen, they can mobilize collective action against the crises, offering a beacon of hope for a more sustainable future. Governments are already rethinking antitrust rules to encourage this collaboration.

Some business leaders may think now is the wrong time to push for sustainability given that the movement for ESG investing has suffered strong pushback, especially in the United States. On the social side, the much publicized American call for stakeholder capitalism, with dozens of prominent signatories in 2019, largely fizzled out in the pandemic as many of those same companies resorted to layoffs and other actions that harmed stakeholders.

We see the pushback as a temporary and natural resistance to an inevitable corporate transformation, especially with the continuing introduction of new regulations by governments in this area. And as we pointed out in the previous chapter, sustainability is quite different from calls for investing in companies with superior ESG policies. The ESG movement was about companies recognizing their vulnerability to external risks. Sustainability is about what companies are actively doing to minimize their deleterious impact and pioneer new approaches for their sectors. ESG thinking focuses on risk management in a defensive way, while sustainability involves going on the offensive to benefit both society and the bottom line.

Even the recent European movement back to fossil fuels came about less from sustainability blowback and more from inadequate investment in low-carbon energy before Russia invaded Ukraine. When Europeans lost their access to cheap Russian natural gas, they weren't prepared. Sustainable economies, and sustainable businesses, are ready for volatility in conventional energy markets.

RISING PRESSURES FOR DECISIVE ACTION

In numerous industries, businesses are already confronting threats from extreme weather events, droughts, flooding, or geopolitical instability. These risks can manifest in supply chain disruptions, market fluctuations, or threats to employee safety. According to a recent Deloitte survey, 97% of more than 2000 C-level executives have already noticed the effects of climate change on their business, and half say these have disrupted supply chains and business models. Climate change and the water crisis are no longer far-off problems, and these risks are only getting worse.

As for material inequality, companies have been seeing its effects with the waning of the COVID-19 pandemic. From the "great resignation" and "quiet quitting" to shrinking labor forces, companies are getting less effort and engagement from their talented employees. They're also facing increasing criticism on the social front when they abstain from taking a stance on significant societal issues, such as the #MeToo movement.

Executives don't have to believe in "late capitalism" or reject "neoliberalism" to recognize that stakeholders demand a different approach from companies. As the three crises call for an all-hands-on-deck response, companies must contribute as well – and even take the lead in some areas.

In addition to mitigating their adverse impact on these crises, companies have five compelling opportunities from establishing goals and strategies on sustainability.

Civic and Consumer Engagement

Fridays for Future, Extinction Rebellion, and other social movements are gaining momentum, demanding ambitious climate action from companies as well as governments. Activists are questioning companies' social license to operate. Climate litigation is spreading worldwide, with companies brought to court for failing to integrate climate considerations into business models, for "failure to adapt" to requirements of the climate crisis, for pollution, and increasingly for "climate-washing."[1]

Consumers are increasingly opting for sustainable choices or expressing a preference for more environmentally friendly products. While their purchasing behavior may not yet mirror their intentions due to factors such as limited knowledge or financial constraints, the intention-behavior gap is closing.[2]

---

[1] Setzer, Joana and Higham, Catherine. "Global Trends in Climate Change Litigation; 2023 Snapshot." June 2023 <https://www.lse.ac.uk/gran thaminstitute/wp-content/uploads/2023/06/Global_trends_in_climate_ change_litigation_2023_snapshot.pdf> (accessed 14 September 2023).

[2] Deloitte. "How Consumers are Embracing Sustainability." 2022 <https:// www2.deloitte.com/uk/en/pages/consumer-business/articles/sustainable- consumer.html> (accessed 14 September 2023) Globescan. "Healthy and Sustainable Living; 2022 Highlights Report." November 2022 <https:// globescan.com/wp-content/uploads/2022/11/GlobeScan_Healthy_and_ Sustainable_Living_Highlights_Report_2022.pdf> (accessed 14 September 2023) NielsenIQ and McKinsey. "Consumers Care about Sustainability – and Back It Up with Their Wallets." February 2023. <https://nielseniq.com/ wp-content/uploads/sites/4/2023/02/Consumers-care-about- sustainability%E2%80%94and-back-it-up-with-their-wallets-FINAL.pdf> (accessed 13 October 2023) World Economic Forum. "The Global Eco- wakening: How Consumers Are Driving Sustainability" 18 May 2021. <https://www.weforum.org/agenda/2021/05/eco-wakening-consumers- driving-sustainability/> (accessed 13 October 2023).

They are increasingly aware of sustainability and expect the companies they purchase from to take responsibility.

Younger generations, the market of the future, trust companies more if they seek sustainability.[3] But older generations are also taking note, including a group of elderly Swiss women. They successfully argued at the European Court of Human Rights that the Swiss government wasn't doing enough to prevent climate change, putting them at high risk of death from heat waves.

Companies that actively move toward sustainability, exceeding what's required or expected, will get a reputational boost from these current and future consumers. They could see both commercial and political gains.

Regulatory Imperative

The shift to mandatory disclosures and regulations on sustainability is intensifying. Companies operating in the European Union must now comply with the Corporate Sustainability Reporting Directive (CSRD), which requires a double materiality assessment to report on the sustainability topics most relevant to stakeholders. This assessment helps ensure that companies acknowledge issues of great impact. Companies also face a growing array of regulations on labor standards, chemical pollution, emissions (including from suppliers), and the end-of-life management of their products.

These regulations typically give companies some time to adjust their operations. But companies that begin the shift ahead of regulations can better invest in changes according

---

[3] Reichheld, A., Peto J., Ritthaler, C., "Research: Consumers' Sustainability Demands Are Rising." HBR, 18 September 2023 <https://hbr.org/2023/09/research-consumers-sustainability-demands-are-rising> (accessed 13 October 2023).

to business opportunities. They have more control over the transition, so they can direct it according to their strengths and their commercial context. These complex regulations are also likely to stymie some firms. To avoid expensive retrofitting and remain compliant with these evolving regulations, businesses will need in practice to stay ahead of governments. Better to take the lead rather than passively be directed to act.

New Markets

Across industries, business leaders see that it is possible to provide value and reap profits by setting goals and developing strategies to benefit society. Companies that proactively integrate sustainable practices into their operations can enhance their brand reputation, attract environmentally conscious consumers, and foster long-term customer loyalty. On the climate side, McKinsey & Co. estimates the annual demand for net-zero businesses across eleven value pools at US$9–12 trillion by 2030. (See Chapter 3 for details.)

Technology

Many new technologies are emerging to promote sustainability, and we need companies to develop and implement these advances. From recycling infrastructure to geothermal equipment, companies have an array of possibilities to reduce their ecological footprint.

Renewable energy has perhaps advanced the most and is now cost-competitive with fossil fuels in many applications. According to the International Energy Agency, "Annual capacity additions [for renewable energy] have more than doubled from 2015 to 2022, rising by about 11% per year on average."

Digital tools have the potential to boost organizational performance. When used effectively, they not only contribute to protecting the planet but also enhance the quality of people's lives. For instance, the World Economic Forum and Accenture estimate that digital technologies can decrease global greenhouse gas emissions by 20% if scaled worldwide. Moreover, according to a study by PwC, leveraging emerging technologies such as artificial intelligence (AI), blockchain, and the Internet of Things (IoT) could enable the attainment of 70% of the UN Sustainable Development Goals targets.

Like governments and individuals, businesses can help to guide these technologies to make our economy sustainable. Some companies are adopting blockchain technology, in connection with AI, to better track, measure, and improve the environmental footprint of their products throughout the value chain. Beyond the visible developments in every sector, technology is lowering the material footprint, boosting recycling materials, improving efficiency, and helping to feed back positively to the earth.

GAINING MOMENTUM

Finally, now is a good time for companies to embrace sustainability simply because of the foundational work they must do anyway to comply with regulations and changing social expectations. Companies are going to have much more information on their performance around sustainability, which is essential for embracing this issue. After all, most big changes require two changes: first, to start really seeing the challenge, and second to start doing something about it. With all the regulatory, not to mention social pressures, companies have no choice but to make a great deal of headway in seeing the challenge.

Virtually every company is now compelled to move toward sustainability. Even if they operate in regions without stringent regulation, they're likely a supplier or seller to a country or consumer that is. And if you're going to be doing something, there's a payoff to doing more than the minimum as long as you're at it.

Real-world business dynamics don't adhere to a simplistic two-step process of achieving compliance and then innovating. While some may be tempted to settle for compliance, doing so risks squandering the momentum and organizational expertise accumulated during the compliance process. It's less costly, and less risky, than getting started on sustainability and just waiting for the next regulations.

We are at a renewal moment for companies. Sustainability may have receded from the spotlight, overshadowed by topics like AI, elections, and geopolitical conflicts. And it's easy for leaders to get sidetracked and focus on immediate concerns.

Yet the recent weather extremes, rising water shortages, and social unrest all underscore the urgent need for change. Companies are increasingly feeling the pressure to act from society, government, and investors. Forward-thinking companies are leveraging their expertise, resources, and global reach to develop innovative products and strategies that not only mitigate negative impacts but also unlock new markets and opportunities. For businesses yet to embark on the sustainability journey, the time is ripe to engage and take action. As Jesper Brodin formulated it, "If anyone is still on the platform, it's time to get on the train."

FURTHER READING

M. Birshan et al., "Playing Offense to Create Value in the Net-Zero Transition." *McKinsey Quarterly*, 23 April 2022 <https://www.mckinsey.com/capabilities/sustainability/our-insights/playing-offense-to-create-value-in-the-net-zero-transition>

L. Cozzi et al., "Tripling Renewable Power Capacity by 2030 is Vital to Keep the 1.5 °C Goal Within Reach." *IEA*. 21 July 2023 <https://www.iea.org/commentaries/tripling-renewable-power-capacity-by-2030-is-vital-to-keep-the-150c-goal-within-reach> (accessed 6 September 2023).

Deloitte. "How Consumers are Embracing Sustainability," 2022 <https://www2.deloitte.com/uk/en/pages/consumer-business/articles/sustainable-consumer.html>

EUR Lex (n.d.) Corporate Sustainability Reporting Directive law, <https://eur-lex.europa.eu/eli/dir/2022/2464/oj>

Globescan. "Healthy and Sustainable Living; 2022 Highlights Report." November 2022 <https://globescan.com/wp-content/uploads/2022/11/GlobeScan_Healthy_and_Sustainable_Living_Highlights_Report_2022.pdf>

IFRS Sustainability Standards Board (n.d.) <https://www.ifrs.org/groups/international-sustainability-standards-board/>

George Manju, Karen O'Regan, and Alexander Holst, "Digital Solutions Can Reduce Global Emissions by Up to 20%. Here's How," *World Economic Forum*, May 23, 2022.

McKinsey & Company, "The Value of Net Zero" 29 August 2022 <https://www.mckinsey.com/featured-insights/sustainable-inclusive-growth/chart-of-the-day/the-value-of-net-zero>

NielsenIQ and McKinsey. "Consumers Care about Sustainability – and Back It Up with Their Wallets." February 2023. <https://nielseniq.com/wp-content/uploads/sites/4/2023/02/Consumers-care-about-sustainability%E2%80%94and-back-it-up-with-their-wallets-FINAL.pdf>

PwC, "Over Two-Thirds of Sustainable Development Goals Could Be Bolstered by Emerging Tech, Including AI and Blockchain," January 17, 2020.

A. Reichheld, J. Peto, C. Ritthaler, "Research: Consumers' Sustainability Demands Are Rising." *Harvard Business Review*, 18 September 2023 <https://hbr.org/2023/09/research-consumers-sustainability-demands-are-rising>

For more details on these challenges, see: Setzer, Joana, and Higham, Catherine. "Global Trends in Climate Change Litigation; 2023 Snapshot." June 2023 <https://www.lse.ac.uk/granthaminstitute/wp-content/uploads/2023/06/Global_trends_in_climate_change_litigation_2023_snapshot.pdf>

World Economic Forum. "The Global Eco-wakening: How Consumers Are Driving Sustainability" 18 May 2021. <https://www.weforum.org/agenda/2021/05/eco-wakening-consumers-driving-sustainability/>

World Economic Forum. "Keeping the Pace on Climate: Panel discussion with Julia Chatterley, John F. Kerry, Jesper Brodin, Helena Gualinga, and Anna Borg, 18 January 2023. https://www.weforum.org/events/world-economic-forum-annual-meeting-2023/sessions/keeping-the-pace-on-climate/

Chapter 3

Seizing Opportunities Rather Than Managing Risks

Knut Haanaes and Julia Binder

As any executive will tell you, moral suasion will not convince most companies to commit to sustainability. Even major long-term threats will not do it. Companies need positive reasons to undertake significant investments. Fortunately, sustainability offers many opportunities.

The challenge is that realizing those opportunities requires some upfront changes. But if we can engage a company's "animal spirits" – their eagerness to chase after a potential market – then we'll attract the ingenuity and resources necessary to get a better economy and society.

The hurdle lies in the need for initial adjustments to capitalize on these opportunities. By tapping into a company's entrepreneurial DNA – their drive to pursue promising markets – leaders can catalyze that ingenuity and resources essential for fostering a more robust economy and society.

FROM RISK TO OPPORTUNITY

It's easy for companies to see sustainability as a nice-to-have, even a must-have, but not a foundation for true success. They can see it as part of the cost of doing business, with thoughts along these lines: "This is what regulators, nonprofits, commentators, and even employees want, so let's grudgingly give it to them – as long as it doesn't interfere with what our company is really about. We'll complain about the risk and uncertainty in order to buy time, and maybe some subsidies, and we'll get to it eventually. Meanwhile, we'll stay focused on how we make money."

Many companies consider sustainability an optional or obligatory activity instead of a fundamental driver of genuine success. They may even perceive it as an operational expense, for example, complying with regulatory requirements, societal expectations, or workforce preferences. This will lead to a lack of enthusiasm to fully embrace sustainability, fearing potential risks and uncertainties, which can delay action while seeking short-term advantages. Consequently, the primary focus remains on core revenue-generating activities.

But sustainability offers enormous opportunities to companies with some imagination and flexibility. Any discussion of sustainability should start with the future market for goods and services that reduce or reverse dangerous impacts on climate, water resources, and inequality. In 2022, McKinsey & Co. estimated the total market for environmental sustainability alone at US$3 trillion in 2030. Whereas the overall infrastructure investments until now have been driven mainly by fossil fuels, the investments from now on will go toward a low-emission economy. That in itself opens enormous opportunities.

That same year, rival BCG assessed climate as an imperative for innovation, estimating the annual green-tech market at US$45–55 billion. That's the current market; the firm expected those revenues to grow 25–30% annually.

Sustainability is perhaps unusually risky as a corporate area. There's much we don't know about how the economy and markets will develop. Companies risk getting stuck in outdated businesses and stranded assets – with angry stakeholders to boot. They learn the wrong lesson from Lego, which faced intense criticism after declaring it couldn't develop a fossil-fuel alternative materials for its product after all. The better response is not to become cautious, but to treat sustainability as a megatrend that will support a variety of risky initiatives. Some initiatives won't pan out, but that's how business works. After all, one reason we as a society favor capitalism is that it energizes organizations that seek risk – unlike government and other institutions that try to minimize risk.

CAPITALISM FOR SUSTAINABILITY

On that note, leaders in government and nonprofits are increasingly realizing that they can't assemble the resources needed to achieve sustainability. Most of the capital must come from private investors, with taxes and philanthropy supplying only a small share. For the foreseeable future, to reduce carbon emissions to non-catastrophic levels, the world likely needs to invest in the order of US$5 trillion every year. Given political realities, the lion's share of that funding will almost certainly come from banks and other private capital intermediaries. To attract those funds, companies need to show a reasonable likelihood of return on investment.

As Ray Dalio, the founder of Bridgewater Associates, told the COP28 meeting in Dubai, "You have to make it profitable." Adair Turner, who heads Britain's Energy Transitions Committee, emphasized the need for supportive regulation, pointing out that climate change is "an economic externality, and you can't expect a free market to deal with it voluntarily." Most of the transition toward greener business models "will be financed by private institutions making profit-maximizing decisions." We don't really know how the financing will work out – here's where we definitely need some innovation – but it's increasingly clear that most of the resources will come from the private sector.

The corporate focus on profitability is already driving some of the backlash we've seen on ESG and related movements. Banks that had enthusiastically committed to net-zero goals are now pulling back. Many countries, and therefore clients, are still entrenched in fossil fuels, from South Africa to Poland and Indonesia. After much fanfare, even BlackRock, the giant investment fund manager, has dropped the use of ESG and scaled back its participation in climate investing.

It's not just a matter of funding. Long experience and economic theory has taught us that only decentralized, private-sector markets can mobilize the talent and initiative we need to transform our economy and society toward sustainability. Governments and nonprofits can nurture fundamental research, set the playing field, and redistribute investment and rewards when the likely winners are clear. But they can't know or decide which paths or technologies to follow to overcome those three giant challenges of sustainability: climate change, dwindling freshwater, and income inequality. Their focus on rational deliberation also discourages the creativity essential to solving tough challenges.

We need entrepreneurs coming up with wacky ideas and making them workable, including ideas that the "smart" people dismiss. We need companies developing and scaling that innovation to minimize disruption to the current economy – otherwise we'll get such a strong backlash we may go backwards. The history of semiconductors points the way. American military spending was crucial in convincing companies in the future "Silicon Valley" to experiment with a new approach to computer transistors. However, once those initial experiments succeeded, the federal government wanted to focus on one narrow application for semiconductors. The companies rebelled, and began attracting capital and selling on the commercial market. The broad interest convinced them to keep developing, enabling an unexpected but crucial decline in chip prices over the years.

In short, we need the power of capitalism, properly overseen, to address our big economic and social challenges. And to unleash that power, sustainability has to be profitable. It won't happen if we expect to move to sustainability from only a moral imperative. "Social entrepreneurship" and stakeholder capitalism have their place, but they won't be enough to meet the challenge.

That's not to say that sustainable investments require short-term returns. If that were so, we'd be in big trouble.

Companies still need to do the work of attracting patient investors willing to forego immediate returns. Plenty of such investors exist – just look at the shareholders who stuck with technology-based companies that took decades to become profitable. But companies must do the upfront work to attract them.

Decentralized markets have another vital advantage over top-down solutions. We can see this in the debates over what to do with the many coal-burning electric generating plants recently built throughout the developing world. Governments and nonprofits based in affluent countries are pushing to retire those plants early on the reasonable grounds that coal is the worst offender in carbon emissions.

Banks that helped finance those plants, and continue to draw fees from clients in those emerging countries, are pushing back. While they argue partly from self-interest, they are much closer to people in those countries than the coal critics. Attempts to shut down the plants would help with climate change but exacerbate income disparities across countries, not to mention invite backlash. Decentralized markets tend to be far better at adjudicating these tradeoffs, and coming up with innovation to transcend them, than top-down solutions. Those markets are also better at mitigating risk and moving quickly as opportunities shift.

THE REGULATORY ASSIST

Governments are acknowledging they can't lead the way with innovation and development. But they can and are taking two essential steps: subsidizing basic technology and construction and regulating to make sustainability more attractive for everyone.

In particular, governments are allowing flexibility in the transition. Carbon credits are a case in point: many governments are now requiring big companies to reduce not just their carbon emissions but those of their suppliers – Scope 3. But if some suppliers can't or won't, companies can buy carbon credits to offset the continuing pollution. Carbon trading markets haven't arisen as broadly as many observers expected, but regulators are encouraging companies to find paths to improvement that match their specific context and capabilities.

Another kind of flexibility is in antitrust. Sustainability involves complex, ecosystem-dependent challenges that often require extensive collaboration across rival companies. Pioneering by one company, such as Logitech's clever labeling of carbon emissions in products like calories in food, can fall flat without rivals following suit. But zealous governments could hinder this collaboration by warning against or even prosecuting this collaboration as a violation of pro-competition policies. Fortunately, federal, national, and international governments are increasingly making an exception here for collaboration around sustainability. Companies, for their part, need to ensure that collaboration doesn't move into collusion or erecting barriers to entry. Greater transparency and voluntary disclosure will also help.

THE GEOGRAPHICAL ADVANTAGE

Even with rising protectionism, most companies can reach a variety of markets, enough to match their capabilities and resources. Emerging markets offer enormous opportunities to develop sustainable infrastructure, housing, electricity, logistics, and healthcare services. As with mobile phone service in eastern Africa that skips the expensive phase of laying out wiring, economies can "leapfrog" into facilities that make it easier to reduce emissions, conserve water, and even minimize class disparities.

In developed economies, the challenge is different. These countries have already built out most of their infrastructure, and their stable or declining populations reduce their demand for significant infrastructure projects. (Just look at the slow pace of installing electric vehicle charging stations.) But many of their affluent consumers put a high value on sustainable products and services and provide substantial markets for innovation in these areas.

Essential in both areas, but especially in developed economies, companies can achieve profitability with multiple business models. Most sustainability challenges involve interlinked, systemic issues. They cannot be solved by just one product, service, or business. The energy transition, for example, requires not only windmills and solar panels – the familiar products that everyone can see – but also experts to help with building and deploying those products, networks to move the energy to where it is needed, storage to keep energy flowing continuously, and recycling for obsolete products and infrastructure. When companies look broadly at possibilities, sustainability becomes not a constraint but fertile ground for inspiration, innovation, and collaboration.

EXPLORE AND EXPLOIT

To make a difference, either in the economy or their own returns, most companies will need to resist the easy categories of the present. Some companies revel in pioneering a technology or market, while others are content to commercialize or scale up the advances of others. We need companies to do both because sustainability is not a normal corporate opportunity. It takes both pioneering and scaling in the same organization.

That's because most pioneering in sustainability is going to take several years before showing any results – and often those results depend on broadly scaling. That means not just building up a division but transforming the ecosystem of companies to support a new approach to business.

For example, many garment companies are keen to develop a "circular economy." They're looking to invest in facilities to recycle or reuse discarded clothing rather than dump it into landfills. The result would be substantial reductions in freshwater consumption and carbon emissions. Yet individual companies, even giant retailers, aren't strong enough to supply those facilities at the needed scale. Technology isn't the issue – we already largely know how to make the facilities efficient and effective. The companies need partnerships not just with each other and with distributors and collectors but also with local and national governments and nonprofits. Only with these arrangements in place can the numbers pencil out.

A company that merely pioneered would likely conclude the sustainability wasn't profitable and move on to other opportunities. A company that merely scaled up might resist doing anything in sustainability because it's hard to find advances with a satisfactory risk-return ratio. Sustainability is so risky that the same company that pioneers the novelty probably needs to scale it up as well, so the animal spirits drive the new product or service to full acceptance.

Fortunately, companies can draw on the example of a number of long-lived companies that have managed to succeed in both exploring and exploiting; 2% of a recent sample of firms. Doing so requires three conditions. First, sustainability must be part of the strategy – it has to be a pervasive, extended, and multifaceted commitment from the entire organization. Instead of delving into a variety of attractive initiatives, companies must pursue a focused program of mutually supportive investments. Only then, over time, will the company develop the business models, capabilities, connections, and experiences to keep those activities going over time – combining both innovation and scaling up. (Centering sustainability in strategy is a good idea for several reasons, including avoiding the traps of greenwashing and never putting enough money in an idea to truly test its potential.)

Second, companies must align their strategy to a megatrend. That's what Umicore, a longtime mining operator, did in switching its strategy toward recycling. In 2022, it rebranded itself as a "circular materials technology company." Instead of digging into the ground for high-demand metals, it extracts them from existing markets.

Such a radical change isn't essential, but some shifts are necessary. Schneider Electric doubled down on its industry, sensing that the energy transition would force a big expansion – but with special attention to the dynamics of renewable sources of electricity. The company established networks for distributing this energy to high-demand areas and helped develop technologies to hasten the transition from fossil fuels.

Third, and something especially difficult for long-lived, determined companies, they must stay outside-driven even after initial success. There's still much we don't know about what sustainability really involves – the fuels, materials, and markets that will help prevent catastrophe while enabling continued growth. Outside-driven companies stay agile and attentive enough to respond quickly to external developments – including those that make some past investments obsolete. Rather than stick with what they've done, they pivot to what markets want now. Again, the drive for profitability is essential.

NECESSITY AND INVENTION

Rather than a burden, the crisis of sustainability can ignite innovation. Just as mobilization in World War II forced companies to adopt a variety of efficient practices, and just as the race to the moon led to major advances in computers and materials, embracing sustainability will stimulate corporate innovation generally. After all, most companies have plenty of ideas on how to do things better, but they rarely invest in those ideas because of the immense pressures of the status quo. Sustainability has the potential to lead to a new innovation age in areas we can't even imagine now. The necessity of making our economy and society sustainable can become the virtue of a new spur to improvement.

Most industries will need to replace much of their existing equipment. For companies that consume a great deal of energy, replacing fossil-fuels with low- or zero-carbon alternatives by 2050 will require an estimated 70% of their capital outlay over that period. By studying the evolving needs of society, companies can uncover new markets and customer segments.

As companies work to reduce carbon emissions, for example, they are making energy infrastructure lighter, smaller, circular, or cheaper. If green hydrogen, for example, becomes a major source of energy, it will create all sorts of opportunities that have nothing to do with sustainability.

Presently, the food industry is a major driver of carbon emissions and freshwater depletion. Making the industry sustainable is already forcing companies to develop plant-based products with regenerative agriculture that uses less water and chemicals – perhaps eventually amounting to another Green Revolution, this time to feed an increasingly affluent world.

Some industries are leading the way. Look at the transportation sector, where companies are developing technologies and structures to provide carbon-free offerings at scale. Digital solutions, especially involving AI, can reduce energy consumption, increase efficiency, or improve product offerings but need development and scaling to prove their effectiveness. Once we do that hard work, we'll reap the benefits in many areas.

Unlike other corporate imperatives, sustainability efforts can benefit from a moral drive even as these pay off commercially. Here we can work from the analogy of rocketry. Elon Musk founded Space Exploration Technologies (SpaceX) out of impatience with the slow pace of rocket development. He wanted humanity to land on Mars and even colonize it, and he attracted other talented engineers to the cause. With reusable rockets and other wild-eyed advances, not to mention overcoming governmental resistance, they ended up radically reducing the cost of getting into space. As a result, we can now send up far more objects, and most of SpaceX's work actually involves the highly profitable launching of satellites into space. Talented engineers who signed up to "make our species interplanetary" are finding themselves working mostly on near-Earth transport and don't seem to mind. The privately held company is now worth more than a hundred billion dollars.

If Musk had started from the goal of reducing satellite launching costs, he would have attracted far less talent and enthusiasm. Sustainability projects can benefit from a similar passion, especially among the many young people now looking to make a difference in the business world. They can put their drive into innovations that also end up being highly profitable.

The key to motivating efforts in sustainability is to look at the big, long-term picture. Companies that address concerns specific to their industry and develop solutions, however imperfect at first, will gain a competitive edge. Their proactive stance not only wins customers and helps them stay ahead of regulatory changes but also positions them to develop sector-wide standards that fit their investments. By shaping their industry's development, they achieve strategic as well as operational benefits. Instead of waiting for the future to emerge, they shape it.

FURTHER READING

Peter Tufano, Chris Thomas, Knut Haanaes, Matteo Gasparini, Robert Eyres, and Chris Chapman, "To Earn Trust, Climate Alliances Need to Improve Transparency," *Harvard Business Review online*, Nov. 29, 2023.

Knut Haanaes and James Henderson, "What Should Your Sustainability Strategy Look Like," *I by IMD*, April 2021.

Alastair Marsh and Natasha White, "UBS Banker's Frustration Exposes Cracks in World of Climate Finance," *Bloomberg*, March 27, 2024. https://www.bloomberg.com/news/features/2024-03-27/ubs-banker-s-comments-highlight-challenges-facing-green-banking?cmpid=BBD032824_OUS&utm_medium=email&utm_source=newsletter&utm_term=240328&utm_campaign=openamericas&sref=bsFVYL6k

Chris Miller, *Chip War: The Fight for the World's Most Critical Technology*, Scribner's, 2022, especially Chapter 5

Chapter 4

The Geopolitical Context

Richard Baldwin and Simon J. Evenett

Companies don't operate in a vacuum. Corporate leaders have to navigate political dynamics, and in Chapter 12 we discuss nonmarket strategies. But there's a global dimension to sustainability that's worth a separate discussion. Will rising geopolitical tensions between America and China, and broadly between the West and emerging adversaries such as Russia, Iran, and North Korea, hinder efforts to boost sustainability? Or could the tensions even boost those efforts? Both stances have some merit, as well as a third position that the net effect of these tensions will be minor.

Let's unpack them to better understand the complex nexus between geopolitics and sustainability.

In our assessment, considerably more thought has gone into the nexus between geopolitical rivalry and the environmental dimensions, especially climate change mitigation. In what follows, we will focus there. It's worth bearing in mind that climate change adaptation may itself have a significant geopolitical dimension. Failure to comprehensively address adaptation might induce millions of individuals to move to hospitable climes within and between nations. Let's not forget that sudden migrations to Europe in the 2010s were a source of tension between governments. So, although the focus of much of what follows is on how tensions influence likely sustainability outcomes, in some cases the causation runs the other way – from the disruption created by a failure to attain sustainability.

TENSIONS ARE BAD FOR SUSTAINABILITY

The starting point for this perspective is that geopolitical tensions have little to do with environmental or social challenges. The issues are familiar ones of great powers maneuvering and attracting allies, and sustainability is a largely tangential issue. Yet in quarreling over spheres of influence or trade barriers, and forming antagonistic blocs, the tensions could preclude the global cooperation necessary to promote a sustainable future. Bickering between the United States and China, in particular, might undermine worldwide attempts at "climate rescue." And if big countries and blocs won't cooperate to address sustainability, small countries probably won't either.

It seems more people lean toward nationalism now than in previous decades, less willing to cooperate internationally or think about "one planet." They are more concerned about their national or group loyalties than about sustainability. When the Global Financial Crisis hit, it briefly pulled the whole world together, but that's no longer true – as witnessed by the free for all for personal protective equipment during the COVID-19 pandemic.

In that context, geopolitical tensions all too often underpin mounting calls to restrict international trade. But free-flowing international trade, besides boosting economic growth in poor countries, is essential to mitigating and adapting to climate change and other pressures. Companies will be less inclined to innovate if we limit their potential markets. The more entrepreneurs believe they can scale up their advances, the greater their willingness to devote creativity and financial resources to making those advances in the first place.

Trade spreads technology quickly around the globe, encouraging further improvement, and often works to reduce pressures on people to emigrate from struggling areas. It can also promote environmental and social justice in ways that are more palatable than outright redistribution. In any case, developing countries won't be able to afford climate mitigation and adaptation technologies unless their firms can earn revenues on world markets. Allowing goods to cross borders will take the edge off the worst aspects of the current crisis. There will be no climate rescue without trade, so geopolitical tensions are a danger here.

Those tensions can also directly undermine goals on sustainability. Soon after Russia invaded Ukraine, Europeans boycotted Russian natural gas – and then restarted several old carbon-intensive, coal-fueled generating plants. Environmental and social goals adopted in times of peace and prosperity might fall away with these tensions.

Geopolitical rivalries are also dangerous for humanity overall. Warfare itself damages the environment and society, but beyond that, some worry about those tensions leading to World War III. On this view, a 1930s-style protectionist spiral and retreat from globalization would presage actual fighting that spreads widely. Climate change would be a rounding error if the world reached that point.

TENSIONS ARE GOOD FOR SUSTAINABILITY

On the other hand, perhaps counterintuitively, geopolitical competition could help promote sustainability. In the 1960s, most Americans were only mildly interested in putting a man on the moon. But as a way to beat the Soviet Union, that goal became a national imperative. The space race greatly sped up investments in rockets and space travel. The same might happen with the United States and China now as they burnish their internationalist credentials. Already the world is getting into a bit of a subsidies race on green technology, as multiple countries vie for green jobs and industry. We may even have overcapacity now in solar cell production, which is bad for Western solar panel manufacturers but good for the world as a whole. If the price of solar panels continues to drop, we'll be able to speed up the transition from carbon-emitting fossil fuels. That overcapacity might hurt Chinese producers as well, but energy buyers everywhere will benefit.

The climate crisis may even benefit from some otherwise problematic dynamics. Geopolitical analysts tend to see government subsidies as a "beggar thy neighbor" policy. It's essentially a form of "stealing" jobs because with subsidies, companies shift production to one country rather than elsewhere. What's good for the first country is bad for others and likely bad in general. But we can flip that narrative when it comes to technologies that might help save humanity from environmental and social disaster. Just as the Americans and Soviets engaged in a space race with subsidies – with the result that humanity got to the moon much faster – China's solar subsidies have spurred a faster ramp up of solar power.

Even geopolitical tensions with allies can help with sustainability. The United States, through its Inflation Reduction Act, and Europe through its Green Deal, are essentially subsidizing the transition from fossil-fuel driven vehicles to electric cars. US–China tensions may sour efforts to liberalize trade generally but speed up this particular transition. Electric vehicles made in the United States, in Europe, and in China will likely get cheaper and therefore be adopted more quickly. And that's one of several technologies behind emerging industries, all scaling faster from government inducement.

A few governments are heavily subsidizing sustainability-related investments, with perhaps hundreds of billions on this energy transition over the next several years. What might look like a race to the bottom on subsidies, with "everybody doing it," might, on this view, end up being good for the world – a race to the top for humanity.

Certainly that government spending is risky. When governments start subsidizing production, they almost always make mistakes. White elephants are inevitable, resulting in overproduction and industrial restructuring. For example, when semiconductors first came out in the 1970s and got popular in the 1980s, many firms around the world started producing chips, often with subsidies and promotion from their national governments. South Korea ended up dominating memory chips, and the United States and Taiwan in high-end processors, while companies elsewhere went out of business. With any push for industrialization, we will see failures and abandoned projects. The lure of subsidies led a Taiwanese company to promise the United States to build a semiconductor plant in Wisconsin. But that plant still is an empty shell because the underlying economics didn't work.

Just because governments make mistakes in seeking to create industries doesn't necessarily mean they shouldn't do it. If governments do nothing, and society relies on the private sector, then on this view energy transition won't happen fast enough to make our economy and society sustainable. Wasteful projects and bankruptcies are inevitable, it seems.

The same is true for overproduction, where critics say that governments pushed too hard for electric vehicles and now some car companies are scaling back from EVs. They say governments gave an artificial boost that may actually undermine sustainable technologies in the eyes of consumers. Even if true, actual damage is likely to be smaller than feared. It can be difficult to get companies to invest, but once they do, costs tend to fall, and consumers come around eventually. We've known for a while that most buyers operate from pocketbook concerns such as price and reliability, not big ideas on sustainability, laissez-faire, or anything else. By helping to scale up the production of electric vehicles, governments are moving the needle on those prosaic issues, and, so the argument goes, that's going to pay off for the planet in the long run.

The critics advance another larger argument about innovation. They reckon sustainability is a huge problem solvable only with technological breakthroughs. Governments are good at promoting incremental innovation and scaling up proven technologies. But as governments grow due to geopolitical tension and industrial policy, they'll inevitable discourage the pathbreaking innovation needed to truly reach sustainability. With big governments, these critics reckon we'll get less free market entrepreneurialism than we would have otherwise.

That criticism flies in the face of history. Some of the greatest breakthroughs have been driven by government spending, often in wartime. The aircraft industry in the United States got a huge leap forward from massive production in World War II. Semiconductors came out of Cold War–driven US spending in the Defense Advanced Research Projects Agency. Yes, innovation is hard to do, and government shouldn't be directly involved. But frequently, government purchasing is what pushes people to innovate in the first place. It provides the assurance for the private sector to invest.

The most recent example was the vaccines for COVID-19. The US government guaranteed that it would buy billions of them, so it created a market. It also directed companies and resources via the Defense Production Act, legislation enacted during the Korean War. In this case, a subtle mix of incentives and resource direction worked.

Government has tended to be involved in great innovations. Take Alexander Graham Bell making telephones work. Without government subsidizing the telegraph, electrical, and then telephone wires throughout the country, his innovations would have stayed in the lab. So government has an enormous role in pushing certain pathbreaking innovations faster than these would have otherwise emerged. Government should not decide on the research to pursue, but it needs to be involved with commercializing the breakthrough. And geopolitical competition can spur that involvement.

As for any retreat from globalization, that actually started back in the mid- to late 2000s, when we had far less geopolitical tension. Deglobalization is happening mainly in manufacturing goods, not in services or in commodities, and is actually due mostly to automation. Westerners started in the 1980s buying a lot of manufactured goods from Asia, mostly because labor there was much cheaper. But the more companies automate production, the less they need labor, so the incentive to make things far away disappears – hence the greater localization and regionalization of trade since the 2000s. Producing close to home just simply makes economic sense because the cost differences aren't as large as they used to be. So geopolitics, whatever deglobalization has occurred, and trade tensions are separate, if related, dynamics with different implications for advancing sustainability.

CHINA PLUS ONE

Moreover, it isn't clear how geopolitical tensions will affect sustainability. Now let's delve into specific challenges. A consequence of this tension is "China plus one." That's a newish approach to supply chains. Even with automation and falling labor costs, many companies that sell worldwide are reluctant to end their profitable production in China. But with rising geopolitical risk, they are now looking hard for a second source: factories in Vietnam, Indonesia, Mexico, or other emerging industrial centers with low labor costs. That's distinct from reshoring, where production is so automated that the rich countries are now assembling some products at home.

This second-sourcing is happening especially in the fast-growing industries, where companies are considering new plants – including green technology with green jobs. Solar production still isn't deep into its industrial life cycle, and now there's green hydrogen and other decarbonization technologies. This shift, where people are no longer content to have everything made in China, creates opportunities for companies outside of China, and even Chinese companies operating elsewhere, as in Vietnam. Total Chinese production may not fall, but it won't grow as fast it did before.

This is happening even with China subsidizing those green industries because China Plus One is fundamentally an insurance policy. Sourcing less from China might actually increase costs, green or otherwise. But if tensions between the United States and China flare up, companies will be happy to have alternative production facilities. And diversifying the supply chain can help with other potential disruptions, including climate related.

China Plus One actually helps with sustainability overall because these industries rely less on a single country. And the competition may encourage China to invest more in sustainability as well. But so far the effects aren't large.

These and other adjustments make it likely that the net effect of geopolitical tension on sustainability is only slightly positive at best. We still need companies to help lead the way.

Companies and their business ecosystems don't operate in a vacuum – they must work within the political and geopolitical context they face. Geopolitical tensions are rising relative to previous decades, and these will surely affect efforts on sustainability. Because geopolitical rivalry can take many forms and can unfold in different ways, sweeping generalizations that geopolitics are good or bad for sustainability are unwise. Better to recognize the opportunities and constraints presented by rivalry between big countries and identify ways to advance sustainability efforts within that context.

We focused on the climate-related and broader environmental dimensions of sustainability only because the thinking here is farther along. Geopolitics may have implications for social sustainability, but less has been written on this topic. Indeed, the social aspects of sustainability may actually command support across the geopolitical divide, prompting cross-border cooperation that can be a useful counterpart to economic and national security competition. Alternatively, national differences in perspective on social matters – such as the legal treatment of different genders and sexualities – could become a wedge issue as geopolitical rivalry intensifies.

TAKEAWAYS

1. Geopolitical tensions are rising, but the net macro effect on the world's move toward sustainability is unclear. Rivalry between states could undermine or encourage this effort.

2. Some governments are putting a lot of money on the table for firms willing to advance the clean energy transition. They could promote breakthrough innovations, but many factors need to fall into place. Executives need to be mindful of durability, uncertainty, and strings attached to state support.

3. The impact of geopolitics on advancing social sustainability is harder to discern than in the case of clean energy and other environmental imperative. This could be good news for companies making plans that promote social change – especially if geopolitical rivalry in other spheres puts a premium on governments worldwide finding other goals in common.

FURTHER READING

Richard Baldwin and Dmitry Grozoubinski, "The 'WTO Rising' Imperative, *VoxEU*, 3 June 2022 https://cepr.org/voxeu/columns/wto-rising-imperative-0

James Bordoff and Meghan O'Sullivan, "Geopolitics – Not Just Summits – Will Shape the Transition to Clean Energy," *Foreign Affairs*, Jan. 18, 2024. https://www.foreignaffairs.com/united-states/geopolitics-will-shape-transition-clean-energy-climate-bordoff-osullivan

European Parliament (2022). Sustainability in the age of geopolitics. https://www.europarl.europa.eu/thinktank/en/document/EPRS_ATA(2022)679092

Shameen Prashantham and Lola Woetzel, "To Create a Greener Future, the West Can't Ignore China." *Harvard Business Review*, May–June 2024. https://hbr.org/2024/05/to-create-a-greener-future-the-west-cant-ignore-china

PART II

The Strategic Imperative

Julia Binder and Knut Haanaes

In a world where change is the only constant, the strategic imperative for sustainability is not just a theoretical construct – it's a call to action. This section of the book delves into the core strategies that will enable businesses to thrive in a future where sustainability is no longer a choice but a necessity. We invite you to explore how visionary thinking, innovative business models, and strategic foresight come together to form the foundation of sustainable business transformation.

The journey begins with envisioning the future – a critical exercise that challenges us to break free from the constraints of the present and imagine new possibilities. Have you ever found yourself constrained by the status quo, wondering how to break free from the limitations of the present to create a compelling strategy for the future? With methods such as **future-back thinking** and **scenario planning**, businesses can craft strategies that are not only resilient to change but also capable of shaping the future. These approaches are essential for developing a strategy that is forward-looking, enabling organizations to navigate uncertainty with confidence and creativity.

However, envisioning the future is just the starting point. To truly lead in sustainability, businesses must innovate at their core. This requires rethinking traditional business models and embracing **circular economy principles** that prioritize resource efficiency and waste reduction. Companies like IKEA have pioneered in this area by launching a secondhand marketplace, enabling customers to buy and sell used furniture, thereby extending the lifecycle of products and reducing waste. But innovation doesn't stop there – it extends into how we build socially inclusive businesses. IKEA's "Welcome Home" program in Belgium, for instance, addresses housing insecurity among single-parent families, demonstrating how businesses can contribute to **social impact and inclusion**, thereby tackling pressing societal challenges.

As you consider these strategies, think about the trade-offs you've faced in your own business decisions. How often have you struggled to balance short-term gains with long-term sustainability? The strategic imperative also demands a holistic view of the entire business ecosystem. From reimagining **end-to-end supply chains** to developing **sustainable brand strategies** that resonate with today's values-driven consumers, every aspect of the business must align with the principles of sustainability. Pricing sustainable products appropriately, for instance, is not just a financial decision but a strategic one that ensures these products are accessible and reflect their true value.

To fuel this transformation, **financing strategies** must evolve to support sustainable initiatives. This means not just securing capital but doing so in ways that align financial goals with sustainability outcomes. It also requires a deep understanding of **nonmarket strategies** – where agile companies play offense, not just defense. Consider Airbnb, which in the wake of the 2021 Taliban takeover of Afghanistan quickly mobilized to offer free temporary housing to 20 000 Afghan refugees. By leveraging its platform and host community, Airbnb responded to a humanitarian crisis faster than many governments and aid organizations, demonstrating the power of active, socially responsible business practices.

When it comes to managing performance, have you ever questioned whether your key performance indicators (KPIs) are truly capturing the impact you're making? The strategic imperative calls for a rigorous approach to **managing performance**, where KPIs are redefined to capture the full spectrum of sustainability – environmental and social as well as economic. The importance of clear KPIs cannot be overstated. Transparent reporting and accountability mechanisms ensure that sustainability is not just a lofty goal but a tangible reality that drives continuous improvement.

Finally, consider the role of **digital technologies and artificial intelligence** in your current strategy. Are you leveraging these tools to their full potential? They offer the potential to revolutionize how businesses operate, from optimizing supply chains to enabling real-time decision-making that enhances sustainability. By integrating these technologies into their strategies, companies not only improve efficiency but also create smarter, more sustainable business practices.

As you engage with the chapters that follow, you'll find a rich tapestry of insights and strategies that together form a comprehensive approach to sustainability. This is not a linear journey but an interconnected one, where each element – whether it's innovation, finance, performance management, or technology – contributes to a cohesive strategy that prepares your organization for the future.

The strategic imperative is more than a blueprint; it's a mindset. It challenges us to think beyond the immediate, to innovate boldly, and to act with purpose. As you explore this section, we hope you'll be inspired to not only envision a sustainable future but to lead the charge in creating it. The journey may be complex, but with the right strategies, it's one that promises not only success but lasting impact.

Chapter 5

Roadmapping with a Future-Back Approach

Knut Haanaes

Moving toward sustainability is a daunting task. There's so much your company could do, from reducing harms from its operations to bettering the lives of customers, employees, and local communities, not to mention the entire planet. But you can't do everything, and you still have to make the business work. Where to start?

Tackling any big task requires not just a plan but a roadmap that charts an effective course of action. Your path, and even the landscape, may change, but at least you know where to start and where to invest. That roadmap is essential to any strategy for successful business transformation. Conventional strategic planning can work well for high-certainty investments and actions, as planners can be reasonably confident of success and can generate a detailed course of action. That same approach won't work for sustainability, which involves enormous uncertainty. Understanding the roadmap matters more than knowing a precise path.

A roadmap is also the essential insight for figuring out what's practical for your company. Imagine where you'd like to be at a certain point in the future, and then work out the steps needed to get there. That's the essence of the "Future Back" tool pioneered by Thomas Malnight, professor emeritus of strategy and general management at IMD. It's similar to the "working backward" approach used at Amazon and other prominent companies.

I've found the tool particularly valuable for sustainability. Many of the solutions for companies to pursue might not yet exist, and it can help identify where innovation and collaboration are needed. It can also reveal opportunities for creating new value for customers and differentiating the company in the marketplace.

The tool encourages business leaders and colleagues to temporarily disengage from the complications of daily decisions and project their company into an aspirational future. From there, they can work back to the present and chart a path to far-reaching change.

HOW FUTURE BACK WORKS

How does Future Back differ from the usual corporate strategic planning? The difference starts with the time horizon and the scale. The value generated from sustainability is achievable only in the middle to long term, and it usually involves widespread change in a company, not just a new initiative here or there. Most companies have great processes and tools for short-term improvements, but few have them for bigger, longer changes.

It also differs from scenario planning, which typically looks ahead only five years (see Chapter 6) and considers multiple possible futures. Future Back is not an exercise to broaden executives' perspective on possible developments. It's a tool for creating a definite plan of action into an unclear future, usually 10–20 years ahead.

That longer horizon is crucial for sustainability. In the short term, the kinds of changes required might seem impossible. But over a decade or two, companies can pivot toward major change. Thinking that far into the future frees executives from what needs to happen today; it liberates them from current concerns to think creatively about their goals. It gives them the space to set challenging and absolute goals rather than incremental ones.

When executives think from the present forward, they become linear and traditional. Caught up in present possibilities, they compromise on timing and targets. Future Back enables them to be ambitious and leaves no room for excuses. It asks them how they will reach their target, not whether they will achieve it.

For every company, the aspirational future will look different. It will depend on company and industry realities. No company can address every, or even many, areas of sustainability. Drawing that future picture requires understanding the needs of various stakeholders. How will we prevent or mitigate climate change? What about reversing our consumption or degradation of freshwater supplies? How do we support social equity and inclusion? How do we give our employees meaningful work?

Here are examples of goals to kickstart action:

"We are in 2034, with no more virgin plastic packaging. How have we satisfied customers and still made a business?"

"We are in 2036, and our business has gone fully circular, with all our products reused into the system. How did we get there?"

"We are in 2038, and our suppliers have managed to pay their employees a living wage for families. How did that come about?"

I have carried out Future Back exercises with numerous executive teams, setting different goals depending on their industry and company. With groups of diverse participants, the following prompt can be a useful starting point: "By 2034, we turned the corner on climate change. How did that happen?"

Once people are thinking and talking about the future, they can get practical, as follows:

Step 1: Imagining where you want to be in the future

It is best to do this exercise with employees from different backgrounds and functions to get diversity in opinions and ideas. Separate small teams can go off and tackle specific elements with specialized knowledge. Yet Future Back also works individually to encourage people to think creatively and ambitiously. Just make sure everyone understands the benefits and how the process differs from traditional and scenario planning.

This first step is like brainstorming in that there are no wrong statements. Teams can get practical later; first they need to tap into their underlying emotional drive for a sustainable business and world.

Start by setting a date for how far ahead to project. Often it's around 10 years away. Shorter, and people get caught up in present concerns; longer, they risk getting unmoored from practicality altogether. The date should be detached enough from the present to enable significant and innovative thinking but still anchored in the real world.

From a sustainability perspective, determine an ideal future for your company. Where would you like your company to contribute? Think about the areas where your company is already having a special impact, such as supporting communities or setting up recycling systems. Can you take that work to the next level, such as organizing recycling for the entire industry?

Alternatively, think about where your company has a negative impact, such as carbon emissions, water use, or low wages in the supply chain. Can any of those be turned around?

This is the time to think broadly. What about the strengths you have in your company? Any company that succeeds beyond the startup phase can draw on a range of assets and people. Could you contribute to solving local or global issues? In an ideal world, where would you like your company to be leading in 10 years' time?

Based on this analysis, set one ambitious objective to reach. Make the goal absolute and without compromise, such as the examples above. Make sure it's truly ambitious and will inspire you and others to work with passion. As Paul Polman and Andrew Winston note in *Net Positive*, if you set a target for 60% renewable energy, you are also saying that 40% will still be energy from fossil fuels releasing carbon. Is that the goal you want to reach? A stretch goal, say to 80%, will also push you and your colleagues to think creatively. Choose a goal that excites the team and that you would be proud to contribute to.

If yours is a construction company, how about imagining a future without waste going to landfills or incineration? If a retail business, how about stores without plastic packaging or where customers can easily return all the plastic packaging they use? If you're in shipping, how about a future with zero net emissions?

Articulate the objective so that it feels real. Does it excite you? If not, you probably need a different goal – either more ambitious, or in a different area.

Step 2: Looking back, how did we get there?

Once the team has a good picture of the aspirational future, it's time to project yourselves into that future. Imagine you're there and you have reached your goal. Now think about what happened that enabled you to achieve it. Try to tell a story *from the future* that leads to sustainability. Encourage people to be *specific* and to think about the steps needed to achieve that outcome. You have two routes to figuring out your path.

Active. Think of the steps to get to the aspired future. Where did you invest? Which frameworks did you build? Which new business units did you create? Which products did you slash or add to your portfolio? How did you get all the employees to contribute to reaching the goal?

Think also about how your ecosystem supported you in reaching the destination. How did your suppliers contribute? Did you build new types of relationships with your customers? Was pre-competitive collaboration required? Did you cross category lines to work with new types of organizations? Think also about the role that external parties played. Did government put up supportive regulations?

Reactive. Think of shocks to the system that might have brought you to the aspired future and how this forced your company to react. For example, were there climate catastrophes that caused governments to shut down parts of the economy, similar to the COVID-19 pandemic? Was there an incumbent that changed the rules of the game? Did a social or political crisis force the company to take a different route? How did the company react to the shock, bringing it to the desired system?

A timeline, or even a visual landscape, can help lay out all the different actions and reactions that are part of the story of that desired future. You can see visually how you got there. Also helpful are frameworks to prod fresh thinking, as well as templates covering the key questions that will help people think through a roadmap.

Step 3: Planning a pathway to the future

Once you have a good picture of the aspirational future, it is time to return to the here and now. Consider which of the steps in the story you could make happen today. Think about products and service models you could develop, ways to leverage your resources differently from today, and possible partners you could collaborate with. Consider how you could influence change at a political or societal level. What other concrete moves, now or soon, could you make to move along the path? Could you adapt, extend, or add to your current business goals? Finally, could you develop new key performance indicators (KPIs) to ensure that your objectives are clear and measurable?

This is a process, not a quick endeavor. Give groups time to discuss and develop a deliverable. Encourage them to work collaboratively and to think creatively. You might have separate groups working on posters that can be shared in plenary for discussion and learnings. Groups come back together and share their narratives, allowing everyone to learn from each other and understand the different approaches.

All of this effort is essential, even the dead ends and rejected paths. Make sure to summarize the discussion. Emphasize what you've learned; don't rush into a solution. Everyone should feel heard. Emphasize the Future Back's "can do" mindset, where almost everything is possible if present realities do not constrain us. Emotionally engaging people matters almost as much as having a "realistic" path. When people are fully engaged, they can overcome even big challenges.

Future Back starts with a long-term perspective, but most discussions focus on that initial path, getting started. Those discussions often include questions on the players. Who are the main participants in moving toward sustainability? What role will stakeholders play? And most of all, how much is on the company, as opposed to those other players. Progress in most areas of sustainability will require a team approach.

FUTURE BACK IN PRACTICE

I've seen many companies shifting their strategy toward long-term goals and acknowledging the need to improve their long-term planning toolkit. They might be adept at short-term goals but lost at sea in approaching visionary gains that require investment over a long period with minimal returns for years.

A construction company used Future Back to expand its attention to emerging opportunities. It aimed to lead in sustainable practice and found potential in building renewable energy plants and collaborating to expand recycling. Its leaders had been aware of these avenues, along with a variety of ecofriendly technologies, but only with Future Back did they integrate them into a roadmap.

An engineering firm had no special commitment to sustainability, but the partners aspired to lead in urban innovation. They were already planning to invest in smart city technologies and to cooperate with urban planners. The Future Back process prompted them to add sustainable construction expertise, as well as specific goals around conserving resources, to those plans.

On the social side, a financial institution looked to lead in drawing in "unbanked" people missing out on the benefits of inclusion. Future Back led it to sharpen its investments in digital infrastructure, community partnerships, and tailored financial products.

WORKING BACKWARD

Future Back might seem a new tool, but versions of it have been around for a while. It's even a mainstay of personal fulfillment. Warren Buffett, among many others, told people, "You should write your obituary and then try to figure out how to live up to it." He then added something relevant to organizations too: "That's something you get wiser on as you go along." Your resources and expertise develop with time as well. The farther you go on your path to sustainability, even with many twists and turns, the better you'll be at tacking the challenge. You'll likely discover new roadblocks, but you'll build confidence, momentum, and yes, wisdom, over time.

Amazon calls this process "working backwards." Employees with an idea for a new product or service don't start with a pitch or budget request. Instead they compose a detailed press release describing the problem that this new offering solves. They explain why existing approaches aren't good enough and how this new solution benefits customers. It's the opposite of popular agile "minimum viable product" thinking that has companies trying out ideas as soon as possible in the marketplace and investing in what sticks. It's hard to argue with Amazon's results: from e-readers (Kindle) to personal speakers (Alexa) to the Cloud (AWS), this seemingly narrow e-tailer has been among the most innovative companies in the past few decades.

Microsoft took a Future Back approach to developing its climate transition plan. The aspiration was to achieve carbon negativity by 2030. Additionally, the company pledged to remove all the carbon it emitted directly or through electrical consumption since its establishment in 1975 by the year 2050. This target was considered innovative by UNFCCC because it was the first corporate goal to commit to eliminating historical emissions, effectively offsetting the company's impact on the climate since its inception. That goal not only aligns with global emission reduction pathways but also introduces the principles of climate justice and equity.

While the rapid expansion of power-hungry AI has affected Microsoft's plans, the company is still working backwards to the long-term goal. It is exploring different technologies and solutions, from abatement to carbon credit, and it is learning and adjusting. The Future Back approach gives optionality, as some technologies will emerge over time.

These examples show the tool helping companies navigate challenges with great risk and uncertainty. That's certainly true of sustainability, an area that will require much engagement and flexibility – but with an eye to a desired future.

Roadmapping for sustainability necessarily requires a great deal of ambition and creativity. Some companies already excel at using the Future Back concept. But all organizations can use it to play a role in protecting our environment, supporting workers and communities, and safeguarding our shared future. The key is identifying the most relevant levers for your business and industry and setting demanding goals.

TAKEAWAYS

1. Climate change and other sustainability pressures involve so much uncertainty that conventional strategic planning won't work here; instead, companies are better off with Future Bank planning.

2. Future Back starts with imagining an aspirational future on sustainability and then planning how to get there.

3. Companies and individuals have used versions of Future Back to develop remarkably innovative and effective plans despite uncertainty.

FURTHER READING

Colin Bryar and Bill Carr, *Working Backwards: Insights, Stories and Secret from Inside Amazon*, New York: St. Martin's Press, 2021.

Knut Haanaes and Bryony Jansen van Tuyll, "Set An Ambitious Goal, Then Work Backward to Achieve It," *I by IMD*, Sept.-Nov. 2023.

Chapter 6

Scenario Planning

Hischam El-Agamy

The last five years have reinforced the imperative for business leaders to incorporate uncertainty in their strategic planning. Doing so requires a paradigm shift in decision-making. This is especially true in the move toward sustainability, which involves enormous uncertainty. While understanding climate change involves learning from the past, it is also urges us to be "forward looking" – to anticipate plausible but unprecedented conditions and expect surprises.

The COVID-19 pandemic and other recent ordeals show that companies remain ill-equipped to confront the uncertainties that the future will bring. Companies need to not merely react but actively prepare for this unpredictable future. Leaders who candidly acknowledge uncertainty can steer their organizations and people through challenges while seizing new opportunities. Scenario planning is ideal for acknowledging uncertainties while still moving forward and committing resources.

HOW CAN LEADERS FACE UNCERTAINTY?

Over a hundred years ago, in 1921, the economist Frank H. Knight distinguished between two types of uncertainty:

1. "Uncertainty risk," in which we know potential outcomes in advance and may even know the odds of these outcomes. Think of rolling a pair of dice, as we know the odds before we roll in a game.

2. "Genuine uncertainty," in which we don't know the possible outcomes in advance, let alone their probabilities. This is often the case in complex systems, where many actors and forces interact over time, such as geopolitics, economies, societal transformations, environmental forces and, undoubtedly, technological changes.

Knight's critical point is this: genuine uncertainty creates opportunities for profit that are not eliminated by perfect competition. Rivals can't assess the odds in advance, so only those that can deal with uncertainty will prevail. In other words, if we want to innovate successfully in business, we must not only deal with uncertainty but seek it out.

In *Mind of a Fox* (2001), Chantell Ilbury and Clem Sunter offer a useful matrix for how people think about events and uncertainty (Figure 6.1). They combine two continua: certainty/uncertainty and control/absence of control.

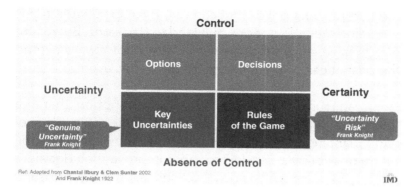

Figure 6.1   How Humans Think about Uncertainty.

At the bottom of this matrix, two areas map to Knight's thinking on uncertainty. "Rules of the game" are for events that are certain but out of our control, like public opinion and demographic factors. They may have knowable odds akin to Knight's uncertainty risk. "Key uncertainties" are uncertain and out of our control, akin to Knight's genuine uncertainty.

Decision-makers prefer the top of this matrix, where they have some control and can make commitments. So the challenge is to use the outcomes of scenario planning to move up to the "Options" quadrant that will drive to decisions. Strategic planning builds on analysis of past and current strengths, but future uncertainty is ignored. As Michael Jefferson, former chief economist of the Royal Dutch Shell Group, wrote, "Traditional economic theory has been developed in relation to general equilibrium, perfect competition, market clearance and other notions which do little to reflect uncertainty and imperfect knowledge."

In most organizations, options come from forecasting methods that consider the future as the extension of the past with some variations. It looks like the analysis performed to forecast product prices that can vary over specified ranges, providing multiple options that lead to decisions. But recent events have shown that the future does not always extend the past; it can bring unexpected disruptive events.

How can companies shake off this assumption that the future will generally be an extension? They can apply scenario planning, which creates options that better match the future possibilities. Leaders can thus improve their decision-making by assessing various scenarios, thereby boosting their organizations' readiness for a range of possible futures.

SCENARIO PLANNING FOR CLIMATE CHANGE

Modern scenario planning comes from the American game theorist and futurist Herman Kahn, who introduced the tool to the US military in the 1950s while consulting for the Rand Corporation. Then in the early 1970s, Pierre Wack adapted scenario planning to private-sector strategy in his job at Royal Dutch Shell. Wack's work was said to help the giant company anticipate two oil shocks in a decade. He described scenario planning as "a discipline for encouraging creative and entrepreneurial thinking and action . . . in contexts of change, complexity, and uncertainty."

In recent decades, scenario planning has enabled many organizations to become more agile, resilient, and prepared for future uncertainties. By drawing on advanced technologies and focusing on sector-specific challenges, businesses can better navigate the complexities of today's dynamic environment.

Since the pandemic, companies applying scenario planning have seen the need for greater resilience in their businesses.

With an eye to sustainability, they are building stronger supply chains and preparing for disruptions.

Scenario planning is not a solution; it is a method to help organizations envision and prepare for potential future events. Unlike traditional forecasting, which attempts to predict a single likely outcome based on current and past trends, scenario planning considers a range of plausible futures. This approach allows organizations to develop flexible strategies that can be adapted as the future unfolds.

Scenario planning is particularly valuable in the context of sustainability. It enables organizations to anticipate and mitigate risks associated with environmental and social challenges, such as water stress, inequality, and climate changes.

Forecasting and scenario planning are often confused, but they serve different purposes. Forecasting uses historical data and trends to predict a single likely outcome. It's a linear process that works well in stable, predictable environments. Especially in the context of sustainability, we need to apply more scenario planning, as the future is highly uncertain and influenced by numerous variables, making traditional forecasting less effective.

The International Panel on Climate Change pointed out that "a scenario is a coherent, internally consistent and plausible description of a possible future state of the world. It is not a forecast; rather, each scenario is one alternative image of how the future can unfold." (IPCC 2000)

For the Global Business Network, "scenarios are stories about how the future might unfold for our organizations, our communities and our world. Scenarios are not predictions. Rather, they are provocative and plausible accounts of how relevant external forces—such as the future political environment, scientific and technological developments, social dynamics, and economic conditions—might interact and evolve, providing our organizations with different challenges and opportunities." Global Business Network, What If? The Art of Scenario Thinking for Nonprofits (2004).

SCENARIOS FOR SUSTAINABILITY

By applying scenario planning, organizations can boost their move to sustainability. This strategic approach not only protects the organization but also contributes to broader efforts to create a resilient future for the enterprise and the society.

Scenario planning embraces uncertainty by exploring multiple, diverse future scenarios. It considers a wide range of possibilities, from the most optimistic to the most pessimistic, and helps companies prepare for each.

The first phase is to identify the primary factors that will influence future conditions. Climate-related issues, for example, might involve greenhouse gas emissions, regulatory changes, technological advancements, and social attitudes towards sustainability.

While analyzing the driving forces, leaders need to resist the temptation to focus on internal dynamics. With an "outside-in" approach, they can start with megatrends on social change, disruptive technology, economic shifts, environmental drift, urbanization, and regulations. These trends influence the industry ecosystems where companies operate, encompassing industry dynamics, market shifts, new consumer behaviors, new competitors' moves, and stakeholders' developments. From there, the analysis will focus on the enterprise level, analyzing the trends

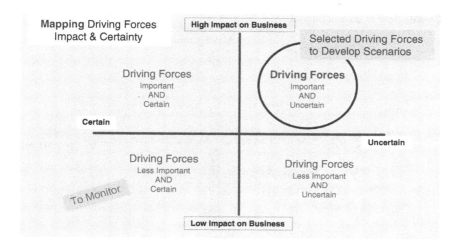

Figure 6.2   **Mapping Driving Forces**

around products, services, operations, financial structure, branding, and business models. This approach ensures that scenarios are relevant and responsive to the changing environment.

Once leaders identify these factors, they can translate them into driving forces and map them by their potential impact on the business's degree of uncertainty (Figure 6.2).

Successful scenario planning comes from the driving forces that are both important for the business and highly uncertain. Selecting these forces is a critical phase in developing scenarios.

The two most important drivers, with high impact and high uncertainty, become the basis for building scenarios. Leaders can display these on vertical and horizontal axes, with low and high values for each, to create four scenarios (Figure 6.3). They can then develop a narrative, or story, to

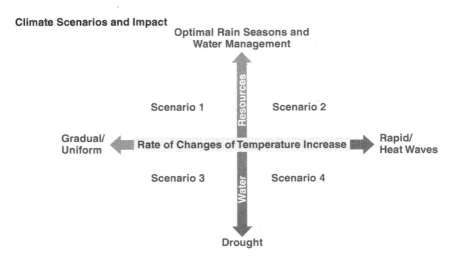

Figure 6.3 Examples of Climate Scenarios

fit that scenario. The process enables them to imagine various plausible futures and revise mental models of the present based on those futures. They can then use those models to reinforce or change the organization's strategies, and increase its readiness to face the various futures.

The scenario teams will assess the potential impacts of each scenario on the organization. Consider how issues such as water stress and climate change could affect operations, supply chains, and stakeholder relationships. Also uncertain is the level of technological innovation in, say, renewable energy or low-carbon materials over the next few years.

The scenarios can help managers develop strategy but also become part of ongoing analysis about the future, with regular monitoring of outside trends. As conditions change and new information is developed, analysts may wish to create new scenarios with additional or different variables.

This technique can also help in projecting those trends. In studying climate change, scenarios enable scientists to convey the potential impacts of uncertain factors, offering decision-makers clear, actionable insight.

In the interpretation phase, the scenario team develops strategic responses for each scenario to mitigate risks and capitalize on opportunities. This might involve investing in new technologies, diversifying supply chains, or advocating for favorable regulations.

As the team analyzes the impact of each scenario, it is crucial to recognize the interconnected challenges between climate change and essential resources: food, energy, and water (Figure 6.4). The effective management of these resources is closely tied to environmental protection.

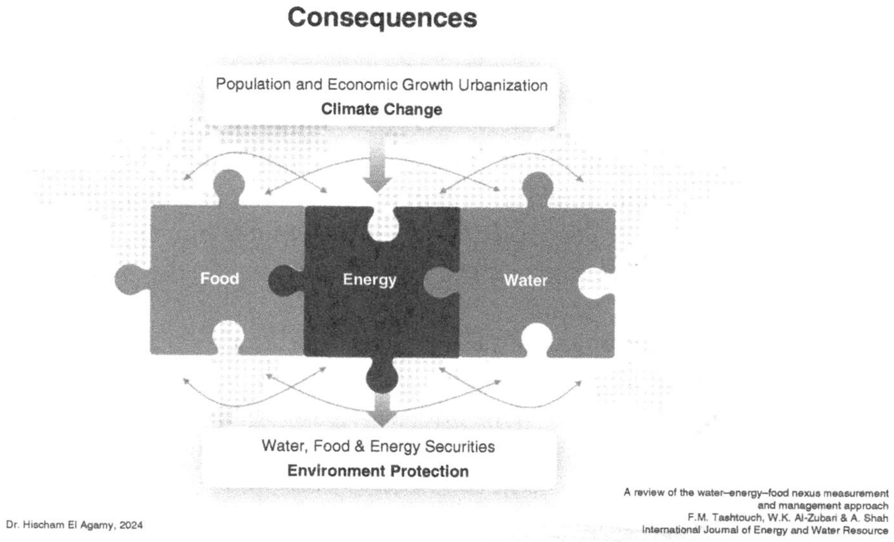

Consequences

Population and Economic Growth Urbanization
Climate Change

Food   Energy   Water

Water, Food & Energy Securities
Environment Protection

A review of the water–energy–food nexus measurement and management approach
F.M. Tashtouch, W.K. Al-Zubari & A. Shah
International Journal of Energy and Water Resource

Dr. Hischam El Agamy, 2024

Figure 6.4   Interdependency of Essential Resources

LEARNING FROM SCENARIO PLANNING

Indeed, business leaders can learn from government agencies and nonprofit organizations that are already applying scenario planning on climate change. Natural reserves and protection organizations use it to anticipate future challenges and develop strategies to safeguard their assets and biodiversity. The United States's Yellowstone National Park, for example, has worked to address potential impacts of climate change, including shifts in ecosystems, fire regimes, and water availability. The park's management explores different future scenarios to develop adaptive strategies that ensure the protection of its diverse habitats and species.

South Africa's Kruger National Park employs scenario planning to address climate change, poaching, and habitat fragmentation. By exploring different future scenarios, the park develops strategies to maintain its wildlife populations and biodiversity.

The World Wildlife Fund (WWF) uses it to address global environmental challenges such as deforestation, climate change, and species extinction. By exploring various scenarios, WWF can prioritize conservation efforts, develop adaptive strategies, and advocate for sustainable policies.

As for companies, Shell has continued to develop scenarios since the 1970s. In recent years, it has used scenarios to explore future energy pathways, including a transition to lower-carbon energy systems. The company's "Sky" scenario outlines a vision of the world meeting the goals of the Paris Agreement by 2070.

Unilever Group uses scenario planning to anticipate and prepare for future environmental and social challenges. The company's "Sustainable Living Plan" integrates scenario planning to address issues such as resource scarcity, climate change, and sustainable sourcing. Unilever's scenarios help in making strategic decisions that align with long-term sustainability goals.

Nike uses scenarios to evaluate the impact of climate change on its supply chain, particularly focusing on water scarcity and material sourcing. Mars, Inc. uses them to address sustainability challenges, particularly in its agricultural supply chain. The company explores scenarios related to climate change, water scarcity, and deforestation. These scenarios guide Mars in developing strategies to ensure the long-term sustainability of its raw material sources.

General Electric's Vernova spinoff uses scenario planning to explore the future of energy systems and the transition to renewable energy sources. The company's scenarios help in understanding how different policy, economic, and technological trends might shape the energy landscape and affect its business strategy.

The recent evolution and events of the last five years have underscored the importance of actively preparing for unpredictable futures. The increasing complexities of sustainability demand a forward-looking approach to anticipate and manage unprecedented conditions. Scenario planning is increasingly adopted as a vital tool to enhance decision-making by preparing for various potential futures and understanding an ever-changing environment.

Companies are now increasingly applying scenario planning to sustainability challenges. With this tool, they can better anticipate and mitigate related risks, ensuring more resilient and sustainable operations. By incorporating scenario planning into strategic frameworks, companies can identify potential threats and opportunities, and develop adaptive strategies. They can better manage risks while seizing opportunities from evolving environmental and social landscapes.

FURTHER READING

Thomas Chermack, *Foundations of Scenario Planning: The Story of Pierre Wack*, Routledge, 2017.

Hischam El-Agamy, "Back to the Future: The Case for Scenario Planning," *I by IMD*, 26 January 2024.

Intergovernmental Panel on Climate Change (IPCC), "Special Report on Emissions Scenarios: Summary for Policymakers," 2000.

Peter Schwartz, *The Art of the Long View: Planning for the Future in an Uncertain World*, Currency Doubleday, 1991.

Pierre Wack, "Scenarios: Uncharted Waters Ahead," *Harvard Business Review*, September 1985.

Chapter 7

Innovating Toward New Business Models

Julia Binder

Innovation is often surprisingly underemphasized in the realm of sustainable business transformation. To truly transition from the traditional "take-make-waste" model to one that thrives in a resource-constrained world, we need to embrace transformative innovation. Incremental improvements are insufficient for achieving long-term sustainability. Gains in efficiency, equity, or reductions in emissions and water use are vulnerable to changes in mindset, regulations, or market prices. Instead, companies must adopt business models that generate new kinds of value and drive growth through their operations.

The circular economy offers such a transformative new model, one that promises to redefine value creation by focusing on sustainability and resource efficiency. It is an economic system aimed at eliminating waste and the continual use of resources through principles of reuse, repair, refurbishment, and recycling. Several companies have already demonstrated the transformative potential of these models to generate both environmental and economic value. We describe five circular business models and some compelling company examples in this chapter.

Adopting these models requires future-ready and aware business leaders who recognize the potential of circular business models not only to address sustainability but also as a significant market opportunity. Many companies are currently experimenting with various innovations, but often these efforts are more about satisfying regulatory requirements or public expectations – essentially maintaining their license to operate – rather than truly transforming their operations to make a significant societal impact. Much of what passes for innovation today is merely business as usual with a sustainability veneer.

We also observe a second major challenge: excess caution. Even when companies pursue serious experiments in sustainability, they frequently fail to scale them up. Due to widespread uncertainty, businesses tend to spread small investments across many initiatives rather than focusing resources on the most promising ones. This approach prevents substantial progress and transformation.

How can companies do better? The solution is not about overhauling current operations. Instead, it's about supplementing or adjusting existing business models to generate value in new ways. This requires a disciplined approach to innovation, where companies prioritize scalable and transformative initiatives over incremental and superficial changes.

By embracing transformative innovation and learning from the successful models of leading companies, businesses can navigate the challenges of a resource-constrained world and contribute to a truly sustainable economy. This chapter highlights the strategies and models that hold the greatest promise for meaningful and lasting change.

CIRCULAR BUSINESS MODEL ARCHETYPES

In a truly circular economy, it is no longer enough for businesses to just focus on making a profit. Instead each organization aspires to make a positive difference in the world. Business models must create both environmental and economic value. Circular business models are uniquely positioned to achieve this dual objective by decarbonizing, dematerializing, and supporting the regeneration of damaged natural systems, while also being commercially viable and contributing to profitability and resilience.

This convergence of environmental and business impacts – what we refer to as "net impact" – can lead to improved customer experience and loyalty, access to new value pools and price premiums, enhanced cost competitiveness, and overall supply chain resilience and risk reduction. Organizations can

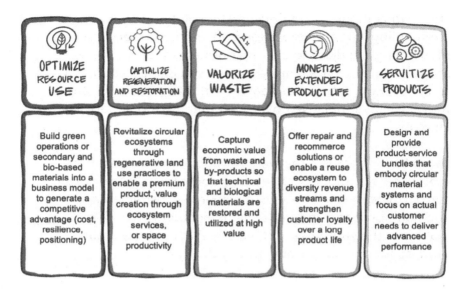

Figure 7.1   Circular business model archetypes by Binder and Braun, 2024,
The Circular Business Revolution.

start the strategic journey to circularity by exploring, developing, and scaling commercially viable, circular business models. This means seeking out ways of doing business that capture economic value by prioritizing resource productivity, circularity, and regenerative design.

1. *Optimize resource use.* This business model archetype focuses on greening operations and replacing problematic materials with sustainable ones to generate a competitive advantage. It goes beyond boosting efficiency to reduce carbon emissions or freshwater consumption. For example, BMW uses recycled aluminum, plastic, and other secondary material inputs for many of its car parts instead of "virgin" materials, promoting circularity and reducing costs as they scale up. Additionally, this model includes using bio-based alternatives to fossil fuels input materials. Although this approach may be a stepping

stone to more innovative models, it is still a crucial part of the journey toward circularity.

2. *Capitalize regeneration and restoration.* As businesses increasingly recognize the importance of nature's services, a new model is emerging that integrates ecological revitalization into economic strategies. This approach encourages investment in projects that not only drive economic growth but also contribute to environmental restoration and ecosystem revitalization. Companies are discovering that regenerating natural systems can boost their economic success and bolster natural capital simultaneously.

   Slow Forest Coffee exemplifies this regenerative approach by combining agroforestry-based coffee production with a direct business-to-business (B2B) model. Instead of relying on conventional industrial farming methods, which often deplete soil and reduce biodiversity, Slow Forest Coffee integrates trees and crops in a way that enhances soil health and ecosystem resilience. By supplying artisan coffee directly from the farm to businesses, they maximize their positive impact on the environment. Trees provide essential shade for coffee plants, reduce erosion, and create habitats for wildlife, demonstrating how sustainable practices can align with economic success.

   Similarly, Veja Shoes has made significant strides in incorporating regenerative practices into its operations. Founded in the early 2000s, Veja invests in a natural rubber value chain in Brazil, where they purchase native rubber from Acre's tappers. This support for traditional rubber tapping helps protect forests and supports local communities. Veja's commitment includes paying above-market prices and implementing a Payment for Social Environmental Services program that encourages adherence to environmental standards, thereby discouraging deforestation and promoting forest conservation.

By doing so, Veja not only advances sustainability but also meets the growing demand for ecofriendly products.

These examples illustrate how businesses can capitalize on the services of nature, integrating ecosystem preservation into their models and thereby creating new revenue streams through premium pricing and enhanced brand value.

3. *Valorize waste.* Beyond the traditional approach of recycling, companies are increasingly exploring ways to close the loop by capturing economic value from discarded items, materials, and byproducts. This business model is at the heart of the circular economy. Can companies create new possibilities from elements that would otherwise just add to the cost of disposal?

Consider McDonald's, which faces significant waste management challenges due to its large volumes of cooking oil. Disposing of this oil is costly and environmentally problematic because it cannot simply be poured down the drain – it would clog pipes. However, McDonald's has turned this challenge into an opportunity by selling their used cooking oil to Neste, a Finnish company specializing in renewable fuels. Neste refines the oil into renewable fuel, which McDonald's then purchases to power their vehicles. In this case, waste transforms into a valuable resource, demonstrating how companies can effectively close the loop and create new value streams.

Another example comes from the Netherlands, where tulips are a major industry. Tulip production generates substantial waste not only from wilting flowers but also from the removal of flower heads to harvest the bulbs. Traditionally, these heads were composted, but now farmers have found a more profitable use. By selling the flower heads to processors that extract valuable pigments, they turn what was once a waste product into a marketable bio-based ingredient for paint. This shift has created an additional revenue stream for tulip farmers and demonstrates the potential for waste valorization in agricultural sectors.

In both of these examples, success hinges on collaboration and infrastructure. McDonald's relies on Neste and other fast-food chains to aggregate enough used cooking oil to make the process viable. Likewise, tulip farmers depend on a specialized exchange platform and pigment processors to create a market for their discarded heads.

Sometimes, valorizing waste requires an initial investment but can lead to significant returns. For instance, large pig and dairy farms often collect manure in lagoons. Traditionally, this waste was sprayed as fertilizer, but covering the lagoons to prevent odor has led to an unexpected benefit: anaerobic digestion produces methane gas. With an upfront investment in methane capture technology, farmers can convert this gas into energy, powering their operations or selling it to local utilities. This transformation of a waste problem into a revenue source highlights how even environmental challenges can become opportunities with the right investment.

It seems simple, something companies should already be working on. But most companies have settled into relying on their traditional value chains, linear product designs, and minimal logistical infrastructure. Valorizing waste often requires rethinking the entire production process. If a material can't be made valuable after initial use, then the company can explore alternative inputs.

4. *Monetize extended product lives.* This model involves offering repair and re-commerce solutions that enable broad reuse of a product. Most companies have narrow revenue streams. By extending the lives of their products, they can diversify those streams.

Extending product lives typically means repairing, refurbishing, updating, and modularizing products to make them fully functional for years to come. But manufacturers can also directly resell a product through a "take back and reuse" process. Or they can cooperate with resellers and build relationships with secondary buyers.

For example, Siemens Healthineers offers an extensive refurbishing program for its medical imaging and therapy systems under the Ecoline brand. These systems are refurbished to certified standards, ensuring performance and value. This program allows Siemens to provide high-quality, cost-effective equipment to markets that might not afford new devices, thus tapping into secondary markets. This approach not only diversifies Siemens's revenue streams but also strengthens customer relationships and market presence. By offering refurbished products, Siemens gains valuable insights into the full lifecycle of their equipment, which can inform future product design and innovations. The strategic move into the refurbishing and resale market exemplifies how extending product lives can be both environmentally beneficial *and* commercially viable.

Similarly, Vestas refurbishes old windmill blades for reuse in new or existing windmills, maintaining customer relationships and learning about usage trends to offer tailored solutions. This practice exemplifies how extending product life can support sustainability and business growth.

5. *Servitization.* This business model can be seen as the ultimate goal of a sustainable business model transformation because it shifts consumption from ownership to access. Why should consumers (companies and individuals) own something if they can have reliable and convenient access to the products whenever they like? At its core the circular economy is about less ownership, less production, and greater circulation of everything we do

make. Instead of focusing on selling the product, companies make money by handling access to the product – with lower costs and higher margins.

A familiar example is ride sharing. Instead of owning a car, consumers can use services like Uber or Zipcar, gaining reliable transportation without the need for personal vehicle ownership. This model benefits both consumers and providers by reducing the number of vehicles needed and promoting more efficient use of resources.

However, servitization extends far beyond sharing economy models. Companies now offer a wide range of products-as-a-service, either for a certain duration, or aligned with certain performance requirements. A family might purchase a performance service, say air conditioning in its flat at 25°C in the summer months. The family pays only for the service, and the provider takes responsibility for delivering it in the most efficient way.

Servitization also delivers a competitive advantage to providers willing to take the step. They gain some leverage in the marketplace, as customers rely on them, rather than cheaper rivals, because only they offer the full service package.

In some cases, servitization can even lead to reduced consumption. Since the 1990s, Interface has offered carpeting as a service. Instead of purchasing carpets outright, companies subscribe to carpeting services. Interface is responsible for maintenance and replacement. By inspecting carpets regularly, Interface realized that only high-traffic areas wear out quickly. They developed carpet squares, allowing for the replacement of only worn-out sections, thus reducing overall consumption and minimizing disruption for clients.

Servitization is the most powerful ally of circularity. Producers can design products for disassembly and take-back, knowing when and how they will reclaim their products. This foresight changes the traditional linear model of production and disposal, promoting a more sustainable, circular approach to business. By rethinking their entire production processes, companies can explore alternative inputs and design products with end-of-life considerations in mind.

EMBRACING SUSTAINABLE BUSINESS MODELS

Adopting sustainable business models involves some inherent risk. What if customers or suppliers resist the new approach? Small-scale experiments often fail to predict large-scale outcomes. Most companies prefer low-risk, incremental changes and may hire consultancies for insights. However, knowledge alone isn't enough; companies need to make strategic investments to mitigate risk and drive success.

Perhaps the most crucial investment is in design. Studies show that 80% of a product's environmental footprint is determined at the design stage. No matter how efficient operations become, design remains paramount. Most designers are trained to optimize for cost and performance, not sustainability. By incorporating sustainability into the design process, companies can expand their innovation potential. Upskilling the design team to consider environmental impacts can lead to more sustainable offerings.

Another crucial investment is in digital technology. This investment isn't solely about boosting efficiency, though that's always beneficial. It's primarily about uncovering valuable information. Digital sensors can provide insights into pricing and cost dynamics, revealing effective business models. They also offer visibility into product materials and customer usage patterns. While many companies already invest in digital technology, directing these investments towards sustainability is essential.

Customer centricity is also critical, particularly in the context of sustainable innovation. While focusing on environmental value is essential, it is not sufficient for success. Sustainable products or services must address customer needs better than existing alternatives. An intense focus on customers has two main advantages. First, it helps companies understand what customers genuinely need and how they use products, informing new business models. Second, it ensures that sustainability innovations align with customer preferences. Too often, brilliant ideas fail because they don't resonate with customers. Companies must start with what customers care about and design sustainable products that meet those needs effectively.

Investment in people is equally important. This involves upskilling existing employees and hiring new talent with the necessary expertise in circularity and sustainability. Companies need a workforce that understands the principles of sustainable design, digital technology, and customer-centric innovation. Leadership must also foster a mindset and behavioral changes that prioritize sustainability. By investing in training programs and creating a culture that values sustainability, companies can ensure that their teams are equipped to drive and support sustainable initiatives.

Another necessary investment is in creating an ecosystem. Sustainable business models almost always require collaboration with partners – willing suppliers, collaborators, customers, and sometimes all three. Sustainability is rarely achieved by a single company; it requires optimizing the entire value chain to use fewer resources and reduce pollution. Companies must build or join ecosystems to innovate effectively.

Fortunately, many knowledge-based, sharing-based, and platform-based companies have emerged to help create and facilitate these ecosystems. From Schneider Electric on energy, to Johnson Controls on building, and Trove on used garments, companies don't need to recreate the wheel with these models.

That's the biggest advice here: companies can't innovate in isolation; they must do so in collaboration. Piecemeal improvements are certainly important. But embracing a new business model adds the discipline and resources that companies often need to make the moves that pay off in big gains for sustainability.

Investing in sustainable business models not only reduces the risk associated with these new approaches but also positions companies for success. While many companies proceed cautiously, sustainability is no longer a mere option; it is crucial for long-term economic viability. As sustainability becomes the defining growth area of the coming decades, businesses that decisively pursue sustainable practices will be at the forefront of this transformation.

These companies will not only improve efficiency and reduce their carbon footprint but will also drive substantial advancements that lead to increased revenue and margins. By embracing sustainability, companies can unlock new opportunities, foster innovation, and build resilience against future challenges. The companies that take bold steps towards sustainability will set themselves apart, becoming leaders in an increasingly eco-conscious market and ensuring their prosperity in a rapidly evolving economic landscape.

The time for cautious optimism is over; the era of proactive, sustainability-driven business is here. Leaders must champion the necessary investments in design, digital technology, customer-centricity, people, and ecosystem collaboration. By doing so, they will earn their "license to innovate," unleashing their potential to create groundbreaking business models that deliver the highest net impact in both environmental and economic value.

TAKEAWAYS

1. **Move Beyond Incremental Improvements**
   Push beyond quick wins to focus on challenging the status quo and opening up transformative market opportunities

2. **Focus on Scaling the Right Innovations**
   Prioritize the most promising initiatives instead of spreading resources thinly across numerous small projects.

3. **Build Collaborative Ecosystems for Sustainability**
   Develop and strengthen partnerships across your value chain, to promote collaboration. Leadership in building these ecosystems is essential.

FURTHER READING

Julia Binder and Manuel Braun, *The Circular Business Revolution: A Practical Framework for Sustainable Business Models*, London: Pearson/FT Publishing, 2024.

Knut Haanaes et al., "How to Make Money on Sustainability," *I by IMD*, 2 September 2024.

Chapter 8

Models for Social Sustainability

Sophie Bacq, Vanina Farber, and
Patrick Reichert

With climate change and economic inequality intensifying global challenges, the imperative for companies to create social impact and foster inclusion has never been more critical. Firms can offer a pathway to a more prosperous, equitable, and sustainable future. But while climate change may be the greatest challenge of our time, it is also most likely to affect people already suffering from social and economic exclusion and other disadvantages.

Indeed, the lowest-income countries produce only one-tenth of the world's greenhouse gas emissions, yet they are hurting the most from climate change. Vulnerable populations in these countries suffer from shortages of appropriate solutions in terms of health, food and water, education, and more.

Worldwide, in recent decades, the income gap between the wealthy and everyone else has widened. Too many citizens still lack the means to thrive in their economies, whether developing or developed. Yet while many feel excluded, the success of climate change actions depends on changes in human behavior. To create a sustainable future for society, there is no shortcut but the necessity to include more people.

Business models geared toward inclusion and social impact come with a great deal of complexity and uncertainty. Social impact refers to a significant, positive change that addresses a pressing societal challenge. Creating social impact means taking care of stakeholders – especially employees, customers, and local communities – by sharing with them, along with investors, some of the economic and noneconomic rewards (such as better health and a sense of pride). How to do that, with satisfactory returns for both investors and broader stakeholders, is no easy task.

Social impact is also notoriously tough to measure, as it is inherently complex and context-dependent. Nevertheless, frameworks such as Theory of Change and Social Return on Investment (SROI), and standards such as IRIS and the United Nation's Sustainable Development Goals (SDGs), provide structured and widely adopted methods to assess and report on impact.

The fundamental idea is that when companies include stakeholders better, they are more productive and innovative, while also contributing to the longevity of our people and planet. Conventional business models are generally good for economic growth, and over time, some of those gains are shared with stakeholders – yet that is often an afterthought more than a commitment. Stakeholder inclusion, by contrast, is an investment that pays off over time, requiring a long-term perspective. It creates wealth for companies and their investors, for stakeholders, and for society as a whole.

CIVIC WEALTH CREATION

Inclusion is not simply about giving stakeholders more of the pie. It gives all individuals, particularly those marginalized or disadvantaged, equitable access to opportunities, resources, and decision-making processes within a society or organization. Getting there is about co-creating wealth and developing solutions *with* stakeholders, including local communities and innovative agents. The idea is to create not only economic but also social and communal wealth. This is, collectively called civic wealth. According to Lumpkin and Bacq (2019), civic wealth creation is the process of creating wealth that goes beyond money and material possessions and is shared with multiple stakeholders.

Take the retail giant IKEA, which in recent years has laid out a global sustainability strategy. The strategy focuses on healthy and sustainable living, climate-positive circularity, and fairness and equality. In order for the company to thrive in the future, its leaders have said they need strong societies and economies buttressed by good environmental conditions. For the social pillar of fairness and equality, they firmly believe that the company's size and scope provides both responsibility and great opportunities to create positive change for multiple stakeholders. So the company collaborated with nonprofits and engaged its local communities, with an eye toward vulnerable groups. While initially relying on financial donations, the vision soon shifted to applying its business strengths to tackle social problems.

One such program was "Welcome Home," launched by the company's Belgian subsidiary in 2021. A cross-functional team selected a unifying and compelling project that drew on its members' expertise in home furnishing. They identified a specific and underserved social group suffering from housing insecurity: single-parent families.

Ikea Belgium began by donating funds to La Ligue des Familles, a nonprofit organization, to collect and analyze data. With that analysis, the team, with employees from individual stores, carried out two kinds of projects. The first involved working with charitable organizations to fund "starter kits" for essential furniture for the families. The team emphasized the decision-making authority of these nonprofits, which worked with families to access the kits from non-IKEA as well as IKEA stores. The second project involved IKEA stores donating furniture to outfit single-parent-oriented shelters throughout the country. Within months, the stores were supporting seven shelters, with one shelter receiving both financial and technical assistance in developing communal spaces for single-parent families.

The next phase came a year later: encouraging (not requiring) store employees to devote some working hours to volunteering. Only 5% did, and the low turnout was due partly to the difficulty of contacting employees in warehouses and other non-desk jobs. Each volunteering session lasted three to four hours, usually helping to assemble furniture, paint, and organize living arrangements in shelters and homes. Another initiative later that year deployed IKEA interior designers to help shelters make better use of their space in welcoming the families. A side project helped run a free clothing store, furnished by the subsidiary, where single-parent families could obtain goods in exchange for volunteering a few hours of their time.

The third phase, also begun in 2022, was advocacy, where the subsidiary used its size and influence to promote positive change in government. It convened a diverse group of political consultants, social innovators, single parents, nonprofits, and other social innovators to formulate proposals and then discuss them with political leaders.

As a business decision, the results show up mostly at the stakeholder level: the subsidiary gained a reputational boost in the Belgian market, as well as greater engagement from employees. But the main purpose of the initiative was to fulfill the company's commitment to apply its size and scope to a major social problem – the lack of affordable and decent housing – with substantial noneconomic wealth created. The company's global sustainability department sees the Belgian program as a successful initiative that has inspired replication elsewhere, depending on each market's unique characteristics.

IKEA's example illustrates four key points for social impact and inclusive projects. First, large or prominent companies are more likely to feel the necessary societal imperative. Small companies are often just trying to survive and lack the resources to tackle social problems. Second, even big companies should target carefully. Rather than address a major problem entirely, they can go after only one segment of it and scale up only after success – expanding the scope of social impact over time. Third, business leaders should look for projects that match what the company already knows how to do well. Partnering with outsiders – mostly nonprofits but also for-profit enterprises if relevant (or what we call social enterprises) – enables companies to take on tasks beyond their expertise. Indeed, entrepreneurial startups often have the advantage of being more agile and prone to innovative solutions. And fourth, leaders should engage the entire workforce, not just a select team or a few volunteers. That is essential not only to achieve substantial impact, but also to spread the word about the program and gain the reputational advantage as a socially engaged company.

A targeted approach on deeper social impact also helps with learning and overcoming the inevitable problems. When the subsidiary saw the low turnout of employees for volunteering, for example, the team doubled down on recruiting. They worked to convince colleagues that anyone could volunteer, not just home furnishing experts.

Another example comes from a global food company with extensive operations in Latin America. Cheap imports were devastating one rural area, as low-income farmers gave up and fell into unemployment. The company worked with local nonprofits, providing funding and expertise to develop new crops. Together they helped the farmers not just to try out the new crops, but also to update their cultivation practices. The new crops succeeded, reinvigorating demand for local produce as well as reviving incomes throughout the region. By working with the community, the company built civic wealth. As a bonus, when the new farming practices strained the region's environment, the company then worked with the community to implement sustainable farming practices.

Rural-based Bush Brothers & Co., the largest provider of baked beans in the United States, was even more committed to the success of its community. With a shortfall in primary healthcare for nearby residents, including its own employees, the company led the conversion of a historic but vacant school building into a clinic. The move had the side benefit of reducing the company's own healthcare costs, which had been rising due to that shortfall in primary care. But the main goal, fitting the company's social impact strategy, was collective action to build up the local community.

FINANCING SOCIAL IMPACT

Impact investing finances social impact initiatives by directing capital toward projects that generate measurable social and environmental benefits alongside financial returns. This deliberate alignment ensures that social objectives remain at the forefront of investment decisions, creating sustainable models where impact and profitability go hand in hand. Although we discuss financing for sustainability in Chapter 11, it is important to highlight how multistakeholder partnerships help firms reduce the risk of impact initiatives.

One such solution is blended finance. Just as social impact projects usually require collaboration with nonprofit organizations – while drawing on for-profit resources and practices – blended finance creatively combines the work of markets (companies and investors) and nonmarket actors (governments and nongovernmental organizations). De-risking occurs through three mechanisms: identifying material social issues for firms, trust brokering from civil society and public sector actors, and catalytic capital aligning incentives through blended finance instruments.

For example, many chocolate companies were concerned about the heavy reliance on child labor in many of their cacao suppliers. As this was a material social issue for them, they had already donated money to various initiatives in the Ivory Coast and other cacao-growing countries. But these donations were too fragmented and scattered to make a difference. Nor could the companies simply switch suppliers, as child labor was pervasive on the farms, and without the work, many families might put their children into prostitution.

Jacobs Foundation, a nonprofit organization, came up with a solution. It worked with the World Cocoa Foundation, an association of large chocolatiers, to make a substantial investment in primary education in the Ivory Coast. Jacobs used $50 million of its own funding to bring in $35 million from World Cocoa Foundation members through matching grants to pay for piloting. In total, $85 million went to building a network of rural schools. Under a "pay for success" plan, the capital has gone out only as the program realized its enrollment goals.

The Transforming Education in Cocoa Communities program has so far seen rising enrollments. To date, it has helped 200 000 children. Although we won't know the full social impact until the program ends in 2030, its interim results are already being evaluated through randomized control trials, the gold standard for measuring impact. Monitoring the trials is Innovations for Poverty Action, a nonprofit that measures impact in developing contexts, including outcomes across literacy and numeracy skills as well as material, physical, and social well-being.

Blended finance is a promising path for social impact precisely because it brings together private and public actors. If transaction costs steadily decline as partnerships gain experience with various financial instruments, blended finance might eventually offer liquid securities. With $90+ trillion in capital controlled by institutional investors in Organisation for Economic Co-operation and Development (OECD) countries alone, the world can't move the needle on social impact without devising ways to de-risk these projects and offer at least satisfactory monetary returns. Of course, blended finance can't do it alone – it is part of the larger investment trend of impact investing, integrating both financial return and social impact into decision-making.

Although blended finance and impact investing offer promising avenues to finance social impact initiatives, they are not without challenges. The industry is still working on impact measurement, scalability, and potential mission drift. These issues must be addressed to ensure the financing mechanisms truly serve their intended purpose.

MANAGING TRADE-OFFS

As for building business models for social impact, companies will face different tensions. First, social and business goals may conflict. Microfinance lending, for example, has a ready trade-off between financial returns to investors and low interest rates to borrowers, who often live in remote areas and only need small amounts to borrow (providing limited opportunities for economies of scale). Early solutions to alleviate these tensions, and lower operational costs, built on the core innovation of microfinance: loans to groups of borrowers that are jointly liable for repayment of each other's loans. Achieving scale through digitalization helps as well. Kenya's M-PESA, an African mobile money service provider, took less than 10 years from its 2007 launch to reach 96% of households.

Second, a company's environmental and social goals may conflict. In Indonesia, for example, companies (with governments) have been working to shut down polluting mines and factories, in some cases before the end of the facility's useful life. Most of these operations are in remote areas and form the economic basis of local communities. Shutting down the facility is good for the environment, but it leaves many people unemployed, often with few resources to fall back on.

Similar conflicts are happening around the world as it makes the environmental transition from carbon-intensive industry. The European Green Deal aims to make Europe climate neutral by 2050, boost the economy through green technology, create sustainable industry and transport, and cut pollution. Public funding, and integrating the private sector, are critical components of the just transition. EU programs such as the Just Transition Mechanism provide targeted support. It will mobilize €55 billion from 2021 to 2027 in the most affected coal and mining regions to alleviate the socioeconomic impact of the transition.

A final trade-off is the risk of "impact washing," where stakeholders perceive actions taken to promote social and environmental impact as insincere or misleading. This risk not only threatens the credibility of the company but can also undermine trust with stakeholders. To manage this risk, companies can ensure transparency in their reporting, adopt third-party verification standards, and align their practices with their stated values.

To effectively manage these trade-offs over time, companies must adopt a systems-thinking approach. Successful companies will consider the interconnectedness of social and environmental issues, anticipating potential unintended consequences, and designing strategies that create positive feedback loops across multiple dimensions of impact. The broader umbrella term of social innovation also provides a powerful approach to navigate trade-offs. By reimagining products, services, processes or even business models, companies can create solutions that simultaneously address social needs and generate business value.

In today's interconnected world, the challenges faced by society – be it environmental degradation, social exclusion, or economic inequality – demand market-based solutions that are innovative and collaborative. Social innovation thrives not in isolation but through the collective efforts of businesses, nonprofits, governments, and communities. As the world increasingly shifts toward a stakeholder economy, it is not enough for companies to simply achieve returns for investors. Companies must also support stakeholders – employees, customers, and local communities – to overcome their challenges. With this new sense of responsibility, creating social impact and fostering social and economic inclusion becomes a central part of most companies' agendas.

WHAT LEADERS CAN DO

- *Identify material social issues.* Focus on social challenges that align with your company's core business, and address them through targeted strategies.

- *Integrate social innovation.* Involve stakeholders to find market solutions to address social and environmental challenges that are more efficient and effective.

- *Embrace civic wealth creation.* Prioritize co-creating wealth with stakeholders that extends beyond economic gains.

- *Foster strategic collaboration.* Partner with nonprofits, governments, and other businesses to leverage diverse expertise and resources for greater impact.

- *Adopt intentional financing mechanisms.* Use tools such as impact investing and blended finance to de-risk social impact projects while balancing social and financial returns.

TAKEAWAYS

1. Companies can help build civic wealth through programs that use their expertise and resources to address social needs in their communities.

2. Managing trade-offs is crucial for social impact and inclusion: companies must balance potential conflicts between social and business goals, environmental and social objectives, and the risk of "impact washing." Social innovation helps navigate these trade-offs by creating novel solutions that address the needs of multiple stakeholders simultaneously.

3. Companies can drive impactful innovation that creates wealth for multiple stakeholders while tackling pressing social and environmental issues by leveraging business expertise, resources, and collaborative partnerships.

4. Blended finance, among other kinds of social impact investing, fosters innovation and collaboration to finance pressing social needs by combining governmental, NGO, and corporate funds and networks.

FURTHER READING

Sophie Bacq and Valerie Keller-Birner, "Ikea Belgium's Welcome Home Project: From Ad Hoc to Deep Social Impact," *IMD Case Study,* May 3, 2024.

Sophie Bacq and Tom Lumpkin, "Building Bridges and Restoring Hope: How civic wealth creation is strengthening local communities through commerce and collaboration," *I by IMD,* December 2023.

Vanina Farber and Patrick Reichert, "Blended Finance and the SDGs: Using the Spectrum of Capital to de-Risk Business Model Transformation," chapter 5 in *Measuring Sustainability and CSR: From the Reporting to Decision-Making,* ed. by Slobadan Kacanski et al., Springer, 2023.

Vanina Farber and Patrick Reichert, "How to Measure Impact Using the Theory of Change," *I by IMD,* January 5, 2024

Tom Lumpkin and Sophie Bacq, "Civic Wealth Creation: A New View of Stakeholder Engagement and Societal Impact," *Academy of Management Perspectives,* 2019.

Chapter 9

An End-to-End Perspective

Carlos Cordon

Few companies nowadays match the ambitions of the early Ford Motor Company in America, which vertically integrated to control nearly every product it sold. It owned not just car part factories, but also rubber plantations for tires, steel mills for chassis, and even mines for iron ore. Instead, most companies focus on their core competence and outsource most of the activities that contribute to the final product or service. Overall, that's been good for efficiency, but it makes sustainability harder because now companies must assess not just what they do in house but also what their suppliers (and distributors) do.

This focusing, and outsourcing, has certainly added to the challenge of making a company sustainable – companies usually can't simply tell their suppliers what to do. But leaders increasingly have little choice. The European Union has begun requiring companies to assess their "scope three" carbon emissions. Scope one emissions come from a company's own operations, while scopes two and three come from suppliers. Scope two is a narrow category covering only the energy the company uses in its operations. Scope three covers everything else, including energy a supplier uses. These usually amount to the vast majority of a company's total emissions, including those caused by small firms not otherwise covered by regulation.

By requiring companies to assess their scope three emissions, regulators are effectively putting all firms, even small ones, on notice to calculate their emissions. That's harder than it looks because of this rampant outsourcing. And that's only one of the three areas of sustainability addressed in this book – we also need companies to assess their activities with regard to freshwater resources and social inclusion. But this end-to-end perspective is essential for understanding whether companies are advancing or not in promoting true sustainability.

WHAT END TO END MEANS

Given the importance of suppliers, many companies have already worked on gaining an end-to-end perspective. Instead of putting scheduling in the planning department, procurement in finance, logistics in sales, and delivery in manufacturing, they've started centralizing the purchasing function. Some of them, such as Unilever, have created a C-suite chief supply chain officer to better coordinate this major part of the operation. But even this broader look often neglects the extended supply chain, including the suppliers' own suppliers and the customers' customers.

This gap matters for sustainability when we start looking at numbers. For simplicity, let's focus on emissions of carbon dioxide. At most companies, the extended supply chain makes up over 90% of CO_2 emissions, in some cases 99%. What a typical company does to reduce its scope one or even scope two emissions is largely irrelevant – the main opportunity is in the supply chain. Some executives are disheartened to learn that, even after helping a supplier renovate a factory, the emissions from that supplier's own supplier dwarf what the first-level supplier did. But that's the reality. The big part is somewhere else – where the assembling company has even less control.

Take Henkel, the German chemical and consumer goods company. It has made some excellent investments in sustainability. But its 2022 annual report admitted that 99% of the CO_2 emissions associated with its product took place outside of the company. Henkel has worked hard to reduce the 1% of emissions that it controls but now is shifting to an end-to-end perspective.

In particular, the company is influencing its consumers to use a lower temperature in washing machines or to buy lower-emission machines. That includes people who started washing clothes before they even had machines, so they think they know how to get clothes clean. It is also reaching out to suppliers, but that's harder. It's a big challenge.

Likewise, Inditex, the fashion company whose main operation is Zara, relies heavily on suppliers to make the garments it sells, and it emphasizes tight coordination between designers and factories. The company has worked hard to reduce its emissions, but its scope three accounts for 99%

of carbon emissions and water usage. They've done a great job but with little real impact.

Nestlé, the world's largest coffee producer, has worked hard to boost inclusion as well as reduce carbon emissions with its farmers in Latin America. The company, with 300000 total employees, claims to have trained 200000 farmers. That's a big undertaking, and even then, the growing of coffee represents only 5% of the company's emissions – the rest is in transportation, processing, and related activities. And we can't tell about results yet.

These are tough challenges with all sorts of complexities. Here's a noncorporate example, but it could easily involve a company's efforts on sustainability. The Hunger Project is a Kenyan nonprofit worried about many fishermen falling into unemployment because of depleted stocks. Several organizations, including the Kenyan government, decided to give the fishermen some land as well as training in farming. The program seemed to be going well until the Hunger Project saw that these new farmers were using their income to buy alcohol, not for educating their kids. It was good that the fishermen now had work, but at what cost? The solution implemented was to give the money in installments and to involve the wives.

What if the Hunger Project was a Western multinational? Should it impose its standards of equality and development on those families? This is a big issue with child labor. As discussed in Chapter 8, if you forbid children working in farms or factories, the children might end up in prostitution. And if a few thousand kids, out of millions, actually get to school instead of work, is that significant progress on sustainability? Is that really fair?

There's an even larger issue. In order to influence extended supply chains, including lots of little companies, we might need aggressive interventions from governments. Could those interventions disrupt the slow progress the world has been making up to now? We want to speed up that progress, but could we kill the goose that lays the golden egg? Could those interventions lead to so much resistance and unintended consequences as to actually make sustainability worse?

LIMITING CAPITALISM RUN AMOK

Supply chains involve one more discouraging dynamic in promoting sustainability: companies need to overcome an important bias. Think about it as reversing or at least limiting a major trend of the past several decades. Ever since the early twentieth century, companies have dedicated themselves to reducing costs. That was one reason for pushing outsourcing in the first place: to gain efficiency. The buyer companies could then invest in their negotiating teams and push relentlessly for lower prices as the supplier reached scale and moved down learning curves. With lower costs, companies would lower prices, which increased demand, which in turn generated scale economies. Everyone prospered. Capitalism at its finest.

But while companies have excelled in minimizing costs, which is generally good, they've sometimes created problems. We saw this vividly in the COVID-19 pandemic, when many suppliers simply refused to sell to companies that had become too tough on cutting costs. Tesco, the big British grocer, had to ration lettuce and tomatoes in 2023 because farmers had decided not to plant as much acreage due to the low prices Tesco offered. Tesco's silo thinking, relentlessly pushing on costs, led to shortages, not to mention farmers losing income. With an end-to-end perspective, focused on the needs of the extended supply chain, companies can rethink some of their practices and promote sustainability.

The good news here is that these practices weren't intended to undermine sustainability. Instead, it was capitalism run amok, where each practice makes sense in each individual instance but has the unintended consequences of creating shortages, fragility, difficult lives for suppliers, or at least a lack of progress for suppliers.

The pandemic actually helped to draw attention to the problem. Markets were extraordinarily efficient but also much less resilient. In the mismatch of pricing, suppliers of crucial components just reduced their operations. Better negotiation isn't enough; companies need to think about the needs of their suppliers. Rather than use its heft to demand the best price, which might push many suppliers out of business, a big company can work to build up a healthy long-term supply. They might even resort to some vertical integration, which would increase their span of control on sustainability.

Supplier relations are always in flux anyway, so companies need to watch those relationships carefully. In the global car industry, most manufacturers either owned their main suppliers outright or strongly influenced them through shares of stock. Then in recent decades, they embraced focus and spun off most of their suppliers. And now they're rethinking some decisions. If 10 years ago you asked the leaders of General Motors if they needed to make batteries, they would have said no. But with electric cars expanding, the company understands that batteries are now a big part of the value proposition.

Control doesn't have to come from actual ownership of the production; the design may be enough. Apple used to outsource the microchips in its products, but instead, it is increasingly designing its own chips. Apple doesn't actually make the chip for its line of Macintosh computers – an outsourcer does that – but it creates the design and owns the intellectual property. Owning the design gives a company not full control but enough to move the needle on sustainability.

Companies are already pulling back a bit on outsourcing for strategic reasons – either to ensure a steady supply of materials or to minimize problems that hurt the brand. Many consumers pay $5000 or more for a Swiss watch, partly for emotional reasons – the dream of excellence, or at least of luxury. What if they hear that making their watch relied on child labor? There goes the emotional connection. So it makes sense to acquire certain suppliers even if that reduces efficiency a bit. This is going to happen with many other products, from pharmaceuticals to clothing to cars. All sorts of seemingly rational steps to save a few cents are going to be reversed.

Some of this shift is already happening with deglobalization and renewed political instability. Companies are reevaluating the risk and cost profiles in their supply chain. Saving a few pennies won't help when your product is stuck in the Suez Canal or has to take a longer route to avoid the Red Sea. Trade wars will affect these calculations further. Adding the sustainability concerns, many companies will either reintegrate or buy more locally, where suppliers are also easier to influence.

All of this is to say that while the supply chain challenges are enormous and serious, companies can still achieve a great deal on sustainability. They just need to look at the potential risks and take advantages of shifts in their span of control.

We aren't going back to the nineteenth century, with much shorter supply chains. Suppliers will always have the lion's share of most companies' total operations. But we can expect a gradual shift back from extreme outsourcing, fueled only partly by concerns over sustainability.

WHAT EXECUTIVES CAN DO

Instead of throwing up their hands and focusing on what they actually control, companies can do better. The key is to set realistic expectations and match investments with pay-offs. If influencing suppliers to reduce emissions yields a much bigger payoff than whatever you do in house, then you should talk to suppliers.

Instead of trying to bring all suppliers along, a company can favor its more sustainable partners, including those with second-tier sustainable suppliers. At least at first, it's going to be a small impact, but if other companies in the sector follow along, the work will add up. It will take years and lots of collaboration, but it can move the needle. There's also a market opportunity to add to the incentive for this work as long as sustainability isn't the main selling factor. (We're learning that now with electric cars.)

Are we going to make everybody buy from sustainable farmers? No. But we can still improve the lives of many farmers and other people. It helps that the amount of sustainability contribution rarely matches the total costs or margins. If you go to Starbucks and pay $5 for a cup of coffee, only about five cents goes to the grower, but half or more of Starbucks' total emissions comes from growing. Even if the farming costs double, that's still only 10 cents. For a long time, companies worked relentlessly on costs, regardless of other consequences. So they have some wiggle room. They can pay more without raising the final price to consumers. And if they do need to raise the price a bit, they can at least point to their progress on sustainability.

Some companies will be tempted to stay small, in order to reduce their potential responsibility for sustainability, but that seems unlikely given the benefits of scale. More likely is that other companies will use their leadership in sustainability to become the dominant providers in their industry. That's because sustainability is becoming a positive consumer good. In the 2010s, for example, the UK Post began offering a service where delivery was more sustainable, but the consumer either paid extra or the delivery was slower. Initially, hardly anyone signed up, but by 2024 the rate exceeded 10% of the mail volume. There's a significant segment of consumers actively seeking sustainability even with higher prices, which is an opportunity for companies that boost the sustainability of their supply chains.

The leadership challenge here is to seek sustainability while understanding issues in their complexity. That includes taking seriously the ongoing need for competitive advantage. Reducing waste, for example, now amounts to low-hanging fruit in most companies. When Toyota and other pioneers worked hard to eliminate waste, they got a big edge. Now, with 80% of companies following their lead, or at least claiming to do so, it's hard to stand out among the competition. Cutting waste becomes just a hygiene factor, table stakes.

Leaders need to drop the idea that sustainability inevitably makes money for the company over the long term. Yes, if one car company is a good deal more sustainable than others, it will make extra profits. But if most or all of them are fairly sustainable, none gets an advantage. And demand is not shifting as fast as predicted. Car companies must plan years in advance, so now their electric-vehicle forecasts are looking problematic, including for return on investment.

Indeed, in 2022, Toyota's board essentially kicked its CEO upstairs for his conservatism – he said the future was not only in electric vehicles but also in electric-gas hybrids and in hydrogen. Now in 2024 he looks prescient, but timing is everything, and going against the grain is risky too.

Sustainability is especially difficult for supply chains because corporate buyers had that single objective of minimizing costs for years. Buyers are now working with multiple objectives, even the 17 United Nations SDGs. If a company claims it is achieving sustainability but doesn't meet all those goals, it gets accused of greenwashing. So some leaders will prefer not to explain what they are doing to avoid the controversy.

Of course, companies are essentially tools for taking risks with economic resources. Companies need to embrace risks and just find opportunities for managing the risks and creating new kinds of value. Here it helps to offer a niche product, as Tesla does, or at least to specialize. General Motors has to build a variety of drive trains and employ different engineers. Covering a broad market is inherently risky. In fact, at the end of the day, maybe a General Motors or Ford should just decide, "We're going to working only on gas engines. We know how to do that, we're really good at it, and we're just going to cede the rest of the market." Many of their investors will hate that approach, but it may be their future. And it may be easier to maintain what they're doing now.

So specialization can help but not in every industry. It's still best to simply to pay attention to your full value chain, and look for the big opportunities to boost sustainability. Look for the steps that are relatively easy to take, but with a big payoff. Most companies actually have many opportunities that are easy to achieve but involve their suppliers, not their own operations. By working with suppliers, they can reduce their total carbon emissions or water usage substantially for much less effort than improving their own operations. It's true that companies can't tell their suppliers what to do, but they do have substantial influence, and the payoff can be enormous. Looking only at what you control cuts off some big opportunities.

Go back to Henkel, which has now established partnerships with suppliers in most areas of operation, from raw materials and packaging to logistics and recycling. Those partnerships stop short of vertical integration, but they give the company some leverage in pressing for sustainability. Of course, the company has to back down on relentlessly lowering cost too. But given how little the company's own operations matter for sustainability, it's not a hard decision.

Another innovator is the Toks restaurant group, with 192 sites in Mexico. Coffee is a selling point for the company, and it wanted to simplify its coffee supply chain. At the time, that chain involved 10 different intermediaries, encompassing all aspects of coffee production and procurement, from growing, processing, and milling to roasting and distribution. Toks decided to buy a milling operation, which meant it could shrink those intermediaries down to 3. Most suppliers were small farmers, and Toks used the milling connection to offer them technical training (both agricultural and financial). The training not only boosted the farmers' revenue, but it broke up the supply chain's focus on buying at the lowest possible price. As Toks got more involved, it offered coordination that ensured most farmers would earn a living wage. Now their children would be more likely to get educated.

Companies can also work with regulators on incentive regimes. Take methane emissions, a big problem in agriculture. In the Netherlands, regulators told farmers to reduce their cow herds by a third. Meanwhile in the United States, in the state of California, farmers got a different message: manage your herds to reduce methane emissions, with a view to getting revenue from carbon credit markets.

Europeans are skeptical of credit markets for carbon, but so far these markets have worked well in most cases, and shutting them down just takes away a tool for promoting sustainability. So companies can promote progress with regulators, too, in a way that affects broad supply chains.

That includes the burden of reporting, especially with the move to scope three. A leader in a big company recently said that if they dedicated as much resources to pursuing actual sustainability as they dedicate to reporting on it, they would make a lot of progress. Regulators say they want to get a complete picture, which is fine, but that means a company going to its suppliers, to their suppliers, and even to a Mr. Jones, a farmer, asking, "What is your CO_2 footprint?" Regulators have worked to ease the burden of reporting with the use of average or hybrid data. And extensive regulation can even prompt pioneering companies to achieve a competitive advantage in reporting. But every requirement has the potential consequence of diverting some resources from actual sustainability.

An open mind also helps. We tend to fall into simple formulas around sustainability, but the true payoffs are fuzzy. One company decided it was using too much plastic, and it pushed its suppliers accordingly. The result was that the company switched to glass bottles. It saved on plastic but added emissions from the energy to clean or recycle the bottles. And glass, being heavy to transport, added fuel costs and carbon emissions in that stage.

So companies have a lot of potential improvement but cannot be net-zero in every activity. Airlines, for example, won't be net zero for a long time, but they want to contribute, and isn't it better if they buy offsets that expand or protect forests while still working for carbon-free jet fuel in the future? Every company has different battles to pick, especially with their diverse value chains.

Real progress on sustainability requires companies to look beyond their own operations. Doing so can be discouraging at first because suppliers and customers often account for the vast majority of damaging activity, and companies can't control them. Instead of just focusing on what they control, companies can pick their battles and invest in areas with the greatest sustainability payoff. They can also factor sustainability into decisions on making in house vs. outsourcing. An end-to-end perspective will deliver more results for the environment and society than focusing in what happens within the company.

TAKEAWAYS

1. Most carbon emissions and other sustainability issues come from a big company's suppliers, not from in-house operations.

2. As the big companies outsourced most of their activity, they pushed suppliers relentlessly to lower costs – which now makes it harder for the companies to push them for sustainability.

3. To boost sustainability in their value chain, leaders can reverse some vertical integration while strengthening relationships that send new priorities.

FURTHER READING

Carlos Cordon, "Securing Supply Chains through Vertical Integration," *I by IMD*, March 28, 2024.

Ralf Seifert, Richard Markoff, and Alexander Schmidt, "Carbon Accounting is Going Broad and Granular. Are We Ready?" *I by IMD*, April 11, 2023.

Chapter 10

Brand Strategies

Goutam Challagalla and Frédéric Dalsace

As with most business opportunities, branding is essential to pioneering in sustainability. Only with branding can a company resist commoditization and obtain a premium price to compensate for the upfront investment and risk in making a major change. Sustainability has a second powerful advantage for branding: it appeals strongly to a set of customers who will eagerly accept that premium price to support that pioneering.

That appeal, however, has led many companies to ignore the basic reason customers buy anything: to get a job done. They present sustainability as a key selling point, when in most cases it is at best a low-cost add-on to what customers mainly care about: getting that specific job done. Few customers make purchases in order to promote sustainability. As a result, companies fail to develop brand power in this area. They'll do better if they understand what branding is all about.

WHY BRANDING?

Most products and services can be divided into two groups: branded offerings, which provide a superior result for a premium price, and commodity offerings, which give customers what they want at a relatively low price. In order to keep attracting that higher price, a company needs to maintain the superior quality (on at least one dimension) of its offering. As soon as the product or service no longer seems to offer a superior result, customers will shift to the commodity offering.

With rare exceptions, branding is not something easily achieved with clever marketing or luck. Branding is essentially a promise to customers: you will pay more for this item, and in exchange you will receive more value than you would get from the commoditized version. Sometimes that superior quality is ephemeral or indirect, but customers perceive it as valuable. In order to keep that promise, companies must continually invest in their branded goods so that they deliver greater value than the commoditized versions. Fortunately, the necessary added investment declines over time, while the revenue from higher margins persists, giving companies a good return on the brand investment. That ability to count on higher margins is brand power.

The possibility of branding is therefore what enables companies to invest heavily in improvements to a product or service. If customers insisted on buying only commoditized versions of any offering, then most innovation would stop because companies couldn't charge the premiums necessary to recoup the cost of the innovation. With the possibility of branding and thus higher margins, companies are more willing to invest in future improvements.

That's especially true for sustainable products and services, which are going to be risky and require a great deal of upfront investment. Companies will need the promise of brand power to reduce this risk. The good news is that some customers are already willing to support brands with a credible commitment to sustainability. To take one datapoint, many homeowners in Britain and the United States pay extra for electricity from renewable energy. The actual service is no different – the electricity, including availability and reliability, is the same – but the market supports a premium price for a sustainable offering.

MARKET ACCORDING TO THE PRODUCT OR SERVICE, NOT THE CUSTOMERS

To achieve brand power, however, companies need to start by assessing their market. Every product or service category has customers varying by their likelihood to pay extra for sustainability. Just how many high-likelihood customers are in your pool of customers? It might be lower than you think. In most industries and sectors, what matters is not whether customers prefer sustainability – people usually say they favor it to some degree – but how willing they are to accept it relative to the offering's traditional benefits, those primary buying factors.

That leads to the three key categories. First, is the sustainability gain largely separate from, independent of, those existing benefits? That's the electricity example, where the source of the power has no bearing on how customers actually experience the offering; it's an add-on with at most a slight increase in price. Second, does the sustainability gain somehow detract from, diminish, or be dissonant with any of the existing benefits? The item might show lesser performance, lower availability, dropped features, or a much higher price, so buyers must accept trade-offs to go with the sustainable offering. Third, does the sustainability gain improve on, enhance, or resonate with those existing benefits? It might actually reduce cost, boost access, or add features, as Tesla drivers have found with electric cars that accelerate faster.

From there, marketers need to estimate their market by customers. "Greens" are buyers willing to pay extra for sustainability. "Blues" are on the fence, interested in promoting sustainability but unwilling to pay much or to weaken those traditional benefits. "Grays" are skeptical: not only are they uninterested in sustainability, but they suspect that it undermines the benefits they do care about. Greens are the main market for dissonant offerings, while grays will favor only resonant ones, and blues might buy from any category. Different markets of the same industry can have different mixes. We know a multinational based in Germany that intended to market a product globally as sustainable. Germany has a lot of greens, but the US executives were doubtful, as most Americans are blue or gray.

It's tempting to classify customers according to fixed attributes (green, blue, or gray), but marketers have found that preferences vary across products and offerings. Take a company that provides energy-efficient milking machines for the dairy industry. One customer showed little interest in the environmental message even though the customer was under some regulatory pressure to reduce carbon emissions. It turns out the customer was focused on its animal feed and supplements suppliers because it saw cows, not farm equipment, as the main source of problems. The offering, more than the customer's intrinsic preferences, proved decisive in purchasing.

Marketers must also deal with the phenomenon of moral licensing. This is when customers spend heavily on a sustainable offering (such as an electric car) and therefore feel free to buy a nonsustainable item. They think they've earned a pass on buying decisions because of that big purchase. So there's no absolute preference for any customer; it depends on the offering and even on timing.

Marketing segments for sustainability must therefore start with the offering, not the customer. Is sustainability an independent, dissonant, or resonant gain? The immediate practical results are clear: independent and resonant offerings can be marketed broadly, while dissonant items need special care. But how to market those items, and achieve brand power, is worth some attention. If you can't appeal to all three customer groups – green, blue and gray – then you're going to struggle to get to scale. You'll have to market your offering as a niche item, which will diminish your brand power – especially your revenues – considerably.

MARKETING FOR INDEPENDENCE, RESONANCE, AND DISSONANCE

The main challenge is with dissonant offerings. If you've spent years cultivating blue and gray customers, you're going to be reluctant to invest in a switch that might alienate them. For an independent offering, sustainability is an add-on, so if you offer it for free, you will get the blue and perhaps gray customers too. If you raise the price more than slightly, then the offering becomes dissonant; you lose the grays and likely some blues as well.

If you must raise the price, or if sustainability reduces performance in one way, then you need to offer offsetting benefits – otherwise you get dissonance. Performance is many things; it can involve holding a bottle easily without slipping or carrying a package without it ripping apart or being noisy. It can even come indirectly through conspicuous consumption – such as Toyota's cleverly arched Prius hybrid cars, which attracted consumers looking to signal their virtue on sustainability.

Some companies have embraced dissonance and successfully scaled up, but that's difficult. Oatly, the plant-based milk, started off in Europe in the 1990s as a lactose-free alternative to cow's milk. Sales were slow because of dissonance: potential consumers disliked the taste. Then in 2014, the company repositioned the product as a lifestyle brand for the "post-milk generation," with the slogan "It's like milk but made for humans." The shift, which quietly promoted sustainability while emphasizing trendiness, enabled the company to expand into the United States and other markets, and total annual sales have grown to $800 million. Yet consumers have been fickle in Asia and elsewhere, and total sales of all vegan milk is still a fraction of the trillion-dollar global dairy industry.

Another possibility is a product extension. Instead of changing the main branded product, offer a sustainable version oriented to green consumers. That's harder to pull off operationally since you have to separate production, adding complexity and reducing economies of scale. Better to see it as an experiment, to learn internally what sustainable production involves, and to test the marketplace externally. If you see a rising demand for the niche product, you may have more green consumers than you thought.

As for independent items, you can scale, but tread carefully. Promoting sustainability could turn off those suspicious grays.

Georg Fischer makes polyvinyl chloride (PVC) piping, and it developed a process using waste oil rather than petroleum at minimal extra cost. The company can pitch this piping in the traditional way to grays, while highlighting the environmental benefits to greens and blues.

Also, especially for add-ons, these advantages are likely to be temporary since others will soon copy the result. So the brand power will depend on continuing investment. Charging a high price to the greens is likely to draw rivals doing the same, so be conservative with pricing. Brand power will be limited.

Of course, if you have a resonant product or service, then you can appeal to all the groups with a strong message. Resonant items also usually offer more new benefits over time, so the advantage continues. But you should still segment that message – play up sustainability when pitching to greens while ignoring it for grays and selectively using it for blues. You can build up brand power, but do it carefully.

CHANGING THE BRAND

Even the strongest brand has to work with customers where they are. And most markets, especially in the United States, have a substantial number of gray customers who will be intrinsically skeptical, even hostile, to brands that emphasize sustainability. Grays instinctively believe that sustainable brands offer less value, at least in the short term, than traditional brands. So they actively avoid those brands.

That's the lesson from Unilever, an otherwise impressive pioneer in sustainable brands. The company decided, in the early to mid-2010s, to give all their consumer brands either a social or an environmental purpose. In effect, the company broke the promise of its traditional brands. In the past, the company focused on superior functionality or another traditional value, but now it announced to its customers that all of its brands had a broader purpose. It was repositioning its brands in the minds of consumers.

In some cases, the new positioning fit well onto the old positioning, or at least overlapped substantially. The result was a fresh, improved brand promise. Lifebuoy soap, for example, had always had the added benefit of a disinfectant because it included antibacterial elements. Now, as the company pointed out, it also improved the hygiene of young parents in Kenya, India, and other countries with high rates of premature birth and infant mortality. Unilever worked with local groups to boost hygiene in the schools in hopes of building habits that would improve habits in families generally. Studies have shown that greater handwashing reduces diarrhea, dysentery, and other diseases that adults can tolerate but babies can't. Because Unilever put feet on the ground in these countries, promoting handwashing with any soap, it was a serious effort, not greenwashing. Brand power went up.

In other cases, such as Dove soap and girls' body image and self-esteem, the connection was minimal. The images were powerful, but the purpose felt arbitrary, not really compelling. No other self-care company had claimed that space, and Unilever did get people talking – it raised an important social issue. But the effects on the brand weren't clear. And other cases, such as Axe – a deodorant aimed at young men, replacing the traditional sexist marketing with nonsexist images – amounted to a new positioning that confused customers, however well-intentioned that move.

Some cases are tricky. Unilever ran a campaign linking its Hellmann's condiment brand with reducing food waste. The company explained the connection as follows: People feel guilty throwing away leftovers, so they put leftover food in the refrigerator and forget about it, eventually tossing it as it spoils. But with condiments, they could freshen up the leftovers and consume them in a meal. So Hellmann's would reduce food waste – except hardly anybody in the real world made that connection. The move confused the brand rather than enlivened it.

That's the big danger here. If the company's major change here is in communication, in positioning, where the product hasn't changed, and with no new feet on the ground, then it's greenwashing. But if you do change the product, then you risk confusing and alienating consumers, especially those gray and even blue ones. You can't have a purpose that's separate from the brand.

This is not about positioning per se. Early on, Procter & Gamble emphasized how well its Tide laundry detergent cleaned. They couldn't say that other brands didn't clean, but Tide was the first one to claim it. P&G kept repeating that claim, and now they still own it. Consumers might not like Tide for other reasons, but they couldn't deny that it cleaned. They understood the purpose with the brand. When you add a purpose to a brand, then you mess around with the brand promise, and that could undermine your brand power.

It's essential for marketers to start with the product or service, not with the customers segments. Resonant items offer the most potential. Independent items can scale as well, but these are harder and the gains may be only temporary. Dissonance is hardest to overcome, but can be done with a fresh message, at least in some markets.

That focus on products and services, not messaging, is especially important for sustainability. Success ultimately comes down not to creative communication but to innovation. Over time, more customers may shift into the green camp, but human nature is unlikely to change. Companies need to make sustainability good for the business, not just for the planet.

TAKEAWAYS

1. Most consumers pay a premium to buy a branded product in order to get a specific job done well, not to serve a larger cause such as a sustainability.

2. Adding sustainability to a brand will affect consumers' perception depending on whether the addition is independent of the brand (no effect), resonant (improves the value), or dissonant (reduces value). Consumers can likewise be divided into greens (favoring sustainability), blues (neutral), and grays (assumes that sustainable products are worth less).

3. It's dangerous for brands to add sustainability to a product without making sure the result is not dissonance, especially if the target market includes many grays and blues.

FURTHER READING

Frédéric Dalsace and Goutam Challagalla, "How to Market Sustainable Products: Three Paths to Success," *Harvard Business Review*, March–April 2024.

Katherine White, David J. Hardisty, and Rishab Habib, "The Elusive Green Consumer," *Harvard Business Review*, July–August 2019.

Chapter 11

Navigating Climate-Related Financial Risks

Salvatore Cantale and Karl Schmedders

Climate change is no longer just an environmental issue but also a critical financial risk that demands immediate attention from business leaders, investors, lenders, and insurers alike. The increasing frequency and severity of climate-related events, coupled with the global push toward a lower-carbon economy, have introduced complex risks that threaten the stability and profitability of organizations across all sectors. These dangers, collectively known as climate-related financial risks, are now recognized as a significant challenge to the long-term sustainability of businesses and the broader financial system.

As the world rallies to meet the goals of the Paris Agreement, companies are under mounting pressure to disclose their exposure to these risks and to demonstrate resilience through effective risk management strategies. Investors, lenders, and insurers are increasingly demanding transparency, recognizing that climate-related risks can have a material impact on financial performance, risk profiles, and long-term viability. This is where the Task Force on Climate-related Financial Disclosures (TCFD) steps in, offering a vital framework to guide companies in understanding, disclosing, and managing their climate-related financial risks.

Established by the Financial Stability Board in 2015 and disbanded in 2023, the TCFD published a report in 2017 providing recommendations for consistent and transparent climate-related financial disclosures. These recommendations are designed to help organizations identify and manage their exposure to climate-related risks, ensuring that investors, lenders, insurers, and other stakeholders have the information they need to make informed decisions.

This chapter explores the real-world implications of these risks through examples such as Peabody Energy and the European Union's Carbon Border Adjustment Mechanism (CBAM). We also explain that proactive risk management is not just necessary but can also position your company to seize opportunities in the transition to a sustainable economy.

PHYSICAL RISKS, ACUTE AND CHRONIC

Climate-related financial risks have quickly risen to the top of the agenda for companies, investors, lenders, insurers, and regulators. These risks come in two main types, physical and transition. Understanding these risks and their potential impacts is crucial for any business leader aiming to navigate the challenges posed by climate change.

Physical risks involve the direct and tangible impacts of climate change. Acute physical risks are event driven, stemming from extreme weather events such as hurricanes, floods, wildfires, and heatwaves. As climate change progresses, the frequency and intensity of these events are expected to increase. Have you considered how a sudden and severe weather event could disrupt your supply chain or even halt your operations?

Consider the 2017 Atlantic hurricane season, one of the most active on record. It caused widespread devastation across the Caribbean and the southern United States, leading to billions of dollars in damages and lost revenue. Companies with operations or supply chains in these regions faced severe disruptions, and those unprepared for such events experienced significant financial strain, highlighting the urgent need for robust risk management and contingency planning.

Likewise, the 2024 flooding in Brazil's state Rio Grande do Sul closed the international airport in Porto Alegre for more than six months. The impact on regional and international trade, tourism, and the local economy was profound, demonstrating how climate-related events can disrupt critical infrastructure and business continuity.

Chronic physical risks, on the other hand, involve longer-term shifts in climate patterns, such as rising sea levels, increasing average temperatures, and changing precipitation patterns. These risks can gradually erode the value of assets, reduce agricultural productivity, and alter the availability of natural resources. Have you assessed how rising sea levels could affect your coastal assets or how prolonged droughts might impact your supply chain?

For instance, rising sea levels pose a chronic risk to coastal cities and infrastructure worldwide. Real estate in low-lying areas like Miami is increasingly vulnerable to flooding and land subsidence, leading to potential devaluation, increased insurance costs, and expensive protective measures.

In China, prolonged droughts have led to significant reductions in hydroelectric power generation, particularly in the Sichuan province. This has had a ripple effect on industries reliant on stable electricity supplies, such as aluminum production, forcing smelters to cut production and driving up operational costs. Chronic climate impacts can have far-reaching effects on industrial output and economic stability.

TRANSITION RISKS IN MULTIPLE FORMS

Transition risks arise from the global shift toward a lower-carbon economy, driven by changes in policy and regulation, technology, market preferences, and societal expectations. These risks can greatly affect businesses reliant on carbon-intensive processes, leading to asset devaluation, increased costs, and reputational damage. As a business leader, have you thought about how your company will adapt to these shifts?

Policy and Legal Risks. Governments worldwide are implementing policies to curb greenhouse gas emissions and promote sustainability. This means companies may face increased regulatory scrutiny, carbon pricing, and potential legal liabilities. Non-compliance with new regulations can result in fines, litigation, and operational restrictions.

Take the European Union's CBAM. It represents a significant policy risk for companies exporting carbon-intensive goods to the EU. By imposing a carbon cost on imports, it effectively levels the playing field between EU producers and foreign competitors. Companies that fail to reduce their carbon footprints may face higher costs and reduced market competitiveness, leading to potential financial losses. How would your company fare under such regulatory pressures?

Technological Risks. The transition to a low-carbon economy drives innovation in clean technologies, which can disrupt existing industries and business models. Companies that fail to adapt to new technologies may find their products or services becoming obsolete.

For instance, the rapid advance of renewable energy technologies, such as solar and wind power, has disrupted the fossil fuel industry. Companies that have not diversified their energy portfolios or invested in renewable technologies risk losing market share to innovative competitors. Similarly, in the automotive sector, the rise of electric vehicles (EVs) is challenging the dominance of internal combustion engines. Is your company prepared to pivot in response to such technological shifts?

Market Risks. Changes in market demand and consumer preferences toward sustainable products and services can lead to shifts in market dynamics. Companies that do not align with these trends may face declining sales and market value.

Peabody Energy, a leading US coal producer, provides a cautionary tale. The company faced a dramatic decline in market demand for coal due to the global shift toward cleaner energy sources. Despite some regulatory efforts to support coal, the market's move toward natural gas and renewable energy led to a significant reduction in coal demand, ultimately driving Peabody into bankruptcy in 2016. Such are the market risks from failing to anticipate and respond to the changing energy landscape. How is your company positioned to adapt to evolving market trends?

Reputational Risks. As public awareness of climate change grows, companies are increasingly scrutinized for their environmental practices. Negative perceptions of a company's environmental impact can lead to loss of customer trust, decreased brand value, and potential boycotts.

Companies that engage in greenwashing – promoting themselves as more environmentally friendly than they truly are – risk significant reputational damage when their claims are exposed. The backlash can lead to loss of customers, legal action, and a decline in investor confidence. Nestlé, for instance, faced criticism for its 2021 sustainability report, which was seen by some as insufficiently addressing its environmental impact. By 2023, however, the company had made significant improvements, including adopting a materiality matrix to better align its sustainability efforts with genuine climate-related risks.

Together, physical and transition risks form a comprehensive picture of the challenges that companies face in the era of climate change. Understanding these risks is the first step toward developing effective strategies to mitigate their impact and leverage the opportunities that arise from the transition to a sustainable economy.

STRATEGIES TO REDUCE RISKS FOR A RESILIENT FUTURE

As the global economy navigates the challenges of climate change, the concept of being "future ready" has taken on new significance. Companies that fail to recognize and address climate-related financial risks are increasingly vulnerable to disruptions that can undermine their long-term viability. In contrast, those that proactively manage these risks and integrate sustainability into their core strategies are better positioned to thrive in the evolving economic landscape. Are you ready to ensure your company is future proof in the face of climate change?

Mitigation to reduce the root causes of physical risks. This work aims to reduce or prevent the emission of greenhouse gases, thereby limiting future climate change. Companies can transition to renewable energy sources, improve energy efficiency, and reduce waste and emissions across operations. Mitigation is not just about reducing the carbon footprint; it is also about ensuring compliance with increasingly stringent regulations, meeting stakeholder expectations, and positioning as a sustainability leader.

The transition of US utilities from coal to natural gas has not only reduced greenhouse gas emissions but also contributed to a broad reduction in air pollution and the associated physical risks. As utilities worldwide continue to invest in renewable energy sources like wind and solar, they further mitigate the risks of climate-related disruptions, such as heatwaves and wildfires, exacerbated by fossil fuel emissions.

Adaptation to manage the impacts of physical risks. While mitigation addresses the root causes of climate change, adaptation focuses on managing the immediate impacts that are already occurring or are inevitable. Companies can adapt by boosting the resilience of their infrastructure, operations, and supply chains to withstand climate-induced disruptions. Have you thought about how your company can adapt to the physical risks posed by climate change?

BAE Systems, a major UK defense contractor with several production facilities in the United States, provides a compelling example. After repeated flooding at its manufacturing facility in Johnson City, New York, BAE Systems decided to relocate the facility to a safer location in nearby Endicott in 2012. The move not only protected assets and maintained operational continuity but also demonstrated the company's foresight in addressing climate-related risks.

Mitigation to address transition risks. Companies can mitigate these risks by actively reducing their carbon footprint and aligning their business models with emerging environmental standards.

During the last two decades, as many US utilities transitioned from coal to natural gas or renewable resources, they not only mitigated physical risks but also reduced transition risks by aligning with regulatory trends favoring lower-carbon energy sources. This strategic shift has allowed these companies to remain competitive and compliant in a market with some customers increasingly oriented toward sustainability.

Adaptation to navigate the transition. Adapting to transition risks involves rethinking business strategies, investing in new technologies, and developing products and services that align with the demands of a low-carbon economy. Companies that adapt effectively can turn potential risks into opportunities for growth and innovation. What steps is your company taking to adapt to the transition risks posed by climate change?

Consider the automotive sector. A company that invests in EV technology is adapting to the transition risk posed by declining demand for internal combustion engines. By doing so, the company not only reduces the risk of obsolescence but also positions itself at the forefront of a growing market for sustainable transportation solutions.

By integrating mitigation and adaptation strategies, companies can effectively reduce both physical and transition risks, ensuring they are better equipped to navigate the uncertainties of a changing climate. This active approach not only safeguards against potential disruptions but also opens new avenues for growth in a sustainable economy.

A STRUCTURED APPROACH TO CLIMATE RISK MANAGEMENT

As companies increasingly recognize the importance of addressing climate-related financial risks, the need for a structured and comprehensive approach to managing these risks becomes clear. Fortunately, such a framework has been developed by the TCFD. This group explains how companies can disclose climate-related financial risks and opportunities, enabling them to integrate these considerations into their overall business strategy.

The TCFD report is – without exaggeration – a seminal contribution to humanity's efforts to deal with climate change, offering a comprehensive framework with numerous invaluable recommendations. While we highlight some key aspects in this chapter, it is highly advisable for companies to stay on top of the full report and future developments. We strongly encourage senior leaders to ensure that their organizations are well-versed in the TCFD recommendations, whether by engaging with the report directly or by having dedicated experts focus on its thorough implementation.

The TCFD framework is built around four elements: Governance, Strategy, Risk Management, and Metrics and Targets. These elements collectively provide a holistic approach to identifying, managing, and disclosing climate-related risks. They ensure that companies are not only prepared for the challenges of climate change but are also well-positioned to capitalize on emerging opportunities.

Governance: Oversight and Accountability. Governance refers to the oversight and accountability mechanisms that ensure climate-related risks and opportunities are considered at the highest levels of the organization. Strong governance involves the board of directors and senior management taking an active role in overseeing climate-related risks and ensuring that these risks are integrated into the company's overall governance structure. Are your board and senior management prepared to take on this critical responsibility?

The board should have oversight of climate-related risks and opportunities and be regularly informed about these issues. This includes setting the tone at the top and ensuring that climate-related risks are integrated into the company's overall risk management processes. Senior management should be responsible for assessing and managing climate-related risks and opportunities. This involves developing strategies, policies, and procedures that address these risks and ensuring that they are implemented across the organization.

Strategy: Integrating Climate Risks into Business Planning. Strategy focuses on how the company's business model and strategy are affected by climate-related risks and opportunities. It urges companies to consider the potential financial impact of climate change on their business, and to incorporate this understanding into their strategic planning.

Companies should consider different climate-related scenarios, including one consistent with limiting global warming to 2°C or lower. This helps companies understand how various climate-related risks could affect their business and strategy over the short, medium, and long term. Moreover, companies should integrate climate-related risks and opportunities into their strategic planning process. This includes assessing the potential impacts on revenue, expenditures, supply chain, and market demand.

Risk Management. This element involves identifying, assessing, and managing climate-related risks. Only then are these risks fully integrated into the company's overall risk management framework, enabling the company to respond to the challenges of climate change.

Companies should identify and assess climate-related risks across their operations, including physical and transition risks. This process should involve cross-functional collaboration to ensure a comprehensive understanding of the risks. Climate-related risks should be integrated into the company's broader Enterprise Risk Management (ERM) framework, thus providing a holistic approach.

Metrics and Targets. Companies need to measure and track their progress in managing climate-related risks and opportunities. The TCFD framework recommends that companies disclose the metrics they use to assess climate-related risks and opportunities, as well as the targets they set to manage these risks. Companies should disclose these metrics in line with their strategy and risk management processes. This may include metrics related to greenhouse gas emissions, energy efficiency, and resource consumption.

Finally, companies should set targets related to managing climate-related risks and opportunities, such as emissions reduction targets or energy efficiency goals. Progress against these targets should be regularly tracked and disclosed to stakeholders.

The integration of climate-related financial risks into business strategy is no longer optional – it is a necessity for any company looking to secure its future in a rapidly changing world. Companies that actively understand, mitigate, and adapt to these risks will not only protect themselves from potential disruptions but also position themselves as leaders in the transition to a sustainable economy. Are you prepared to lead your company through these challenges?

As we move forward, the need for comprehensive climate risk management will only grow. The TCFD framework provides a robust foundation for companies to build upon, ensuring that they are not only compliant with emerging regulations but also capable of seizing new opportunities in the low-carbon economy.

Are you ready to lead your organization in navigating the complexities of climate-related financial risks? By embedding these strategies into your business operations, you can turn potential risks into drivers of innovation and growth, securing your company's place in the sustainable economy of the future.

TAKEAWAYS

1. Integrate climate risk into governance and strategy: By involving your board and senior management in overseeing these risks, you can set the tone for active climate risk management and ensure alignment with long-term business goals.

2. Focus on both mitigation and adaptation: While mitigation, such as reducing your carbon footprint, is crucial for compliance and positioning your company as a sustainability leader, adaptation, such as boosting your infrastructure resilience, will safeguard your operations against the immediate impacts of climate change.

3. Follow TCFD recommendations for comprehensive risk management: The TCFD framework offers a structured approach to managing climate-related financial risk. By focusing on governance, strategy, risk management, and clear metrics and targets, your company can navigate the complexities of climate change while identifying new opportunities for growth and innovation in a sustainable economy.

FURTHER READING

Recommendations of the Task Force on Climate-Related Financial Disclosures, 2017. https://assets.bbhub.io/company/sites/60/2021/10/FINAL-2017-TCFD-Report.pdf

TCFD, *Implementing the Recommendations of the TCFD*, 2021. https://assets.bbhub.io/company/sites/60/2021/07/2021-TCFD-Implementing_Guidance.pdf

ADDITIONAL REFERENCES

On CBAM, see https://taxation-customs.ec.europa.eu/carbon-border-adjustment-mechanism_en.

On future readiness, see IMD's description at https://www.imd.org/future-readiness-indicator/home.

On the hurricanes of 2017, see https://www.ncbi.nlm.nih.gov/books/NBK556352; and https://www.us-tech.com/RelId/1099381/pagenum/9/ISvars/default/BAE_Plant_Ruined_by_Flood_Back_on_Line_with_Europlacer_s_Help.htm.

On Miami's vulnerability, see https://www.wusf.org/environment/2023-03-11/mimis-hidden-high-ground-what-sea-rise-risk-means-for-some-prime-real-estate. On China's drought, see https://www.wusf.org/environment/2023-03-11/miamis-hidden-high-ground-what-sea-rise-risk-means-for-some-prime-real-estate.

On Nestlé's efforts, see https://www.nestle.com/sites/default/files/2024-02/creating-shared-value-sustainability-report-2023-en.pdf.

On Peabody Coal, see https://dialogue.earth/en/business/8824-peabody-s-downfall-a-cautionary-tale-for-energy-investors and https://www.climatesolutions.org/article/1590119179-mr-peabodys-coal-train-jumps-tracks.

On the Rio Grande do Sul floods, see https://disasterphilanthropy.org/disasters/2024-rio-grande-do-sul-brazil-floods.

On utilities moving away from fossil fuels, see Nadja Popovich, "How Does Your State Make Electricity?" *New York Times*, Aug. 2, 2004, at: https://www.nytimes.com/interactive/2024/08/02/climate/electricity-generation-us-states.html?login=email&auth=login-email.

The Paris Agreement is the 2015 international treaty to prevent climate change, achieved at the 21st United Nations Climate Change Conference (COP21). See the UNFCC's explanation at https://unfccc.int/process-and-meetings/the-paris-agreement.

Chapter 12

Nonmarket Strategy

Michael Yaziji and David Bach

The Swiss start-up Planted makes plant-based meat substitutes with remarkable environmental benefits. Its "beef" requires 97% less CO_2 and 81% less water than meat from cows, while its "chicken," also from pea protein, involves 77% less CO_2 and 81% less water. Sales were strong, yet the company found itself in a legal skirmish. Traditional meat companies wanted the company banned from calling its offerings "beef filet," "chicken," or "schnitzel," triggering a government investigation into whether Planted's product names confused consumers.

Many sustainability-focused companies find that offering attractive products and services is not enough. They must also shape their social and political environment, especially to mitigate risks or secure competitive advantage. This is the domain of "nonmarket" management. As governments and society give increasing attention to business, companies must develop and implement effective nonmarket strategies. They must work with stakeholders, issues, and institutions such as governments, communities, activist groups, and the media. All of these shape the firm's opportunities and risks.

Historically, many companies approached nonmarket issues through philanthropy or simple reputation-building in society or hard-nosed lobbying on the political front. However, as regulations, public policies, activism, and social expectations increasingly affect markets, and as stakeholders increasingly influence one another and thereby make neat domain separation impossible, leading firms are going beyond these basic approaches. They are integrating their market and nonmarket strategies to achieve business goals while boosting their own and society's sustainability.

THE NEED FOR NONMARKET STRATEGY

Let's delve into stakeholder power and regulatory complexity. These, along with internationalization, reputational risk, and shared value opportunities, are elevating nonmarket strategy.

Stakeholder power is rising as social media empowers activist groups, communities, and consumers to address issues ranging from environmental protection to social justice. Firms that fail to engage with these stakeholders risk losing their social license to operate.

The ever-evolving regulatory landscape presents both challenges and opportunities. From data privacy and environmental protection to product safety and healthcare, companies can actively shape the regulatory context to gain a competitive edge. To do so, they need to understand policymaking and build relationships with government stakeholders.

As companies expand their operations to other countries, they are navigating a diverse array of social, political, and cultural contexts. From intricate regulatory frameworks to local cultural norms and expectations, they must engage with nonmarket factors in order to succeed.

In an era of heightened scrutiny and hyper-transparency, firms also face significant reputational risks. From supply chain scandals to executive misconduct, negative incidents can quickly erode trust and damage a company's brand. To build reputational resilience, firms must cultivate robust stakeholder relationships and demonstrate credible social performance. They must move beyond compliance and actively contribute to the well-being of their local communities.

Finally, there is a growing recognition that poverty, poor health, and environmental degradation present immense business opportunities. By aligning their business strategies with efforts to address these challenges, companies can find growth areas while promoting sustainability. Capturing this potential, however, requires a fundamental shift in mindset and an integrated approach to creating both economic and social value.

Consider PepsiCo CEO Indra Nooyi's "Performance with Purpose" strategy. Facing criticism over the role of sugary beverages in the obesity epidemic, Nooyi did not just play defense. She actively reshaped the company's product portfolio, acquiring healthy brands and reformulating products to reduce sugars, sodium, and saturated fat. She also engaged with regulators and public health advocates. As a result, PepsiCo boosted its reputation, gained market share, and averted costly regulation.

INTEGRATING MARKET AND NONMARKET STRATEGY

Nonmarket factors profoundly shape most markets, and some companies have already integrated their nonmarket strategy into their overall business approach. This integration is not a siloed or separate activity but a holistic approach that acknowledges how nonmarket forces affect profitability.

Nonmarket forces, including regulations, public policies, and social norms, can greatly influence market size. The legalization of cannabis, for instance, is rapidly expanding a market expected to reach $43 billion by 2025, while taxes on sugary beverages, implemented in over 40 countries, are shrinking the market for these products.

Similarly, intellectual property rules shape industry structure and competitive dynamics, as these determine the power of industry incumbents relative to new entrants. Pharmaceutical patents, for example, enable pricing power and exclusivity periods.

Moreover, policies ranging from carbon taxes to minimum wage laws to trade tariffs have major effects on firms' cost structures. Engaging in policy dialogues to shape these rules, as Walmart has done for wage minimums, is increasingly important to managing costs.

Finally, nonmarket forces are key drivers of business risk, with climate change directly threatening supply chains and carbon regulations forcing adjustments. Investor pressure and employee activism can affect companies seen as misaligned with social values.

Those values are not static. A generation ago, before the Nike sweatshop controversy, it was seen as acceptable, perhaps even "smart," to arbitrage labor conditions by outsourcing to markets where labor power was weak. Today, activists and shareholders are pressuring Volkswagen to sell its factory in Xinjiang, China over the alleged suppression of the Uyghur minority there.

Given these pervasive impacts, integrating market and nonmarket strategy is not just about defending against risks. It's also about shaping the market context to create and capture value in ways that align business success with wider progress. It is about building trusting stakeholder relationships so the firm thrives in the long term with a competitive advantage.

With a comprehensive, interconnected market and nonmarket strategy, companies can better navigate the complexities of the modern business landscape. This approach not only mitigates their risks and optimizes costs but also enables them to seize opportunities for growth and innovation. An integrated nonmarket strategy thus becomes critical to business success, enabling firms to create value for both shareholders and society.

THE ELEMENTS OF A NONMARKET STRATEGY

Integrating a nonmarket agenda into the larger business strategy requires analysis, formulation, implementation, and evaluation. Companies need to check on their capacity to carry out their agenda, as well as its feasibility. Only then can a company confidently implement its nonmarket strategy.

The analysis involves understanding the nonmarket context, encompassing both issues and stakeholders. *Issue* analysis should map the evolving regulatory, political, and social environment, including:

- What is the issue's stage of evolution: emerging, escalating, mature, or dormant?
- How is the issue playing out in the legislative, regulatory, and public opinion arenas?
- How concentrated or diffuse are the stakeholders around the issue?
- What is the power balance between stakeholders on different sides of the issue? Note that lopsided stakeholder power can lead to unbalanced policies.

The dynamic nature of nonmarket issues is evident in the evolving landscape of climate change policy. What was once a fringe concern has rapidly escalated into a mainstream issue, with a broad coalition of stakeholders – environmental activists, investors, consumers, and regulators – mobilizing for action. Fossil fuel companies long maintained diffuse nonmarket power through their central role in the energy system and political influence. But the stakeholder balance is shifting as the financial risks of climate change become clear and clean energy alternatives become viable. Issue analysis would have prepared energy industry leaders for this shift, enabling them to adapt their strategies and business models in a timely way.

As for *stakeholders*, the questions include:

- Who are the key stakeholders? What resources and influence do they have? Where do they operate?
- What are stakeholders' interests, ideologies, and goals? How aligned or misaligned are they with the firm?
- How susceptible are stakeholders to influence? What dependencies or pressure points could shape their stances? What are the key coalitions and adversarial groups?
- How open are stakeholders to collaboration with the firm or others? What potential alliances could be formed?

When Nike faced criticism in the 1990s over labor conditions in its supply chain, stakeholder analysis was essential to its response. The company mapped key critics, analyzed their interests and networks, and identified a shared interest with some in improving factory conditions. By engaging these stakeholders in collaborative supply chain reform, Nike improved both working conditions and its reputation.

Once they understand the context, companies can formulate the strategy. That involves setting clear goals, building influential coalitions, identifying influence pathways, and planning tactics.

Nonmarket strategy should be anchored in *clear market-related goals*. Besides the regulations and standards affecting market size, costs, and entry barriers, a company can partner with an NGO to build its own or its brands' reputations. Is the firm trying to shape laws, influence regulation, create voluntary standards, or develop a competitive advantage? The goals should be determined by the company's market strategy, its values, and its existing or developing competencies.

From there, the company must define the focal issues and set the geographic scope of the nonmarket strategy. This could involve issues at the local, national, or international level. Once the scope is clear, it's crucial to establish specific objectives, such as creating, supporting, or blocking laws; influencing regulatory interpretations; or shaping voluntary industry practices and standards.

It is good to remember that market choices can also affect nonmarket opportunities. For example, when Walmart set a goal of sourcing 100% renewable energy as part of its market strategy for energy cost resilience, the move enabled the company to build nonmarket partnerships with environmentalists, investors, and local utilities who shared this goal.

Companies also need to build a strong coalition. They must identify potential partners, such as certain competitors, supply chain players (upstream, downstream, and post-consumer), and cross-sector stakeholders like NGOs and governments. The coalition should maximize influence and alignment with the company's goals.

Once forming the coalition, it's important to establish the roles and coordination among members. Each partner should have clear responsibilities and a shared understanding of how their efforts contribute to the overall strategy. Some nonmarket conflicts involve disputes between coalitions.

In the tech industry, for example, Google, Facebook, and other giants have formed coalitions with trade associations, think tanks, and academic institutions to shape public discourse and influence policy on issues like data privacy and antitrust regulation. They face up against progressive coalitions such as "Freedom from Facebook and Google" that push for breaking up large technology companies.

Next, companies should *identify influence paths*: mapping these pathways is critical for targeting nonmarket efforts. Companies need to assess decision-makers and analyze the stakeholder-to-stakeholder dynamics that shape their opinions and actions. By understanding these influence networks, companies can find the most effective ways to achieve their goals. They can exert influence through direct channels, such as lobbying decision-makers, or indirect channels, such as mobilizing grassroots support or leveraging media coverage to shape public opinion.

During the COVID-19 pandemic, Pfizer, Moderna, and other pharmaceutical companies worked directly with governments and regulatory agencies to secure emergency-use authorizations for their vaccines. They also engaged in public education campaigns to build trust and support for widespread vaccination. Similarly, when pushing for legalization, the cannabis company Canopy Growth directly lobbied policymakers to shape regulations; mobilized industry associations to advocate as a united front; partnered with medical associations to build credibility; and funded public education to shift social attitudes.

Finally, companies must choose a *tactical focus*. With clear goals, a strong coalition, and influence paths, companies must select appropriate tactics for their context. They need to decide on the framing of the issue and the mix of formal political lobbying, public influence and media campaigns, participation in standards bodies, and industry group influence campaigns. They should orchestrate the timing and sequence of these moves to maximize impact and minimize risk.

For instance, in the battle over net neutrality, Comcast and Verizon employed a mix of tactics, including lobbying, legal challenges, and public relations campaigns, to shape the regulatory landscape. They also carefully framed the issue around the benefits to consumers and to US overall competitiveness, rather than their self-interest.

Formulating a successful nonmarket strategy requires a systematic approach that integrates goal setting, coalition building, influence mapping, and tactical planning. By adapting these elements to the specific context and stakeholder landscape, companies can shape their nonmarket environment to support their business objectives while creating value for society.

As the examples of PepsiCo, tech giants, pharmaceutical companies, and telecommunications firms demonstrate, a well-formulated nonmarket strategy can navigate complex social and political challenges, and achieve competitive advantage. Of course, nonmarket strategy is only as good as its execution. Effective implementation requires several elements that must be built up before needed:

Firms need *competencies*, distinct capabilities in such areas as stakeholder engagement, policy analysis, and social innovation. That means building the human capital required for nonmarket leadership: hiring experts, training existing staff, and cultivating an externally engaged culture.

The e-scooter rental company Lime, which deals with diverse municipal regulations, has built up a large team to work with policymakers and stakeholders across its market area. It recruits many of them locally due to their relationships and understanding of city-specific political dynamics.

A *values-driven culture* is the foundation for nonmarket leadership. Clear values enable consistency in the face of competing stakeholder demands and decentralized decision-making. When companies embed their values, they empower employees to make judgment calls that advance their nonmarket goals. Patagonia is committed to being "in business to save our home planet," a stance that guides nonmarket strategy from its advocacy for protecting public lands to its embrace of circularity.

Companies also need *agility* to adapt quickly to dynamic nonmarket environments. Close stakeholder connections, decentralized teams, and flexible resource allocation enable them to pivot as issues evolve. Thus Airbnb was quick to offer free temporary housing to 20000 Afghan refugees in the wake of the 2021 Taliban takeover. Drawing on its platform and host community, Airbnb helped out in a crisis situation ahead of many governments and aid organizations.

That's still not enough. After analyzing the context, developing a strategy, and preparing the execution, companies need a robust approach for evaluating it. That includes *ethics*. Given the stakes for society, they should rigorously assess the social, environmental, and political impact of their advocacy. Transparency and consistency with the firm's stated values is critical to maintaining trust. Companies must judge success on social as well as business outcomes.

When Google fired the "ethical AI" researcher Timnit Gebru after she criticized the social impact of Google's AI technologies, it faced backlash from employees and civil society. The ethics of this move can't be addressed yet, as AI is still emerging, but companies run ethical risks if stakeholders see their nonmarket strategies misaligned with their stated principles.

Companies can also assess the *feasibility* of their strategy. Based on past campaigns, they can do war-gaming to anticipate competitor and stakeholder responses, evaluate the resource requirements, and stress-test their assumptions. Given the unpredictability of nonmarket environments, they should also plan for contingencies.

Many firms underestimated the feasibility of action on climate change given partisan gridlock in the US Congress. But Engine No. 1 and other activist investors have used novel tactics to force change via new channels, such as electing climate-oriented directors to ExxonMobil's board. They show the importance of assessing a range of paths to change.

Of course, firms should also evaluate their nonmarket strategy for alignment with their market strategy. Nonmarket initiatives deeply at odds with the business model aren't practical for long. Tensions between market and nonmarket activities must be actively surfaced and reconciled.

A cautionary example is Purdue Pharma's anti-opioid abuse initiatives, including sponsoring an addiction research center and equipping law enforcement with easily administered antidotes. While well-intentioned, these efforts seemed hypocritical alongside Purdue's aggressive opioid marketing. The result was a devastating backlash that ultimately bankrupted the company. Tight alignment between market and nonmarket strategies could have averted this outcome.

That includes assessing the business returns on the nonmarket strategy – both tangible impacts, such as policy outcomes and reputation scores, and intangible impacts, such as stronger stakeholder relationships and enhanced legitimacy. A balanced scorecard approach, considering multiple impact dimensions over different time horizons, can help here.

Unilever's Sustainable Living Plan exemplifies this approach. It aims to decouple business growth from negative social and environmental impacts. Unilever rigorously tracks the plan's impacts on sales, costs, risk, purpose, and performance relative to competitors. By taking a holistic, long-term view of returns, Unilever demonstrated the business case for sustainability.

HOW NONMARKET STRATEGY PROMOTES SUSTAINABILITY

We need substantial shifts in how our economies operate to avoid the worst consequences of climate change and resource depletion, not to mention income inequality. Getting there requires a fundamental rewiring of the economic, political, regulatory, and social contexts for firms. Currently, these contexts often incentivize short-term thinking and a narrow focus on shareholder value, while externalizing environmental and social costs. They create collective action problems where even if an individual firm wants to operate more sustainably, the actions of its competitors and the expectations of its stakeholders constrain it.

This is where nonmarket strategy comes in. By engaging with governments, civil society, and other stakeholders, firms can help shift this context. They can advocate for policies and regulations that internalize the full cost of operations. They can partner with NGOs and local communities to reset expectations for business. They can collaborate with peers to set norms and standards for sustainable practices.

In doing so, firms are not just enabling their own sustainability efforts – they are contributing to a broad systems change. They are helping to create a new operating environment and sending signals to investors, consumers, and employees that prioritizing long-term value creation over short-term profits is not only acceptable but essential.

To help address mounting social and environmental challenges, companies need a new approach to nonmarket action. Simply reacting to social pressures is no longer enough. Firms must actively shape the nonmarket context in ways that align their interests with society. They must shift from seeing nonmarket engagement as a defensive necessity to embracing it as a source of opportunity, innovation, and advantage. Doing so requires building capabilities in stakeholder collaboration, social innovation, and adaptive leadership. And it requires embedding purpose and broad value creation into the core of the business. There is no longer a bright line between market and nonmarket.

As the nonmarket context grows ever more pressing and complex, the imperative for an integrated, strategic approach only grows. Firms that master this new nonmarket environment will be the ones that thrive in the coming age of sustainability. They will not only outperform other firms but also help build a world where business and society can flourish.

TAKEAWAYS

1. Integrating market and nonmarket strategies is crucial for modern businesses. This integration helps firms navigate complex regulations, manage stakeholder relationships, mitigate risks, and create shared value opportunities.

2. Effective nonmarket strategy requires a systematic approach involving analysis, formulation, implementation, and evaluation. This enables companies to shape their nonmarket environment to support business objectives while creating societal value.

3. Nonmarket strategy is essential for promoting sustainability. By engaging with stakeholders, companies can
shift broader contexts to prioritize long-term value creation and sustainability.

FURTHER READING

David Bach, "When CEOs Should Take a Stand in a Fractured
World," *California Management Review online*, April 15, 2024.
Michael Yaziji, "Three Filters for Making Business Decisions in the
Age of Stakeholder Capitalism," *I by IMD*, October11, 2023.

Chapter 13

Navigating the New Era of Sustainability Reporting

Florian Hoos

Sustainability is becoming a mandatory aspect of companies' annual reports around the world – and for some leading the pack, a fundamental aspect of their strategy. Some companies already translate their strategic sustainability considerations into credible reporting documents without any legal necessity. Yet, so far they have done this in a non-standardized manner, leaving room for companies to decide what to disclose and what to disguise. This era of voluntary sustainability disclosures, which makes it hard for investors and other external stakeholders to assess a company's sustainability performance, is coming to an end.

Starting with the financial year 2024, we are entering into a new era of company reporting and performance measurement. Before, we were mostly interested in financial statement information and forecasted financial data. Sustainability reports were just a nice add-on, receiving neither assurance certifications from auditors nor much attention in investors' and other stakeholders' decision-making. Now, we will have unified quantification and accounting standardization of emissions, water usage, land degradation, biodiversity, human rights, executive compensation, and many more topics.

Companies will face myriad new reporting requirements, which will largely standardize what they must report. But beyond meeting these compliance expectations, the real challenge lies in using the window of opportunity that opens up in the next years for a strategic transformation of what sustainability means and measuring and managing dimensions deemed relevant to gain and maintain competitive advantage.

Much has been written about the bureaucratic jungle of sustainability reporting regulations and the challenge of playing the compliance game. This chapter does not focus on detangling compliance, scope, materiality, and timelines. Many (consulting) firms will help companies comply with the regulations, which are specific to geography, size, and industry. Instead, this chapter explores how to navigate the new landscape from a strategic long-term perspective, with an emphasis on pragmatic and value-generating change management.

In any case, companies will have to adapt accounting and reporting systems, data collection mechanisms, internal reporting governance, and potentially upskill employees – from the top to the bottom of the hierarchy – to tackle the new sustainability challenges. So why not use the biggest accounting and reporting change in a hundred years for advancing your strategy and improving long-term performance instead of just complying with regulation?

THE FRAGMENTED LANDSCAPE OF MANDATORY SUSTAINABILITY REPORTING

Sustainability reporting has undergone a dramatic transformation that began with a redefinition of the type and amount of information that companies must report. It was nothing less than changing a fundamental principle of accounting: materiality. The latter had been forever focused on financial information that companies need to report at least annually to their stakeholders. And here is the crux of the new reporting challenge: while worldwide agreement has been reached of what materiality is for financial information, this consensus is yet missing for sustainability information. The world remains divided here, and even from a compliance perspective, what companies report will depend on the mandatory standards.

Leading the pack on ambitious and far-reaching sustainability reporting is the EU with its CSRD. The CSRD obliges all major listed companies in, and many large companies outside, the EU to report on sustainability topics. Based on the CSRD, the EU has cemented its focus on double materiality. In essence, this means that companies have to provide two types of information.

First, companies need to map out all sustainability issues that matter for investors. This so-called *financial materiality* is a concept designed to help companies separate a long list of possible issues from those that affect their financial performance and matter for investors. For instance, freshwater consumption is financially material for an agriculture firm in regions with water stress because it puts the business model at risk, while for a consulting firm, freshwater consumption is negligible.

Second, companies need to add material topics to their list if the company's activities substantially affect the planet or society irrespective of potential influences on firm value. This is *impact materiality*, which applies not to an investor perspective but to a stakeholder perspective. If the solar panels that your company uses need a big surface and you need to cut trees to make space, then this will probably not affect your firm value and thus is not financially material. But your business activities clearly have an impact on biodiversity because you cut trees and destroy the homes of animals. So you would need to report on biodiversity from an impact materiality perspective while ignoring it from a financial materiality perspective. Including impact and financial materiality as the basis for reporting into a double materiality regime is the European way of doing things.

The competing set of mandatory standards comes from the International Financial Reporting Standards (IFRS) Foundation. Historically, the IFRS Foundation has transformed the global landscape of financial information by introducing accounting standards that have become the global language of financial statements. With the creation of a new standard setting board – the International Sustainability Standards Board (ISSB), the IFRS Foundation attempts to provide the global baseline for sustainability reporting. Its sustainability standards are solely based on *financial materiality*. While some try to downplay this fundamental difference between single and double materiality, it does lead to different internal processes and can lead to significantly different sustainability reports.

Furthering this fragmentation is the Chinese approach. The Chinese government aims to establish a mandatory, ISSB-aligned reporting system close to the IFRS sustainability standards but at the same time promotes a double-materiality perspective. China's approach is representative of the fact that major economies around the world that adopt IFRS sustainability standards might adopt versions of the standards that depart from the originally proposed IFRS Foundation versions.

For the years to come, this leaves us with mandatory sustainability reporting in all major economies – with perhaps the lowest standards in the United States – but also with considerable geographical differences in terms of what companies have to report by law.

THE PUSH FOR HARMONIZATION

It is unlikely that shareholders and potential investors, but also activist groups and other influential stakeholders, will accept nonharmonized sustainability reporting in the long run. Just as shareholders once demanded consistent, comparable financial data to make informed decisions, which effectively led to the globalization of one set of financial reporting standards (IFRS), we can expect influential stakeholders to push for the harmonization of sustainability data.

The harmonization will not happen overnight, but there are strong precedents of what will happen with the most important sustainability dimensions. For instance, with the Paris Agreement from 2015 that aims to limit global warming below 2°C, one important set of stakeholders – governments around the world – have shown that they can reach global agreement on a fundamental environmental topic. It then took a few more years until the European Sustainability

Reporting Standards (ESRS) E1 and the IFRS S2 standards made emission reporting mandatory, and more important the obligation to report how companies contributed to reaching the Paris Agreement objective of limiting global warming.

This shift was a game changer in the world of accounting standard setting. The sustainability standards referenced global agreements, thereby effectively holding companies accountable for reaching politically agreed-upon objectives. The result was to harmonize emission reporting around the world. And even if the United States does not make scope 3 reporting mandatory, major investors of US-based firms will likely ask companies to report scope 3 emissions like their European competitors.

We can expect the same mechanism that happened with emissions and the Paris Agreement to happen for freshwater use, biodiversity, human rights in the supply chain, phosphorous, nitrogen, and plastic pollution. It is hard to say how long this will take, but with the Paris Agreement prominently cited by mandatory sustainability reporting standards, we have a precedent that global political agreements enter into accounting standards. Once these enter into mandatory sustainability standards and offer valuable information under one reporting regime to stakeholders, they serve as precedents to ask companies around the world to respect the highest standards.

In this new setting where different stakeholders push for harmonization, companies need to make strategic choices of how to tackle the new reporting regime. As the new era of sustainability reporting dawns, corporate leaders find themselves in two camps. One merely complies with regulations while waiting and watching before going beyond the baseline requirements. The second camp plays an active role in shaping and preempting the emerging standards; it goes beyond regulatory requirements in external disclosures and then takes on a pioneering role. The latter camp is led by companies such as Schneider Electric, which have shown that a clear sustainability strategy and superior reporting practices can lead to outperforming competitors.

Clearly, companies in both camps will play the compliance game to perfection. Being compliant with regulation is a baseline license to operate. Yet stopping there is a long-term transition risk that might backfire. Many companies are already surprised by the fast developments in sustainability reporting. They are overwhelmed by reaching compliance with current standards given the challenges of data collection along the supply chain, setting up new accounting and reporting systems, and figuring out how their stakeholders will react to the additional set of nonfinancial sustainability metrics.

It is by no means surprising that sustainability investing, through ESG, is facing a backlash, that sustainability in general is criticized, or that tensions around sustainability reporting standards increase. We are changing the rules of good company performance, adding a new comprehensive set of metrics. Of course, this puts some companies' stock market prices in danger, might make millions of jobs obsolete and in turn influence voters' behavior.

For leaders, the strategic question is whether you can allow yourself not to prepare for a world where the global baseline is double-materiality reporting. The latter might never happen, but if it happens, it will shake up the current rankings of the most valuable companies around the world.

GETTING READY FOR MANDATORY SUSTAINABILITY REPORTING

Many leaders see the new mandatory sustainability reporting regimes as an exhausting task, requiring time, money, and other resources with unclear outcomes. But it can also be a window of opportunity for change management. This is comparable to a human being with a recently diagnosed chronic disease: You can ignore it and complain about it while living off painkillers, or you can change your life and potentially become more resilient than ever before. Having this in mind, companies can make strategic choices to be at least prepared for a world where integrated sustainability reporting becomes reality.

Prepare for integrated reporting with governance. Until recently, accounting and reporting decisions were the responsibility of the chief financial officer. The rise in sustainability reporting has led some companies to create new roles such as a chief sustainability officer (CSO), serving as an internal and external signal that the company is taking the issue seriously. Many big companies used the new position to create new teams and hired external people with decades of sustainability experience. But new governance structures also bring political gaming and competency fights among the new and old board members, sometimes leading to regress, not progress. In addition, small firms often lack the resources and ability to hire more people to tackle sustainability opportunities. While there does not seem to be a one-size-fits-all solution to the new governance challenge, both new positions and new sustainability competencies are among the most crucial variables that companies must consider.

Vaude, the "European Patagonia," with its CEO Antje von Dewitz, and Ragn-Sells, the Swedish circular economy champion, with its CSO Pär Larshans, are two examples of small- and medium-sized firms where sustainability champions drove change. Both changed the governance and invested in training, collaboration, and internal reorganization, but they did it from different positions in the organizational chart and with different strategies adapted to their industry and seize.

So the need for new governance, people, and knowledge is evident, but the *how* should be a customized path to success. The ideal output of the new mandatory sustainability reporting regimes around the world is an integrated report, where the sustainability and financial metrics speak to each other. The IFRS Foundation and the EU regulation suggest between the lines that this is the end goal, and companies need to make sure that their governance restructuring allows the integration of financial and sustainability reporting. Adding myriad new sustainability metrics after the financial information in an annual report is surely not what will lead to competitive advantage.

Don't overpromise externally, but be prepared internally. For sustainability reporting, companies need to consider the difference between managerial accounting (using financial information for *internal* purposes only) and financial accounting (providing it to *external* stakeholders for decisions based on mandatory standards). They must report according to the mandatory sustainability reporting standards. But in the absence of reasonable assurance audit opinions and little enforcement for correct sustainability reporting for a couple more years, they can provide minimally compliant sustainability reporting (comparable to financial accounting) for external stakeholders while in parallel building up and experimenting with a managerial sustainability accounting system that prepares them internally for future sustainability reporting demands.

If at some point leaders want to go far beyond mere compliance with mandatory sustainability reporting, then strategic materiality is a useful concept. It is an opportunity to think about a materiality framework that translates a sustainability strategy into action. This is far from a one-size-fits-all solution to materiality reporting. It is a company's strategic sustainability approach with wise decisions about what to report externally, and what to use in that company's internal reporting systems only.

The exercise might show you that sustainability is just a mere compliance game for you because you have your competitive advantage outside the sustainability space. But then at least you have made your decision based on a sophisticated materiality assessment and not from a general neglect of the most fundamental shift in reporting in history. Based on this strategic materiality assessment, you might find that you actually have material topics where you can lead the pack and outperform others.

For companies that want to use the one-time change in reporting to their advantage, the search for nonreplicable sustainability strategies is key. What is a material aspect in your industry where you can outperform all your competitors – something that is not necessarily based on any standard but driven by the purpose of your company? Working in the German automobile industry, for instance, has been the dream job for many engineers around the world for decades. The competitive advantage of Porsche and others was built around their human capital in engineering. After the diesel scandal and the shift of the industry from car producers to agents of sustainable mobility, the German automobile industry has lost its human capital material advantage. The new talents that they need (software engineers, AI experts, and electrical engineers) go to companies in sustainable mobility. If the *Economist* is right and Germany stops making cars in the future, then this might be due to the companies no longer topping the list for employee well-being and clear purpose.

Embrace the changing accountability scope and collaborate. Admittedly, many businesses will face significant difficulties in meeting the new reporting requirements. The CSRD requires firms to supply high-quality data along the supply chain. Companies might be accustomed to consolidating financial data within the group of companies that they control, but now they need to collect and make sense of data that concerns their entire supply chain, distribution of their products, and the use-phase impacts.

The automobile industry's shift toward electric mobility is easily explained by 70% of emissions occurring in the use phase of a combustion engine car (upstream Scope 3 emissions), with only 20% in the supply chain (downstream Scope 3 emissions). Similarly, with rulings on corporate sustainability due diligence, companies need to take responsibility and report on what happens in their supply chains with severe litigation risks for misreporting or greenwashing.

The requirement for listed companies to publish non-financial data together with the annual report will shrink timelines to collect the data, ensure alignment to standards or regulations, and publish the whole report. Streamlined processes, digital solutions, and stakeholder engagement will be critical aspects of reporting in the years to come. This requires a collaborative mindset and people who can build trust and coalitions across supply chains. While the financial reporting scope ends when you don't control an asset anymore, the sustainability reporting scope goes far beyond this control. It encompasses what suppliers do, how they affect communities and nature around them, as well as what will happen with products once in use. This is a dramatic shift in scope for accountability.

Mitigate in the short run and innovate in the long run. Mandatory sustainability reporting does not force companies to do what is good for the planet or society. It simply forces companies to report on what they have done based on predefined metrics and to forecast what they want to achieve. It remains the company's responsibility to explain to stakeholders that the numbers they report show respect for the planet and that they advance society while boosting the financials. Most companies will try to mitigate material sustainability risks. For example, agricultural firms might reduce freshwater consumption and emissions, improve working conditions in the supply chain, and some more. But there is a limited amount of emissions, freshwater use, and working conditions that you can improve without changing your business model in traditional agriculture. At some point, you will report only incremental improvements.

Here, the new regulatory frameworks also offer a compelling invitation – and, in some sectors, an obligation – to innovate in products and services and to deliver them within "planetary boundaries." By taking advantage of a unique opportunity to embrace strong narratives on material topics, supported by relevant data, successful companies can use tighter regulation and reporting to disrupt their industries on the most important sustainability dimensions. The incredible capital that has gone into vertical farming (which might at the end not be the solution) shows that investors are ready to fund innovative ideas that can disrupt industries.

Sustainability is about future, not past performance. What companies with sustainability-focused governance have in common is that they downplay the role of KPIs focused on past performance. This is a fundamental difference between financial and sustainability reporting. While the former is largely about outlining past performance in the balance sheet, cash flow, and profit and loss statement, the latter is more about contributing to long-term targets such as the Paris Agreement's objectives. Doing so often requires forecasting exercises for the next 25 years, including credible milestones 5, 10, and 20 years from now with, for example, emission reductions. Instead of looking at last year's emission reduction or the number of human rights violation complaints, companies will have to apply a forward-looking and scenario-based approach.

With rigorous sustainability reporting standards, it is also important that companies embrace a "less is more" mentality when it comes to the major KPIs. The CSRD requires hundreds of new metrics in sustainability reports for some companies. Reporting these metrics is a painful compliance exercise. But it has nothing to do with developing a compelling strategic narrative that is backed up by a few credible KPIs.

A common pitfall in sustainability reporting is to introduce many KPIs instead of a strategic narrative, as these are often contradictory or inconsistent. The goal is not to measure every aspect of sustainability but to prioritize a few well-chosen KPIs clearly connected to your company's materiality assessment and strategic narrative. For example, if carbon emissions are a significant material issue for your business, your KPIs should focus on measurable reductions in emissions across scopes 1–3.

Finally, to seize business opportunities based on environmental or social value creation, companies need to align their strategy closer to frameworks such as the planetary boundaries (environment) or the doughnut economy (social). They can then engage in long-term forecasting exercises on those dimensions that matter. Lombard Odier focused early on investment strategies that take plastic waste reduction prominently into account. And those companies that took human rights seriously in the past will be less exposed to due diligence risks in the future. In both cases, a match has been found between what is good for the planet and society and what is good for financial performance in the long run.

THE CHANGING RULES OF THE GAME ARE NOT ABOUT LEGAL SCOPE

Whether big or small, the reporting rules of the game are being changed forever. If you are not in the scope of mandatory reporting, it is likely that one of your clients will ask you to provide sustainability data because you are part of the client's supply chain. Over time, probably no firm will escape sustainability reporting because of being either in the legal scope or the supply chain of a company that is subject to the mandate.

Yet the rules do not change in the same speed and not with the same magnitude around the world. CSRD and similar global initiatives are fundamentally altering the rules of corporate reporting in some countries and for some industries right now. The German automobile industry clearly missed this reporting macro trend, and today, these companies face declining stock market prices due to their lack of clear strategies to drastically reduce emissions. The right timing for strategic changes is fundamental in the new era of sustainability reporting.

What is clear is that sustainability is no longer a peripheral concern. With its uplift into companies' most important evaluation – the annual report – sustainability has gained its place as a fundamental performance criterion. It is becoming as critical as financial reporting in assessing a company's long-term viability and success – not at the same speed in all industries and regions, but it will come to your company if you are not affected right now, slowly but surely.

It is your strategic choice whether you see this one-time change in reporting only as a pain for which you apply costly painkillers to decrease the compliance burden – or you take adaptive action in strategy and governance and make forward-looking investments. Competitive advantage is about adapting quickly to macro trends – and the changing rules of the game can be considered as such.

TAKEAWAYS

1. Embrace double materiality for strategic advantage, fully integrating it into your internal reporting processes. This means assessing how sustainability impacts not only financial performance, but also how your operations affect society and the environment. This dual perspective can help you identify new risks and opportunities and gain competitive advantage.

2. Less is more when it comes to KPIs. Focus on developing indicators aligned with your most material sustainability issues. Ensure that you have a limited number of credible KPIs that support your strategic narrative. This approach will enable you to report credible sustainability progress to your stakeholders and drive meaningful change.

3. Comply with the highest upcoming standards without necessarily reporting based on them. Stay ahead of the curve by adopting these standards internally early, to meet upcoming regulatory requirements and investors' and other stakeholders' requests.

FURTHER READING

Florian Hoos, "Are You Ready for the Biggest Accounting Experiment in 100 Years," *I by IMD*, 4 August 2023.

Chapter 14

The Paradox of Digital Technology

Didier Bonnet and Michael Wade

Promoting sustainability involves reworking much of what companies do and at least some future market opportunities. Digital technologies are powerful enough to help with that reworking, but they can also hinder companies from moving forcefully. Different companies will use this technology differently. Mindset, more than any technological or economic imperative, will likely drive any broad impact.

AI is perhaps the most powerful kind of digital technology now emerging, enough to justify its own chapter in this book (Chapter 15). In this chapter, we focus on the many powerful digital technologies apart from AI, from digital twin simulation to the IoT.

BOOSTING TRANSPARENCY

A 2022 survey suggested that fewer than half of executives believed digital tech would promote sustainability in their companies. But that's misleading. These technologies are well-suited to visualizing, improving, and scaling industrial and commercial processes – which is mainly how companies will actually achieve sustainability over time. The potential is enormous because sustainability is in part a computational problem from added complexity (nonfinancial goals), and digital technology excels at computation.

Executive skepticism may come partly from how companies have used digital technology up to now, mostly to boost profitability in non-sustainable ways. With the crisis of sustainability, companies can now apply many of the same tools to environmental and social concerns, not just financial ones. The technologies have proven their power; companies just need to adjust the goals.

Digital technologies by themselves are not neutral – they generate 4% of global carbon emissions, greater than aviation. Data centers are going up everywhere, consuming enormous amounts of electricity and fresh water. Already Alphabet and Microsoft have backtracked on their commitments to carbon neutrality because of their growing reliance on these centers.

A great deal of digital equipment is also sent to landfills every year, as companies factor advances into a kind of planned obsolescence. The technology industry itself must do more to minimize these direct impacts. So the first challenge is to reduce those emissions and waste, which companies can partly do with digital technologies, as we'll explain below. Then they can promote sustainability broadly by better employing those technologies.

This rapid obsolescence can actually help indirectly with sustainability. Digital technology changes so fast that most of the biases of the pre-sustainability era will be largely removed soon. Even core software in enterprise resource planning systems gets rewritten over time. Some biases will persist, but on the whole, digital technology is less stuck in tradition than other corporate tools.

As for the main task, start with visualizing. Digital technologies excel in giving executives transparency: a clear view into actual operational performance on a variety of sustainability measures. To reduce their impact, companies need to measure it, and increasingly that's through inexpensive digital sensors, digitally connected to data analytics, often in real time. These can yield hard numbers on actual carbon emissions, freshwater usage, and other variables. They can also assess diversity and inclusion in the workforce, as well as other social indices. Armed with that view, executives have the pinpointed knowledge to make improvements throughout the organization. They also have the means for accountability for the different areas of the company.

Those metrics work in the field as well as the factory. Baker Hughes, the oilfield services company, collects data from sensors on its field equipment and combines it with simulation data from a digital twin of that same equipment. Other companies do the same thing for heavy equipment purchased by customers to help those customers collect data. Instead of resorting to a physical crash, you can simulate the damage to the equipment from a likely crash. The industrial internet, or Internet of Things, will enable all of these efforts by digitally connecting sensors and machines.

With all this intelligence, companies can make smarter judgments. Digital tech has shown us that many of the steps we thought would make a big difference for sustainability aren't so effective, while others are.

The results can be astounding. Tony's Chocoloney is a Dutch chocolatier that promotes sustainability. It set up "Beantracker," a cloud-based platform, to monitor the flow of cocoa beans from West Africa to Europe. Chocolate has one of the longest value chains in the food sector: beans grown inland in one country, bagged and shipped off at a port, processed and packaged in at least one, sometimes four countries, before sale in yet another country.

Beantracker, in combination with digital sensors and analytics, provided crucial transparency on Tony's value chain. Besides measuring carbon emissions, it helped the company to ensure that its beans were free from slavery and unfair labor practices as well as environmentally damaging farming. With GPS satellites and drones, for example, the company can now measure a farm's output against typical yields. If the yields are abnormally high, the farm may be relying on exploited labor or deforested land – or stealing from neighbors. If abnormally low, the farm may be planting unsustainably in other ways. Both findings generate a visit from a Tony's inspector in the region.

The people at Tony's started with some assumptions about their biggest environmental impact, but they didn't know. Some suspected it was in freshwater use, especially in the farms. Others said it was the heavy fuel oil used for ships. And others blamed the company's elaborate packaging.

But it turns out the biggest environmental impact came from cows, which supplied the powdered milk in making many chocolate products. So now the company is scrambling to use less milk or to find an environmentally friendly alternative to milk. Digital tools enable companies to dig deep into their value chains. They may be surprised at where the impact really is.

The metrics and analytics will be especially important for visualizing impact beyond what a company does internally. As firms understand their scope-three impact – carbon emissions and other problems from suppliers, distributors, and customers tied to the firm's offerings – they'll need digital technology simply to ease what would otherwise be a heavy computational burden. Digital tools provide visibility, pointing companies to where they can make the biggest difference. And now almost everyone is walking around with a sophisticated digital sensor in their pocket – a smartphone.

Transparency is especially important for initiatives that might otherwise be little better than guesses about future market demands. A company might not know exactly what customers will want, but with this knowledge about actual current impacts, they can confidently predict where markets will be looking for solutions. With transparency, they'll know where they're likely have the biggest payoff.

That data collection can also transform business models, especially in creating products as a service. With the IoT reporting on usage, airlines are buying hours of flight instead of the jets themselves, with the manufacturer handling all maintenance and replacement over time. As customers know more about their usage, they can take steps to conserve energy and other scarce resources.

IMPROVING OPERATIONS

Next, digital technologies can help companies make enormous advances in improving their operations and offerings. Companies are always looking to optimize, but digital tools make this work much easier. If they can optimize for performance, they can optimize for sustainability. But the improvements are not just about optimizing to reduce waste or replacing hardware with software, which are likely to happen anyway. Digital tools can work directly to change how companies operate – not just optimizing their activity but taking it to a new level of sophistication and insight.

As with the crashes, digital tools enable simulation, which enables testing and experimentation with far less need for materials. By monitoring its field equipment and comparing it to a "digital twin," Baker Hughes extends the life of its equipment, protects the environment, and reduces dangers to workers. Digital twins also work well for simulating new operations for that equipment, including ways to boost sustainability. Thus the technology not only increases efficiency for existing processes but also frees the imagination to try out better processes.

Back to earth, agricultural equipment companies such as John Deere help farmers plant productively while using less pesticide, fertilizer, and water. BASF, the chemical manufacturer, combines satellite and ground-level sensor data to tell farmers where and how to plant crops to minimize the ecological footprint. Instead of using these sensors, satellites, and analytics to maximum farm yields by cost, companies can adjust the algorithms and maximize for the lowest environmental (and social) impact. They can still make money from enabling all these savings while boosting sustainability at the same time.

Everything works as before; we just change the software, for qualitative as well as quantitative improvement. Or to take an entirely new product area: companies can use digital sensors combined with weather reports to maximize energy from each wind turbine, in some cases adjusting angles or speeds. Optimizing works broadly. And some applications that didn't make sense financially, such as applying the IoT for predictive maintenance beyond heavy industrial equipment, could now work for companies pushing sustainability – partly for the information it offers along with optimization.

Digital technology has moved into operations in multiple ways. Additive manufacturing, or 3D printing, generates products that require less material. Moving paper-based processes to online formats reduces not just the drawbacks of paper but also the amount of transportation and shipping required. Remote maintenance systems, with local technicians guided by experts at headquarters, reduce transportation and materials as well as equipment downtime. Thus the liquid-packaging giant Tetra Pak uses virtual-reality headsets to enable onsite technicians to conduct complicated maintenance on its equipment. Videoconferencing replaces at least some carbon-intensive travel for face-to-face meetings.

One study estimated that better use of digital technologies would reduce global carbon emissions by a fifth. Note that this isn't just about reducing emissions from current operations. It's also about coming up with innovative ways of meeting current market needs. As more products and services rely on software, it gets easier to adjust the offerings to nudge customers toward sustainable uses.

Optimization and simulation together, when pursued with creativity, could lead to big operational advances. These will

be crucial elements in improving our current levels of affluence and equality without wrecking our ecosystem.

SCALING WITH DIGITAL TOOLS

To get a broad impact, it isn't enough for companies to do
better individually. They need to scale those improvements
and innovations. Scaling is a major challenge, but digital
technologies help here as well. Start with the seamless
connectivity from digital sensors and networks, which provide crucial infrastructure for scaling. Instead of a few disparate innovations, companies can offer customer-friendly
solutions with enormous impact.

The greatest potential lies in cross-company and cross-sector
collaboration. If a company acts in isolation, its impact will be
narrow, no matter how successful. Companies might eventually imitate its success, but collaboration will both speed up
and improve this process.

Tony's Chocoloney didn't keep Beantracker to itself. It now
shares this platform with suppliers, retailers, and even some
competitors so they can work collectively to improve sustainability along the entire chocolate value chain. The results
are too early to tell, but this courageous sharing has the
potential to boost sustainability in the entire industry.

Or farming generally. If John Deere and other agricultural
equipment providers convince most farmers to allow sensors,
they can work together to justify major investment in water
supplies, low-emission tools, or conservation in a region. The
benefit comes from digital networking all this data in real time.

Many companies have talked about sustainability's importance and have made bold statements about their future

impact. But that's the easy part. The main challenge will be in efforts that don't pay for themselves – for economic and social improvements that cost money through at least the medium term. Companies could charge higher prices and justify them on sustainability grounds, but to do that they'll need hard data. And that data comes only from digital sensors and analytics. B2B customers in particular will want to know how much they'll reduce carbon emissions by using the product or service.

THE DILEMMA OF CONVENIENCE

The very power of digital technology can also become a trap for executives. Most consumers seek convenience along with affordability and quality. What happens when this desire for convenience works against sustainability? We've seen this not just in the garment industry, where digital technology has enabled a "fast fashion" approach where consumers wear clothes only a few times before discarding, but also meal delivery and single-use containers. Outsourcing itself can raise issues if the outsourcer is less committed to sustainability. After all, few consumers really see sustainability as a job to be done. Instead they focus on meeting this need affordably and conveniently now. Sustainability-driving buying decisions are still a tiny niche.

It's hard for companies to resist competing on convenience. But companies can seek alternative business models that still give long-term value to consumers as well as producers.

NOT TECHNOLOGY BUT MINDSET

Digital technologies can help with sustainability indirectly as well, pointing to a model of adoption over time. Companies have seen waves of new digital technologies wash over their industries, often with disappointing results. Each new technology goes into a hype cycle of great enthusiasm, followed by merely ordinary results. Often the challenges have nothing to do with the technology itself, which might work fairly well. It's about getting organizations to embrace the technology, altering the relevant processes, roles, structures, and incentives. Doing so requires experimenting, adapting, and being open to change generally. Too many people don't adjust their mindset, so the technology underperforms.

Something similar may be happening with sustainability. Hardly anyone opposes it. But when managers try to change those processes, roles, structures and incentives, they meet resistance, and they move slowly. Most companies tend to act conservatively and to try to minimize risk, which is where regulation and public-private partnerships can help.

Fortunately, even as companies have resisted many digital technologies, most now rely heavily on them. Change has come slower than expected, with many digital opportunities still unexplored. But companies operate very differently from how they did in previous decades. We can expect something similar for sustainability. The only question is whether companies will change fast and far enough to prevent calamities.

Also, companies can make enormous progress without flashy initiatives. From holding virtual meetings instead of flying, to putting a digital service into existing products, or just adding software to extend the lifetime of hardware, organizations will quietly become much more sustainable. Some people say these are just the low-hanging fruit and that much of it might be plucked anyway for conventional business reasons. But cumulatively these will have enormous impact and prepare the way for innovative advances – even as younger generations help to change the mindset toward sustainability.

Progress will also come over time with a gradual redesign, again driven by that different mindset. Most digital tools emerged to address conventional business imperatives, often with minimal attention to sustainability. Data centers and other digital processes use enormous amounts of energy. Eventually we'll redesign those tools, and the teams that implement them, around sustainability. With shared governance for commercial results and sustainability, we'll get better results for the environment and society in many areas of operation. After all the work to develop and manage digital tools with impressive capabilities, companies will gradually reorient them toward sustainability.

Mindset is essential in any case. Companies can have impressive tools but make little progress unless they work diligently to use them. Sustainability efforts will require big capital investments, as well as attention to environmental and social dynamics, and many leaders still hold conventional ideas of short-term business dynamics. If market signals favor sustainability, then digital tools will do great things. But if market signals go in the opposite direction, as with fast fashion, then we need companies to use digital technology to keep going toward sustainability.

Digital technologies bring enormous power to bear on the challenges of sustainability. But they aren't a simple solution. Managers will need to work carefully to apply the technologies to targeted problems and innovations. They'll also need to ramp up the often difficult work of collaborating with suppliers and rivals in order to scale up advances. But with commitment and diligence, companies can use digital technology to move quickly to a sustainable world.

TAKEAWAYS

1. Use digital technology and data to get visibility on your sustainability performance metrics and to educate customers to reduce environmental impact.

2. Use digital simulations to optimize operational performance for sustainability, as with reducing materials and maintaining equipment remotely.

3. Explore cross-company and cross-industry collaboration to widen the sources of information and scale digital solutions, such as gaining full visibility on supply chains.

FURTHER READING

Michael Wade and Julia Binder, "Digital Sustainability for a Better Future," *Stanford Social Innovation Review*, 2024.

Chapter 15

Artificial Intelligence

Öykü Isik and Jose Parra-Moyano

One digital technology, artificial intelligence, has special potential to hasten or hinder the transition to sustainability. The technology is still emerging, especially in its generative form that works with large language models (LLMs). But we know enough so far to see that companies can use it to enable their transition – as long as they avoid decisions that entrench pre-sustainability practices.

THE AI OPPORTUNITY – AND THREAT

AI is essentially an aggressive form of pattern recognition technology that has the ability to learn from data and that can develop tools to automate certain tasks. With enough computation, based on humans' past actions (coded in data form), a machine demonstrates a capability that resembles intelligence. It's still just 0s and 1s manipulated through computer programming languages, but the machine, through pattern recognition and data processing, adds value that companies can incorporate into their work.

Generative AI is simply the branch of AI that generates new content (text, programming code, images, music, voice, slides, etc.). LLMs (one of the latest additions to the AI family) are sophisticated enough to act as if they understand human input in natural form (i.e. text or voice). This enables the AI based on such models to interact with people in their natural, everyday, nonmachine language – a step that takes the computational requirements to another level. And thanks to the computational capacity that companies can access via massive cloud computing infrastructure, AI can be applied to many business activities around the world.

For sustainability as described in this book, AI has two possibilities. The first is that companies use AI to find solutions to sustainability problems. Suppose a company is trying to optimize its energy consumption to reduce its carbon emissions. AI can suggest choices that maintain the business objectives while reducing the burning of fossil fuels. Perhaps the company can proceed in ways that shrink the carbon footprint without affecting the operations or don't bother the clients. The company can use AI to find that out. Many of the improvements discussed in Chapter 14, such as precision agriculture, may get even better with AI.

The idea here is that most organizations want to become more sustainable, but the issues are so complex that only with complex analytical tools such as AI can they make much headway. AI essentially simplifies what might otherwise be a daunting computational burden in moving to sustainability. For example, Alphabet, Google's parent company, recently used AI to optimize its energy usage to reduce carbon emissions – which would have been impossible with human calculation.

Going further, AI can come up with entirely new solutions to a sustainability challenge. Suppose a company is concerned about its consumption of fresh water. Instead of optimizing that consumption, AI might suggest a new way to make a product that uses far less water. It goes beyond optimization and into innovation, with ideas that human developers likely could never have imagined.

This is where generative AI may be particularly helpful. DSM-Firmenich, a Swiss fragrance company, uses the technology with their century-old capabilities on perfumes and flavors to generate new formulae for taste molecules. The augmented creation speeds up innovation and brings solutions to market quickly.

That's the positive view, which often dominates discussions on sustainability. Unfortunately, AI can also hinder the transition. The previous chapter already talked about digital technologies' heavy use of electricity in server processing and cooling. As Alphabet knows all too well, because AI is computationally intensive, it uses more energy than other digital technologies. All of that data needs to be stored, and crunched, somewhere. Alphabet's overall energy consumption has taken off as it invested heavily in AI. Likewise, Microsoft's reported scope three CO_2 emissions rose by almost 30% between 2020 and 2023.

But there's a bigger problem with AI. Every AI program is essentially a model built on those past human actions. Most of those actions happened in a world with little concern for sustainability. So AI in the present might end up being just as oblivious to sustainability as most of us were in the past. A comparable example came out in 2023–2024, when some early versions of generative AI exhibited the same racist and sexist assumptions that were common in past decades.

Even deeper, many of us worry that AI is fundamentally anti-human. In their eagerness to automate and boost efficiency, managers might become desensitized and less connected to stakeholders. Capitalism could run amok, with widespread layoffs and de-skilling. So could governments – already we've seen Australian authorities overtaxing citizens abroad and Dutch bureaucracies demanding child welfare payments paid back due to poorly designed algorithms.

Other digital technologies have been accused of dehumanizing, but AI takes that concern to a high level because of its extraordinary power and broad application. It could develop momentum of its own. AI might excel at a specific task, but if companies rely on it broadly, they could undermine our human sustainability overall.

Except in highly regulated industries, especially with bioethics experience, most companies are paying little attention to governance. Ethics by design, and privacy by design, are established concepts, but companies rarely apply them to AI. Of course, a single company can't alone develop strong governance for this fast-developing technology, but consortia and other groupings could go far in de-risking AI. Yet most companies are moving quickly and trying out AI in many areas with little thought.

DATA AS A RESPECTED RESOURCE

What can companies do to maximize the positive outcomes and minimize those problems? What is really new about AI is the centrality of data. Data reflects reality, so as reality evolves, AI programs will need new data. Companies can maximize positive outcomes by respecting what are called data cooperatives, data commons, or data unions. With powerful AI, data has become a factor of production, like capital and labor. Just as companies need cash and people to generate value, they also need data to automate operations with AI.

That is especially true for the next wave of generative AI. The first chatbots and other programs aimed at plausibility, not so much accuracy. In order to reduce "hallucinations" and make generative AI practical for many corporate uses, AI providers will need more hardware and especially more data. That is likely to come soon.

In the early twentieth century, despite the fragmentation of labor in industries, governments eventually compelled companies to give workers a degree of respect. With that respect, workers could form unions and achieve crucial benefits and a degree of affluence. Likewise, we now need governments to compel companies to give the sources of data, especially data of past human activities, a degree of respect. That won't be easy – the ownership structure of data is more fragmented than that of labor. Also, some companies own multiple datasets distributed across many different platforms. But formal data cooperatives could negotiate with companies to ensure privacy, exercise influence, and gain a share of the monetizing of that data.

Several data cooperatives already exist, especially in health care, where promoting research, privacy, and ethics matter more than monetizing. Midata and SalusCoop work to channel data toward the concerns of the data owners. Driver's Seat caters to the gig economy, giving people insights and tools to better manage and learn from their work-related data. Swash collects and monetizes browser histories for the individual user, while the Data Workers Union advocates for the rights of data producers across multiple sectors. Companies with large data needs may find that working with a data cooperative is less expensive in the long run than may appear.

Data is also difficult to respect because unlike capital and labor, it is not exclusive in its use. A company in Spain can use data at the same time a firm in China uses the exact same data – it's just 0s and 1s. But any artificial intelligence is only as good as the data in its model, so these data co-ops, as gatekeepers, may gain substantial power if they can promise companies a ready supply of good data. The data from any individual is worth practically nothing. But if a co-op put together data from a critical mass of citizens, suddenly this data becomes quite valuable, as AI can better recognize patterns and draw conclusions.

Co-ops will be motivated to collect valuable data and make it accessible for companies. We could even get data entrepreneurs to make that happen and in a way that does not compromise privacy. Techniques such as federated learning – a technique to train AI models across different repositories, combined with hiomomophic encryption – a privacy-preserving technique, will help here. Cooperatives can exercise their influence and even monetize the data of their members, without sacrificing their members' privacy.

Just as regulators are now overseeing the sharing of financial information in open banking, they could oversee the sharing and training of data in a privacy-preserving way. The regulation is essential, to prevent a tragedy of the commons. Anyone who contributes to a data co-op, at least in the early years, probably won't see a big payoff. That is partly because companies often don't know if certain data is valuable, so they'll pay little for the data, but also because the main benefits are likely externalized. Suppose someone contributes to a data co-op, which then makes the dataset usable for a pharmaceutical company. If the company discovers and markets a new drug, based partly on the data set, then every person will benefit from the drug even apart from any contribution to that data. Regulators can help to direct more of that value toward the data contributors; they can also ensure that the data co-ops follow certain principles to avoid overuse of the resource.

That's one way to make AI more sustainable in itself and to mitigate its harms. Another is for companies to resist the temptation to anthropomorphize AI. People can't help but be attracted to a machine that speaks well in many different languages. They expect it to do many things it cannot really do competently.

Take, for example, how it improves English prose for non-English speakers. It generally does this well, but it tends to overuse certain words that were prominent in the database it draws on. Depending on the version used, words such as "delve" and "seamlessly" appear more than they would from a human writer. The result is that writing gets easier, especially for people who have struggled in the past, but the value that people give to texts falls. Maybe human writing will thereby gain in value, at least as a niche product. Maybe editors will matter more, to help filter and improve the abundance of texts coming out. That is especially important for texts that seek to stand out, to catch the attention of customers or clients, or to leave a good impression. Even if future generative AI solves the problem of repeated words, the text may still feel a little artificial.

COMPLEMENTING, NOT SUBSTITUTING FOR PEOPLE

We can't anticipate how AI will develop. But historically, companies have always engaged with emerging technologies, and usually with a mix. They substitute out some labor, while other labor gets complemented by the technology in a way that adds value. With AI, we can expect the same mix of substitution and complementarity, but we don't know the ratio ahead of time. If companies embrace AI so deeply as to substitute nearly all the workers, that is not sustainable – we could have mass unemployment and extreme inequality, and companies will lose consumers, or worse.

If companies use AI mainly as a complement, to enhance the capabilities of the employees and enable them to do more, then everyone is likely to be better off. They can still use AI to boost efficiency, but in a smart way. They'll substitute out some workers, but the remaining employees will solve problems faster and produce more. That's been the overall historical trend with technology, emphasizing complementarity, with some short-term pain from substitution. But AI is so powerful that the long-term gains from complementarity may get overwhelmed by that short-term substitution, pain – and we could get a crisis of sustainability. So we need long-term thinking to escape the bottom-line mentality of just cutting costs with AI.

That goes for developing human capital. AI might actually weaken capabilities in the long run if companies automate tasks that otherwise would have helped junior staff develop. How will people build the skills to take on the hard questions that AI can't effectively handle if AI has deprived them of the training up to that point?

AI will certainly create some new positions altogether. Data reflects reality, so as reality evolves, AI programs will need new data. Even with flourishing data cooperatives, companies will likely need to collect some data on their own. Like the people Amazon hired to hold conversations in fake houses when it was training Alexa, we will have many jobs that essentially serve AI by generating data for it. That is actually better than relying on synthetic data, especially data created by the programs themselves, which is already happening. Synthetic data is cheaper, but it dilutes the quality of the results while dehumanizing them. We'll be better all around with fresh human data, free of the biases of the past. Companies that rely on this data will promote social sustainability while getting more value in the long run.

The underlying assumption in all of this is that AI is a tool to serve a company's needs. The companies themselves are just tools, but to what end? Leaders face a dilemma: they are in a competitive industry, and they need to use AI to some extent just to keep up. Customers are increasingly expecting it. But should a company invest aggressively in AI and maybe even seek some innovation? Often those aggressive investments involve a high degree of complementarity. Or should leaders be cautious and go along with the pack, emphasizing substitution, and try to differentiate in other ways lest they get carried away with AI?

Investing aggressively carries risks, especially with all the uncertainty around its development. It could damage the organization over time, just as much as proceeding cautiously and seeking differentiation elsewhere. Executives need to be prudent and pick their battles – substituting in some areas but complementing in others. Rushing into AI is a mistake all around.

THE COMPANY CONTEXT

Because AI relies on massive amounts of data, the pioneering companies will always be the handful of technology giants with large data sets. They are usually one step ahead of regulators, while other companies often move a few steps behind. Those latter companies cannot advance fast. But they can choose the mix of substitution and complementarity in the AI steps they do take.

Generative AI in particular is likely in a bubble. The very user-friendly aspects of it are leading many companies to put it to uses it cannot perform well, especially without broad, fresh data sets. Most companies still have trouble making sense of their own data with technology that has been around for a decade. As a result, even apart from the substitution/complementarity question, many executives will be wise to hold off on big AI investments and make sure they have enough analytics for their existing data. Data architects, data scientists, and data engineers are still in short supply and have the biggest payoff for many companies. Let your rivals be distracted by the cool kid in the room. In the long run, AI may have the biggest consequence in advancing data science, just as the COVID-19 pandemic jumpstarted remote working. And once companies have full data analytics capabilities, they can make advances in sustainability with the magic of AI that they could never make otherwise.

Company context is also essential for the old build-vs-buy question. Given the massive investments likely to be necessary for accurate AI, most companies will prefer to buy and adapt an existing AI program rather than make their own. That could be good for sustainability because they'll rely on others' investment in these energy-intensive resources. They won't need to do the extensive training to make an AI effective.

The downside is that these companies will risk losing their differentiation in the marketplace.

There's a middle ground between these two choices: many companies may not need as large an AI model as they think. Perhaps they can get what they need from multiple small AI models. How much accuracy do they really need? There's no need to boil the ocean for a few small problems. Many companies may be able to get enough AI differentiation from relatively small investments, which would be good for sustainability as well.

Big companies may want their own large-language-model partly to facilitate knowledge transfer across the organization, with some benefits as well in compliance and privacy. The small firms can fine-tune an off-the-shelf AI program with their own data. It's the mid-size companies that have the hard choices. And however much a company relies on outside datasets, it needs to make sure the data minimizes the biases of past decades that can undermine sustainability in the present.

QUESTIONS TO ASK

AI, especially generative AI, is still so new that instead of case studies of AI in companies, we offer questions for executives to ask before investing in it. Besides the specific areas mentioned above, here are some general questions:

1. What is the value you are trying to create? AI can do many things, often spectacularly well, but most of those tasks will add little value to the company or to customers.

2. What data do you really need for the AI program to work well? Small amounts of high-quality data, perhaps from a data cooperative, may actually end up costing less than a huge volume of middling data.

3. How will the use of AI affect your people and organization? Setting aside the value-adding benefits of complementing rather than substituting labor, AI has the potential to undermine the engagement of human capital. What will you do to minimize the disruption and alienation that AI could cause?

Companies need to treat AI like any other strategic oportunity. It can be an advantage and a threat, for sustainability as well as their bottom line. Much depends on thoughtful decisions and governance.

TAKEAWAYS

1. For sustainability, AI is both a powerful opportunity – greater efficiency and creativity – and a grave threat, entrenching past biases and dehumanizing companies.

2. The value of new data may induce companies to work with data collectives that also take steps to safeguard privacy.

3. In the mix of substituting and complementing labor, companies can promote social sustainability by upskilling employees.

FURTHER READING

Öykü Isik, "When It Comes to AI, You Must Build Consumer Trust," *I by IMD*, April 2, 2024.

Öykü Isik et al., "Four Types of AI Risk and How to Mitigate Them," *Harvard Business Review*, May 31, 2024.

Jose Parra-Moyano, "Data Entrepreneurs of the World, Unite! How Business Leaders Should React to the Emergence of Data Cooperatives," *Capco Journal*, 59, 2024.

Jose Parra-Moyano et al., "How Data Collaboration Platforms Can Help Companies Build Better AI," *Harvard Business Review*, Jan. 26, 2024.

PART III

The Leadership Imperative

Julia Binder and Knut Haanaes

Sustainable business transformation requires more than just a solid strategy – it demands leadership that is visionary, courageous, and deeply committed to change. This third section of the book focuses on the leadership imperative – the essential role that leaders play in driving sustainability within their organizations. The section explores how leadership can turn ambitious strategies into tangible realities, creating cultures that not only embrace sustainability but thrive on it.

Leadership in sustainability begins with the ability to lead and manage change. Have you ever felt frustrated when your well-crafted plans met with resistance or inertia? Many leaders find that despite their best efforts, change initiatives often falter. This is not because the strategy is flawed, but because the human aspects of change are complex and challenging. Effective leadership requires a deep understanding of the emotions, fears, and motivations that drive people's behavior. Leaders must create a shared vision and build trust within their teams, fostering an environment where change is not just accepted but embraced.

But leading change in the present is only part of the equation. To truly succeed in sustainability, leaders must also be **future-ready**. This requires an **ambidextrous leadership** style that balances the need to exploit current opportunities while exploring new ones. Have you ever wondered how to stay agile and innovative while maintaining your organization's stability? Ambidextrous leaders navigate the immediate challenges of today while keeping an eye on the future, ensuring that their organizations are not only surviving but thriving in the long term. Developing this capability is critical for any leader who aims to guide their organization through the uncertainties of the future.

Developing these leadership capabilities goes beyond acquiring technical skills – it involves embarking on both an Inner and Outer Journey. The Inner Journey is about cultivating resilience and mindfulness, essential for maintaining energy and focus amid the demands of sustainability challenges. Leaders who practice self-awareness and emotional intelligence are better equipped to lead with clarity and compassion. The Outer Journey, on the other hand, involves seeking external perspectives to refine leadership approaches. For instance, Skanska's leaders engage in "discovery expeditions" where they visit sites such as a sustainable construction project in Seattle to gain insights that inform their practices back home. This blend of internal and external growth enables leaders to be more adaptive and innovative in their approach to sustainability.

Leadership in sustainability also involves a fundamental shift in how we wield power – from "power over" to the **courage of "power with."** This approach is not just about sharing power; it's about creating entirely new ecosystems where collaboration and collective ownership drive innovation. Have you ever considered how powerful it could be if you could truly mobilize all your stakeholders toward a common goal? In today's interconnected world, no single organization can achieve sustainability alone. Leaders must build and sustain **ecosystem partnerships** that engage a wide range of stakeholders – from suppliers and customers to governments and NGOs – in a shared mission. This is more than just forming alliances; it's about constructing new ecosystems that are resilient, adaptive, and capable of driving systemic change. The most effective leaders understand that by embracing a "power with" approach, they can harness the collective strength of their teams, partners, and broader communities to achieve goals that would be impossible in isolation.

However, many companies face significant cultural barriers to adopting sustainability practices. Often, these organizations have deeply ingrained **cultures** that prioritize short-term gains over long-term impact. Leaders can't simply tell people to think long-term; they must demonstrate the immediate benefits of change. For example, Eneva, a Brazilian energy company, shifted from relying on distant engineers to hiring locally in the Amazon. This not only saved costs but also built local capacity, subtly shifting the company's mindset toward valuing sustainable, community-focused decisions. By addressing cultural biases and demonstrating tangible benefits, Eneva's leaders began to open the door to broader acceptance of sustainability practices.

Effective governance is another critical aspect of the leadership imperative. As sustainability becomes increasingly central to business strategy, the role of governance – particularly at the board level – must evolve. Boards are no longer just custodians of financial performance; they must also oversee the integration of sustainability into the company's core strategy. Have you considered how your board is evolving to meet these new demands? This involves rethinking traditional governance structures and embedding sustainability into every aspect of decision-making. For many companies, this means appointing a chief sustainability officer, integrating sustainability metrics into executive compensation, and ensuring that board members have the knowledge and expertise to guide the organization on its sustainability journey. **Family businesses** often serve as models in this regard, where their long-term vision and legacy naturally align with sustainability goals. By integrating these principles into the governance framework, leaders can ensure that their organizations remain committed to sustainability at the highest levels.

Leading for sustainability also requires a commitment to **inclusion**, ensuring that diverse perspectives are integrated into decision-making processes. While inclusion is crucial, it's also essential that leaders focus on embedding sustainability deeply within their organizational structures and governance systems, making it an inextricable part of the company's DNA.

Finally, effective leadership in sustainability requires mastering the art of communication. **Talking the walk** is about crafting a compelling narrative that engages and inspires. It's not enough to do the right thing – you must also communicate your efforts in a way that resonates with stakeholders. Whether through storytelling, metaphors, or clear messaging, leaders must convey the importance of sustainability in a way that motivates action. A compelling narrative can turn abstract concepts into a cause that people want to rally behind, ensuring that sustainability becomes a shared mission across the organization and beyond.

As you explore the chapters in this section, you'll see that the leadership imperative is about much more than just managing change; it's about inspiring it. It's about developing the capabilities to lead in a complex, fast-changing world and embracing new approaches to power, governance, and inclusion. It's about creating a future where sustainability is at the heart of everything we do.

In the end, the leadership imperative challenges us to think deeply about what it means to lead. It asks us to move beyond traditional leadership models and to adopt a more holistic, inclusive approach. As you engage with the ideas and strategies in this section, we hope you'll be inspired to lead with purpose, passion, and resilience. The journey may be challenging, but with the right leadership, it's one that promises profound impact and lasting success.

Chapter 16

Leading Change

Jean-Francois Manzoni

For companies to become sustainable environmentally and socially, they need pressure and direction to change. Much of that pressure can come from markets and regulators, but people on the inside must focus that pressure in a directed way. Most companies developed in a way that took resources largely for granted, and they now need to proceed differently. Significant change, involving more than a handful of people, almost never happens without *someone* taking the lead and prodding the group into action. Leaders can show the way to sustainability.

This work is not automatic, and companies will need to make the transition to sustainability in different ways – often depending on their leadership. As Sumantra Ghoshal pointed out repeatedly, "Leaders are not paid to preside over the inevitable. They are paid to make happen what otherwise would not have happened." Increasingly, the public says they are paid to do what leaves their companies and society stronger and more capable of facing its next challenges – but how?

Leaders are essential, but for most companies, they will be effective not through blanket directives. They need a collaborative, positive, and energizing approach. This chapter focuses on the how of leading companies toward sustainability.

WHY LEADERS OFTEN FAIL TO CHANGE

Leaders frequently launch change or transformation projects, but most of these fall short of objectives. The projects yield minimal real impact, or realize only short-term, unsustainable gains.

Often that's because leaders manage the change mainly through decree or directives. Decrees can work, but only in some specific situations: emergencies, when the entire organization sees the need for substantial change quickly (which is not the case for sustainability now), or a painful stalemate. Otherwise, a top-down approach rarely works. People simply refuse to implement the directive, or they carry it out only with delay or only for a short while. Or, which may be worse, they carry it out in only a perfunctory, compliant way, without energy or creativity. And over time, decrees weaken employees' willingness to think and act autonomously. Highly respected leaders might get away with some decrees, but only at the cost of heavy withdrawals from their goodwill accounts.

Complex change involving a great deal of uncertainty, such as the transition to sustainability, requires hopeful, confident and engaged employees. Leaders who fail to cultivate those qualities will accomplish less than expected. They need to put as much time and attention into the process of change as they put into the content of the change, and think of their role as contributing to reduce fear and increase confidence.

Another common pitfall is to emphasize the negative over the positive. Many change projects in the past have actually been efforts to reduce cost or boost efficiency. We see companies restructuring to exit failing areas, or cutting head counts, but not really doing much differently. Sustainability does require some boost in efficiency, but most of the work involves reorienting or reimagining what the business does. If a change process aims mainly at cost-cutting, it will not be as engaging and energy enhancing as if the organization is reinvesting some of the gains thus generated into growth and transformation.

WHAT CHANGE MANAGEMENT TAKES

Beyond decrees, management thinkers have written about change management for decades, with versions of the same advice. Here is a checklist of process questions focused on change projects for sustainability.

1. The first question involves the audience to establish urgency and clarity. People won't bother to change unless they understand why this change, why them, and why now. So leaders must start by describing and showing that the status quo can't go on. They need people to be dissatisfied with the present situation – without

sowing panic or disempowering. They need to make the case for change in simple, clear, and impactful terms. People need to find the gain so appealing that they will endure the inevitable pain to get there.

What leaders shouldn't do is emphasize that hardship. Change of any case will disrupt existing practices and habits and create fearful uncertainty. Better to sell the gain than the pain – to position the pain in the context of the future gain that will make companies truly sustainable, less vulnerable to the problems leaders explained earlier. The efficiencies will generate resources to be reinvested for growth but won't inspire people. As Antoine de St. Exupéry said, "If you want to build a ship, don't drum up people to collect the wood and other tasks; instead, teach them to long for the endless immensity of the sea."

This process takes time. The audience will subject what leaders say to three hurdles: is it true? Is it acceptable? And is it actionable? Rational argument is often insufficient, as people will often need to grieve over losing the status quo. They may need time before they can look at the more positive aspects of life. Leaders can minimize this grieving and help people digest the loss by respecting it and listening to them talk about it.

2. What is the clear, credible, and monitorable plan to get there? People won't engage with change unless they see a workable and realistic plan, not just a nice vision. That doesn't mean laying out all the particulars of the plan, which will evolve over time in any case. But employees and other stakeholders must have confidence in the new direction and believe that it includes the discipline and resources necessary to actually happen. Otherwise they'll fight over which of many good ideas or projects to pursue.

3. Whose support do we need, and how will we get it? Leaders need to work on this question in parallel to developing their plan. To do so, they can analyze the full variety of stakeholders for their attitudes toward the change. The usual distribution is for some people to be early adopters, many others in a wait-and-see mode (some joining early, others later), and the rest – hopefully only a few – adamantly resisting the change.

   For sustainability, some groups will likely be entirely sup-portive, perhaps even adopting elements of the plan already. Other groups will be skeptical or downright hostile. How will leaders engage those groups? They can start by identifying those with the most impact on the organization in this area, especially the opinion leaders. Leaders can work to understand their point of view and develop a strategy to gain their support or at least minimize their resistance.

4. How should leaders communicate the plan? What, when, where, to whom, and by whom should the messages go out? This question is about quantity, quality, and timing. Explicit repetition is essential. Leaders may think they've conveyed a message many times, but they need to dis-count the times they've delivered the message in their own heads or to their immediate colleagues. They also need to watch how they deliver the message; if they offer it along with dozens of other points, if they present it unconvincingly or in a way that was easy to disagree with, then they haven't really delivered the message. Skeptics may never agree, but leaders need to win over most of the audience.

5. How to develop momentum? Enthusiasm needs to build, especially to attract the fence-sitters. Quick wins are essential, and they require careful planning and invest-ment. The most brilliant plan in the world won't work if the benefits appear only after several years.

6. What obstacles are ahead, and how to remove them? Leaders should expect problems along the way and prepare remedies to keep those problems from stalling the change or disheartening the early adopters. Leaders don't need a smashing success, but they must keep the change going even with setbacks. Here they need to look at the many determinants of behavior in the company, from incentives to information technology to culture, and predict issues of concern.

   They must also avoid "insanity territory," doing the same thing a little harder and hoping for a different result. Leaders must continually ask, "Why aren't people making the change already," or "Why aren't they doing it often or easily?" Problems could exist at the systems level, in which case leaders need to adjust the system to get a better result.

7. How to keep the change going? Once the issues 1 to 6 get resolved and the company is changing, how can leaders maintain the momentum after, say, 18 months? Even better, how can the new behaviors become part of the culture? Culture is what people do when no one is watching, and the change won't stick unless people start acting that way even when no one is telling them to do it. Leaders can expect culture to change over time, but it will change only if the organization continues to reshape in the desired direction the behavior of enough employees for long enough. Culture expert John Kotter said he used to think that "the biggest impediment to creating change in a group is culture. Therefore the first step in a major transformation would be to alter the norms and the values. But everything I've seen over the past decade tells me it's wrong. Culture is not something that you manipulate easily. . . . you can't grab it! Culture changes only after you have successfully altered people's actions . . . for a period of time."

WHEN TO START

Those are daunting requirements, but leaders don't need all the answers upfront. Investments in sustainability may not pay off for several years, but in the current scramble, if a leader does nothing for three years while preparing, it may be too late to start. Other companies will gain first-mover advantage, or squatter's rights because the efforts take a long time to make a difference.

Several researchers at IMD have looked at what pioneering companies are doing. We see them working on their portfolio, which by itself is not new. Companies are always adjusting the mix of businesses, what they're going to sell or sunset or buy, and especially what they're going to develop. But sustainability is altering those decisions. The pioneering leaders are managing the transition from one set of businesses to another, which is a complicated process – old businesses don't die linearly while new ones grow up linearly. Sometimes an old business drops like a rock, and a new business grows exponentially. In other cases, the old activities can be optimized to last a while longer while the new one(s) develop slowly. Sunsetting a business can free up cash for investing in sustainability, but earnings will take a hit. Even highly predictable trends involve a great deal of uncertainty.

CHANGE IN ACTION

Neste began in 1948 as Finland's state-owned petroleum company. In the 2000s, the company began to shift toward renewable energy, much of it from biomass. By the 2010s, the executive leaders had decided on bold investments for sustainability, but they lacked a clear plan and broad alignment throughout the company. The board of directors therefore sent them back to the drawing board.

After regrouping, the leadership launched a massive effort to gain strategic alignment throughout the organization. They argued that the shift to renewables was inevitable, especially in transportation, and that Neste needed to start building the required capabilities now. They also lobbied regulators for supportive regulation and started learning from clients that were innovating in this area. They linked the why, what, and how, including employee capabilities and the management of the change process, into well-researched narratives. Eventually the board agreed with this big move.

A key strength has been the company's longstanding ability to manage complex supply chains and other systems. That helped to make the plan realistic to employees. Neste also benefitted from clarity of purpose, required capabilities (each with an executive sponsor), and a push for inclusion, away from the traditional command-and-control. Neste's leaders succeeded by working with what the company already did well rather than try to take on many aspects of sustainability.

PARTNERING – FILL GAPS IN THE BUSINESS MODEL

To help address the uncertainty and other problems, leaders can partner with NGOs. These NGOs extend a company's capabilities. To move toward sustainability, companies will have to learn to do things they just can't do, or at least don't know how to do. A company could develop all those capabilities internally, but that's going to take time, and it might disrupt the rest of the organization. Some of these efforts can be taken on by cooperation at the industry level – rival companies could decide to stop competing on packaging and move to a standard package that is more sustainable, perhaps more recyclable, than the array of current packaging choices.

Over time, companies will build more capabilities in house. Pioneers will promote people based on new kinds of expertise and connections, not on the traditional ones. But even the most aggressive shifts in human capital won't be enough to give companies what they need. Partnering with nonprofits and even rivals may be essential.

There's also partnering with stakeholders. Many company leaders have seen employees or communities as neutrals, if not outright adversaries. But to accelerate the transition to a prosperous, environmentally friendly, and socially inclusive future, they need to collaborate with them. Through partnering, companies can reshape employee behavior and ultimately culture in an inclusive direction, not to mention fostering that engagement crucial to innovation and agility. An adversarial approach will backfire in the coming crisis.

RESPECTING THE CULTURE

A company's culture must change over time as well. Consider pricing. Among a culture's assumptions is to raise prices only when adding immediate, tangible value. Sustainability is not so immediate and tangible, so companies are reluctant to raise prices on products that are environmentally favorable. If they stay with that culture of pricing, they'll move too slowly on sustainability.

How do leaders change pricing behaviors? Practically, they can pull levers at the executive and individual team levels. But collectively, they need courageous decisions and long-term perspective. In every significant pioneer scholars have studied, a bold, farsighted leader brought along the rest of the top team. Then they made sure of support through the ranks with working on the structure. They located the pricing expertise, whether at headquarters or in divisions, and acted accordingly. The instincts behind the culture eventually changed as well.

As for any larger cultural move to sustainability, that move typically came later, more as a result of the company's push than a North Star guiding the decisions. Individuals may have been inclined in that direction, but any explicit purpose for the company emerged only after the behaviors had changed, not before. Nor was the stated purpose lofty; it was typically concrete, concerned with specific goals for the company, not for the planet or society. Most important, any cultural change has to work within the existing norms, not drastically modify them.

Schneider Electric, for example, worked gradually to move its strategy and culture toward sustainability. Starting around 2000, its leaders worked with its pragmatic engineering mindset; they didn't try to change it. The company was already strategically shifting from heavy industry to electricity and increasingly to energy management to automate and boost efficiency in transmission and consumption – both trends that support sustainability. Still, at first sustainability was just "the cherry on the cake," recalled Gilles Desroches, now the senior vice president for sustainability.

The change continued to be gradual as it built momentum. The company had two successive CEOs, Didier Pineau-Valencienne and Henri Lachman, interested in the social role of the firm. They sought to create wealth not just for investors but also for customers, employees, and the society at large.

Then in 2005, new CEO Jean-Pascal Tricoire rode the wave of increased electricity demand worldwide but with an eye to transitioning from fossil fuels to renewable sources. He saw both business opportunity and public responsibility in pushing the company to boost the efficiency of energy flows and improve demand management. The company dove into new markets for services and solutions that required less in the way of physical assets and more effort in customer relationships. The company also embraced digital technology, not only for automation but also for an open platform to help customers manage their energy for both efficiency and sustainability.

Even so, Schneider Electric went beyond moves that combined clear business opportunity and sustainability. Especially with its engineering mindset, the company never wanted a flamboyant vision; everything had to translate into factual, measurable accomplishment. So the company began in 2005 issuing the Schneider Sustainability Impact (SSI), a plan for the next three years. Over time, the plan expanded to five areas, each based on a materiality matrix encapsulating the social or environmental issues that could affect the company and its stakeholders, and with specific KPIs. These have been: climate, circular economy, health and equity, ethics, and development. Each quarter, the company publishes the results for each KPI on a scoring scale of 1–10 as monitored by external auditors. To expand accountability, in 2011, the company began including SSI in the variable compensation of employees. In 2019, SSI's weight for the bonus of each of the 60000 employees went from 6 to 20%.

The company now works mainly on projects that either promote sustainability or have a neutral effect. In 2021, the media and research firm Corporate Knights ranked it first worldwide out of 8000 multinational companies for its performance on sustainability. By then, Desroches was calling sustainability "the yeast in the bread" of Schneider Electric.

Or as Tricoire, now chairman, pointed out, "Sustainability is at the core of everything we do."

Leaders may see the move toward sustainability as a daunting task. In the midst of deep uncertainty, how can they transform the company while keeping the current businesses profitable enough to pay for investment? They can follow the lead of pioneers, who moved aggressively and are now in a strong position.

TAKEAWAYS

1. The process of change matters enormously, not just the content of change.

2. Leaders should be aware of the context, stakeholder positions, and potential obstacles for the change they hope to deploy.

3. Momentum matters. Better to move now, without all the answers, than wait for the perfect opportunity.

FURTHER READING

Frédéric Dalsace, "Schneider Electric: Becoming the World Leader in Sustainability," *IMD Case Studies*, March 30, 2022.

Jean-Francois Manzoni and Julia Binder, "A Clear Vision for Sustainable Business Transformation," *I by IMD*, September 18, 2023.

Chapter 17

Managing Change in the Organization

N. Anand and Jean-Louis Barsoux

Moving toward sustainability is fundamentally about changing an organization, altering established practices, and shifting people and resources to new directions. As with any major change initiative, sustainability transformation has the potential to disrupt many people and evoke resistance. Companies can't just switch; they need to pursue a gradual transition that puts the company on a sustainable path while protecting the business and the cash flow.

Management thinkers and executives have been writing about change management for decades. It's a familiar subject, yet many companies continue to carry out the process inefficiently and even ineffectually. Traditionally, many of them stumbled in implementation, which has now improved greatly – yet most change projects still disappoint their proponents. Real change doesn't happen, and in the case of sustainability, many companies resort to greenwashing in order to project a good reputation. Here's a better way, centered on preparing ahead of time for a well-considered quest.

THREE UPFRONT STEPS

Any substantial corporate change involves three clear steps upfront before any actual change happens. The first step is the catalyst, trigger, impetus, or reason for the transformation. Maybe an activist investor points out a problem. If leaders decide to go for a change, they need to articulate why the change needs to happen now and what it will involve. They need to face the reality of the current struggle but also the difficulties of change and how the organization will compete in the future. Leaders will face many problems, and they need to know which are urgent. Why go to this trouble now?

The second step is deciding on the quest itself. Companies have many areas of concern that might justify big changes. We've been tracking these areas for over a decade, and we've seen five of them get most of the attention: gaining a global (or regional) presence, getting close to customers (often with solutions rather products), boosting innovation (especially by widening the source of ideas), becoming nimble (simplifying to gain agility), and moving to sustainability.

Note that these involve goals, not tools – even a digital transformation needs a focused end result. Each of these quests involves different sub-goals and enablers. Any company that embraces multiple quests at the same time is unlikely to succeed. Some companies can straddle two quests, such as innovation and sustainability, as long as they fuse the two quests into a single imperative with one cogent focus. And just getting leaders in a company to agree on the priorities, and therefore the quest, can be difficult.

When asked which of the five quests is relevant to their organization, many executives might say, "All of them." But that would be too much to handle. Typically, the key question is not what needs to change but what needs changing first?

The third step involves communicating the transition process to the organization and securing commitments from its leaders. After thoroughly discussing the priorities and challenges, the leaders advocate for a specific course of action and disseminate this message throughout the organization. It is crucial to clearly explain how the decision was made, what alternatives were carefully considered, and why this particular transformation path is deemed the most appropriate. Additionally, this step includes identifying key executives who will play vital roles in initiating and sustaining the transformation. These strategic personnel choices signal the direction of the transformation far more effectively than initial statements, and they help prepare the entire organization for the upcoming change.

All three steps matter. Taking the metaphor of a hamburger, or a "transformation sandwich," the top bun is the first step, the catalyst, while the quest or second step is the choice of filling. But the bottom bun, which represents leadership capacity (third step), is also essential. Neglecting one of these steps turns the hamburger, and the change process, into something much less effective. Without the first or third steps, like the two halves of the bun, the process gets messy indeed.

LEADING THE TRANSITION TO SUSTAINABILITY

Since the 2010s, we've been conducting informal polls of executives to identify the most common types of corporate transformations. Before the COVID-19 pandemic started in 2020, nimbleness led the way as the most popular quest. Since 2022, sustainability – especially around reconfiguring supply chains – has taken first place, but it's still a real choice. Companies can't transform in multiple directions simultaneously. Adding nimbleness, globalization, customer focus, or even innovation could preclude substantial progress on sustainability. But opting for sustainability alone does not entail sacrificing business success.

Take the case of two similarly challenged companies that chose different paths. In the early 2000s, both Norske Skog of Norway and Stora Enso of Sweden were giant paper companies struggling with falling demand – the same catalyst for change. Norske Skog, an abbreviated version of Norwegian Forest Industries, decided to double down on its main business and become the surviving global consolidator. Only one mainline company would survive, and it would be super-efficient Norske Skog. The leaders emphasized globalization by acquiring the failing mills of international rivals and process innovation with ABB and other partners to boost the productivity of its operations and quality of its paper.

Stora Enso, by contrast, started leveraging some promising experiments in sustainable packaging for the fast-growing ecommerce market. The leaders opted to go on a different quest: to become a sustainable company in paper and adjacent domains, especially packaging and building materials.

It gradually reduced its reliance on the main papermaking business and specialized in those new areas to highlight the renewable dimension. Norske Skog ran similar experiments, but their focus remained on reducing energy consumption and improving existing products.

In the third step, Norske Skog made few management changes other than to shift investment to innovation. They emphasized deep engineering knowledge on efficiency. By contrast, Stora Enso's CEO realized his senior team would struggle to explore prospects for fresh growth. So he worked with human resources to set up a parallel "Pathfinders" leadership team. The team brought together a dozen managers from various parts of the organization and changed every year. At first the team was mainly a way to keep bringing new perspectives to executive decisions. But the idea soon expanded into a program for identifying and developing agents for the change. The two approaches got very different reactions from investors. While Stora Enso's stock price rose, Norske Skog's fell to 10% of its 1990s level. It declared bankruptcy in 2017 and continues to close paper mills – including one in New Zealand that now faces $1 billion in claims over a lake that was filled with toxic sludge. In 2016, it started piloting new products, such as micro-fibrillated cellulose, but it was too little too late.

Stora Enso also overcame common problems in pursuing sustainability. These involve undermeasuring or underreporting progress out of caution for this new area; or the opposite, broadcasting shallow victories (greenwashing) in order to report good news early on. Another challenge is that sustainability can undermine efficiency, still essential for serving most customers. As with many of the examples in the book, the company gained traction on sustainability mainly by turning it into a competitive advantage, as epitomized by the outdoor clothing company Patagonia.

PITFALLS OF MANAGING CHANGE TO SUSTAINABILITY

This three-step setup may seem straightforward, but companies regularly fall short, quite apart from the mistaken bets just described. The first common pitfall involves providing too little rationale or operational detail for the quest. In the case of sustainability, has the C-suite established a materiality matrix guiding their decisions on investments? (See Chapter 13 on materiality in metrics.) Has it won detailed approval from the board?

In 2021, like most of the other major petroleum producers, Exxon Mobile responded to climate change and "peak oil" by committing to a quest for sustainability. But the company failed to move decisively, including on step three of management development. The resulting confusion gave an opening to Engine #1, an activist investor that won two board seats to promote sustainability aggressively. The activists hijacked management's agenda and left the leaders scrambling to respond.

The second, and more common pitfall, is to go overboard. The leaders settle on a single quest, sustainability, but then try to do everything they can in that area. Every input gets questioned, with plans to improve the sourcing as well as in-house operations. Throughputs, structures, processes, customer actions, community impact – everything gets the same attention. The temptation is to do too much because it all seems worthwhile. But then the company lacks the bottom bun, the leadership capacity, to execute on all these issues. Many well-meaning companies will spread themselves thin in transitioning to sustainability.

Doing nothing, however, may be the most frequent response to these dilemmas. Many leaders resist bad news, understandably concerned about needing to address difficult weak spots. Knowledge, competencies, and activities that once provided competitive advantage may have grown stale and become rigid. Leaders will be tempted to ignore challenging developments or react superficially with a call for change. A better approach is to set up a structured way to gain a discrete but cold, hard look at the company. Leadership teams are often less aligned on the big issues than they think they are. That alignment, however painful, is essential for effective change in an organization.

Leaders might talk at length about a catalyst and even shift leadership development accordingly, but little of substance actually changes – the hamburger lacks a meaningful filling. Many initiatives follow but with generic goals such as efficiency and cost-cutting. This is especially common in industries with declining demand, as Norske Skog found. An endless turnaround gets dressed up as transformation but without strategic traction.

A "quest audit" can reveal disconcerting patterns that prompt discussions on transformation – which can be useful even if the leaders don't move forward with major change. As the head of HR at a Japanese food group pointed out, an audit led to team dialogue on issues that were previously off-limits. "It provided 'permission' to reflect on the current reality and how we got to where we are. That immunity led us to frame some breakthrough questions to understand our challenge and what we needed to do to solve it."

Even when everyone in the organization supports the goal of sustainability, managing the transition is still difficult. Transformation of any kind is a challenge, especially in an area as uncertain as sustainability. Before plunging ahead, leaders would do well to set themselves up for success. Otherwise, even flawless execution will just create more problems.

TAKEAWAYS

1. Before proceeding on a major change, leaders should focus on three essential steps: establishing the reason or catalyst for change, deciding on the focus of the change, and then communicating the plan for the change.

2. Deciding on the focus of change is essential, partly to prevent companies from trying to change too much.

3. The common pitfalls in change are doing too little and doing too much, both due to leadership failure.

FURTHER READING

N. Anand and Jean-Louis Barsoux, "What Everyone Gets Wrong About Change Management," *Harvard Business Review*, Nov.–Dec., 78–85, 2017.

N. Anand and Jean-Louis Barsoux, "Raising Your Board's Strategic Game," *Ivey Business Journal*, March–April, 2–11, 2019.

Tina B. Aune and Espen Gressetvold, "Supplier Involvement in Innovation Processes: A Taxonomy," *International Journal of Innovation Management*, 15, 121–143, 2011.

Chapter 18

Leading Transformation

Mikolaj Jan Piskorski and Richard Roi

The next few decades will bring numerous technological advances, new environmental demands, and societal changes, which will call on leaders to develop new business models and new ways of generating revenues and profits. At the same time, they will have to continue driving transformation in their core businesses, to continue to meet customer expectations for short-term results.

Many CEOs we have spoken to call this their "dual transformation" challenge and rank it as one of the hardest problems in their tenure. They say transforming core businesses for tomorrow while also transforming the company for today is a delicate balancing act requiring not only well-considered investment but also a particular leadership style.

This chapter focuses on that style as it examines the core characteristics of "future-ready" leaders – those who possess the unique skills and mindset to lead organizations through this dual transformation. In our research, we found that only a small percentage of leaders possess a full suite of characteristics to be "future-ready." However, with proper exposure, experience, and education, many of them can dramatically improve their future-readiness in a matter of years.

THE DUAL TRANSFORMATION: TRANSFORMING FOR THE PRESENT AND THE FUTURE

Established companies have traditionally focused on achieving commercial goals, generating the necessary cash flow to pay expenses and deliver dividends to investors. But in today's competitive and fast-paced business environment, many established companies are no longer protected by the competitive moats that once shielded them. So they must invest in the core business and transform it to remain profitable in the short term.

At the same time, leaders are increasingly recognizing that the existing business models, regardless of current transformations, will at some point exhaust their profit growth potential. The disruption often comes from startups that scale quickly or aggressive rivals encroaching on long-standing market positions. To protect themselves from becoming obsolete, companies need to invest in creating new sources of value, often using recent advances in technology, such as AI, or new sustainable business models.

These investments are risky, not guaranteed to generate solid returns on investments results, as entering markets with new business models is often costly and time consuming.

Consider, for example, the automotive industry. Companies in that sector must continue to invest to improve the performance of cars based on internal combustion engines – still the backbone of the business. At the same time, they must invest to succeed in the electric and autonomous vehicle market, which, with time, will likely replace the internal combustion engine cars. If they invest too much into improving the existing business model and invest too little in the future one, they might get locked out from later success. But if they invest too little into improving the existing business model and too much into the future one, the short-term profitability might collapse, again locking them out. They must balance present and future in this dual transformation.

Despite the difficulties of dual transformations, many prominent companies have achieved it, and their experiences offer valuable lessons. For instance, under the leadership of CEO Satya Nadella, Microsoft transformed its core business by shifting from a Windows-focused strategy to one centered on cloud computing. At the same time, the company built new growth engines by forming partnerships in AI and launching a new platform in that space. Nadella and his team exemplify a successful dual transformation, running both the core and transformative strategies in parallel.

Similarly, Ping An, a large Chinese firm, began as a traditional property and casualty insurer. The company invested significant resources to improve its existing business but also into the future to enter banking and healthcare. This strategic diversification allowed Ping An to tap into new markets and revenue streams while maintaining a focus on its core insurance business. As a result, the company has grown into the world's second-largest financial services firm, demonstrating the power of dual transformation. Ping An's success highlights how organizations can simultaneously innovate and strengthen their core operations to drive long-term growth.

DUAL TRANSFORMATIONS ARE HARD

Against these two examples, we see several companies that have attempted dual transformation only to realize how difficult it is to realize in practice. The board of directors of Shell directed its leaders to continue improving oil extraction in the short term to maintain profitability while moving away from petroleum in the long term to become a net-zero emissions energy company by 2050. These audacious goals called on Shell's leaders to excel as both strong operators, driving profitability in the core business, and diligent transformers, experimenting and taking risks for the future. Many of them report just how difficult it is to know where to allocate investments and their attention to transforming today's business versus transforming their business for tomorrow.

Similarly, Nike, which distributes athletic footwear and apparel, has employed technology to better understand its customers and make data-driven decisions about distribution. Before, the company operated a push-only supply chain, with decisions on what to produce and where to sell made long in advance – which yielded too many items no one wanted to buy and too few desirable items. With greater visibility into customer demand, the company shifted toward a pull supply chain, improving both the bottom line and the company's sustainability.

Encouraged by success in transforming the core business, Nike invested heavily in new business models based on direct-to-consumer sales, apart from its traditional offline and online sales channels. While the strategy worked during the COVID-19 pandemic, it backfired thereafter, reducing sales and profitability. Management is now slowing down the direct-to-consumer investments and going back to what was working to create a more stable path to long-term transformation.

While dual transformations are essential, they are not easy. First, traditional investment frameworks don't support them. In most companies, the core gets abundant resources, while new areas never have enough money for the experiments people would like to conduct. This gets even harder when the core business comes under pressure. In those situations, leaders often revert to focusing on the present and neglecting the longer-term transformation. After all, corporate expectations and incentives tend to reward short-term performance, thus delaying much-needed future innovation.

Second, most organizations still employ the old structures and separate their investments and their talent into distinct areas: one for optimizing the core business and another for developing future innovations. Today, this separation no longer works. After all, the same digital and AI technologies often help optimize core operations as well as build new businesses. Companies need to carry out dual transformations simultaneously, using shared resources and the same management team.

These two factors, combined, challenge most leaders. Leaders are now responsible for two different changes supported by different resource structures: one with plentiful resources and one where they are scarce. They must behave differently yet carry out these transformations in tandem.

Indeed, our study of senior leaders of 55 large multinational companies found that only 12% managed both transformations. The remaining 88% were either excellent at optimizing the core or excelled at creating new growth engines, but not both. With so few leaders prepared for the task, it is no wonder that dual transformations are so hard.

MAKING DUAL TRANSFORMATION A REALITY

Despite all these difficulties, companies should continue to strive toward dual transformation. The first step is for the board of directors to acknowledge that the core business is no longer invulnerable. It is under attack from competitors, market changes, and technological disruptions, thereby requiring transformation of the existing business. The second step is for the board to call on the company to prepare itself for the future by developing new revenue streams and growth engines.

With this recognition is in place, the executive team must formulate a strategy that addresses both transformations. Most companies are used to running annual business plans centered on the core's profit-and-loss structure. Typically, these plans include a few speculative bets on future innovation, but these are often treated as side projects, detached from the core business. To succeed in dual transformation, companies now need an integrated strategy that transforms its core while advancing long-term ambitions.

We have seen this process work well at Mandiri Bank in Indonesia. Thanks to its corporate governance, the company formulated its dual transformation strategy and executed it. Specifically, it rejuvenated its corporate financing and treasury management business while developing an entire retail banking ecosystem in a short period of time. Through its mobile platform, customers can now purchase cars or begin the process of buying homes, all within the Mandiri ecosystem. This success is particularly noteworthy because retail banking requires a different mindset than corporate finance. Yet Mandiri's leaders pursued both goals simultaneously, strengthening the core while expanding into new markets.

With the dual transformation strategy in hand, the companies need to be specific about ways of working to assure its execution. For example, dual transformation for the future often requires exploring the landscape to become a platform or even ecosystem provider. Thus, leaders leading the process need to ask, "Do we need to build an ecosystem of partners to help accelerate our offerings and outreach to markets? Do we need new capabilities, and if so, can we acquire them?"

Microsoft, again, is an excellent example: Its leaders astutely realized that their business model and structure, which had performed well for decades, no longer worked in the current environment. But instead of aiming to build everything by themselves, they started collaborating with outside companies. That was a big shift, as it forced them to cede some control. And instead of simply giving up on Windows, they sought partnerships to reinvigorate it as a cloud-based system. Meanwhile they invested heavily in AI and video game systems. They revived the core while taking leadership for the future with their investment and partnership with OpenAI.

DEVELOPING LEADERS TO DRIVE DUAL TRANSFORMATION

In addition to the strategic imperative from the board, companies need to develop leaders who can drive these dual transformations. To do that, they must change the way they nurture their talent. Most senior executives arrive at their position with a singular focus shaped by their work experience. Some have spent their careers as dominant performers, excelling at driving operational excellence, while others have made their mark by creating new offerings and entering new markets. Few, however, possess the range of skills needed for dual transformation.

To overcome this problem, companies need to provide leaders with varied career experiences. They must expose future leaders to different roles, companies, functions, and bosses. Research has shown that diverse experiences correlate with the ability to manage both the core business and new ventures. Leaders exposed to multiple industries, roles, and challenges are more likely to possess the mindset necessary for success.

Thus, stretch assignments, cross-functional projects, and job rotations into highly entrepreneurial positions can all help aspiring leaders develop the flexibility and range needed for dual transformation. People need to operate in business environments where they benefit from receiving the lion's share of capital and attention, as well as those where they are left to compete for limited resources. They learn to make the most of scarce resources, activating informal channels and leveraging entrepreneurial instincts to drive transformation. But they also learn to drive change at scale. Both experiences are needed for engaging in dual transformation later in their careers.

A CONVICTION FOR CHANGE

To ensure future success, companies must also develop leaders with a broad cognitive, emotional, and behavioral range. We often hear from managers, "Why would I want to expand my range and change when I already have a playbook that works?" They need to know that generalists are running many companies now, not just deep specialists with single profiles. So they must hone their skills for both the core business and the businesses for the future.

Equally, companies need to go through a fundamental change in how they see talent. Many executives believe that people are hardwired to perform in specific ways – some are operators, others are innovators – and their roles should reflect these strengths. This outdated "horses for courses" mindset no longer applies in today's dynamic business environment, where leaders must be able to pivot between multiple roles and responsibilities.

Fortunately, research has shown that leaders can expand their range through practice, experience, and discipline. Emotional intelligence, for example, can be developed by learning to recognize and respond to a wide range of emotions in others. Similarly, cognitive agility can be enhanced through new ways of thinking and processing information. With training and experiences, leaders can thrive in both stable and uncertain environments. They can master the art of dual transformation by combining operational excellence with a readiness to experiment, pivot, and innovate.

For these development experiences to be effective, we often recommend that companies invest in leadership assessments and simulations that measure cognitive, emotional, and behavioral agility. Equipped with detailed knowledge of leaders' strengths and development opportunities, companies as well as the leaders in question can engage in targeted development opportunities that allow leaders to lead the two types of transformation rather quickly.

Developing leaders who transform for today and for tomorrow is not just a desirable quality – it is essential for managing the complexity and uncertainty that companies face now. Leaders who can simultaneously optimize their core business and drive transformation will be well-positioned to navigate the challenges of sustainability. By fostering a culture of dual transformation and developing leaders who can drive it, companies can secure their place for the future.

TAKEAWAYS

1. With long-time competitive moats no longer protecting them, many large companies must overhaul their core business while transforming the organization to move into the businesses of the future.

2. This dual transformation is hard because management structures favor the core business and because leaders are groomed to focus on either operations or innovation.

3. Companies can succeed with committed governance and with leaders developed from a broad range of experience in both core and peripheral businesses.

FURTHER READING

Mikolaj Jan Piskorski, "On a Long-Haul Mission to Have Meaningful Impact: Interview with Ralph Herbst of Bayer," *I by IMD*, June 11, 2024.

Chapter 19

Developing Leaders' Capabilities

Albrecht Enders and Michael Watkins

Moving an organization to sustainability is a complex and demanding task that challenges leaders far beyond their traditional roles. It requires deeper skills and a broader self-awareness than many leaders possess at the outset. The move demands not only technical expertise and strategic thinking but also a profound shift in how leaders approach their roles, their teams, and the ecosystem in which their organizations operate.

Leaders must navigate two interconnected journeys. The Outer Journey is the visible, action-oriented one – mobilizing teams, driving change, and achieving tangible goals. The Inner Journey, which receives less attention, is equally critical. It involves cultivating resilience, emotional intelligence, and mindfulness to lead with authenticity, clarity, and balance. Those qualities are essential in the transition to sustainability, a highly emotional challenge that can easily overwhelm leaders.

This chapter explores the dual journeys, focusing on the qualities and skills essential for moving organizations to sustainability. To avoid burnout, leaders must focus and mobilize energy within their organization while also developing the inner qualities through meditation, journaling, and adequate sleep.

While most leaders are not fully equipped to succeed at first, they can develop the necessary skills over time through disciplined practice, reflection, and a commitment to personal growth. By understanding and embracing the outer and inner aspects, executives can navigate the challenges with confidence and effectiveness. They can preserve their equanimity while building successful organizations.

THE OUTER JOURNEY OF THE LEADER

The outer journey encompasses what leaders do and are seen to do by the people they lead, both their immediate teams and the organization as a whole. It involves mobilizing and focusing the energy of people, processes, and capabilities, as illustrated in Figure 19.1.

The vertical axis represents the degree of focus – how well leaders define the mission, provide clear direction, make tough trade-offs, and drive accountability. The horizontal

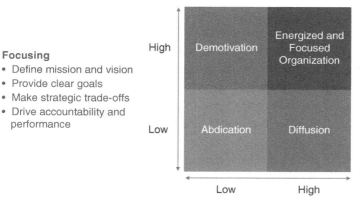

Focusing
- Define mission and vision
- Provide clear goals
- Make strategic trade-offs
- Drive accountability and performance

Mobilizing
- Listen actively and engage empathetically
- Seek out diverse input and perspectives
- Role-model desired behaviors
- Inspire through vision and actions

Figure 19.1   Focusing and mobilizing.

axis reflects how well leaders engage and mobilize their teams, listen to input, show vulnerability, and inspire through their actions. Mobilizing also involves role-modeling the behaviors they wish to see in their teams, setting the tone for the organization's culture, and driving collective energy toward shared goals.

Leaders need to balance these two dimensions and orient their organization toward the top right quadrant, where both high focus and high mobilization create an energized and productive organization. Leaders who excel in one dimension but falter in the other risk falling into states of demotivation, diffusion, or even abdication, where organizational performance and engagement suffer. Moving to sustainability depends on achieving that top right quadrant.

As part of focusing, leaders must provide clear direction and rigorous accountability. They must make the tough decisions that inevitably arise, such as balancing the imperative to reduce carbon emissions with the need to maintain business viability. They have to prioritize initiatives, determining which areas to address immediately and where a longer-term approach is appropriate. Achieving sustainability is not a single event, but a process of picking battles and gradually moving in a good direction.

In navigating these challenges, leaders manage competing criteria, explore options beyond their pre-existing paradigms, and make difficult trade-offs that balance diverse objectives. A decision matrix can be an invaluable tool in this process, helping leaders visualize, assess, and thoughtfully balance the various factors at play to arrive at well-considered, on-balance decisions.

Separately, leaders must engage and mobilize stakeholders, particularly those essential for implementing sustainability initiatives. This involves actively listening to a broad range of voices – including customers, local communities, regulators, and investors, as well as employees – and role-modeling desired behaviors and inspiring action through a clear and compelling vision. Leaders must seek input from these diverse groups and acknowledge their own uncertainties, setting an example of openness and collaboration. This openness is vital, as different stakeholders may hold perspectives or ideas that challenge the leader's assumptions, helping to illuminate blind spots.

Leaders should also strive to engage with stakeholders beyond the usual suspects, actively seeking out nonobvious voices that might otherwise be overlooked but can offer critical insights and alternative viewpoints. By role-modeling the inclusivity and collaboration they wish to instill in their organizations, leaders can inspire broad participation and drive collective action.

Gathering a wide range of perspectives enables leaders to present a balanced view of their decisions, particularly when these diverge from stakeholders' recommendations. Leaders can build trust even when their choices aren't popular by showing they have considered all concerns, weighed the pros and cons, and made a well-reasoned decision on balance.

Many leaders struggle with the humility and openness required to achieve this balance. It's a skill that can be developed through deliberate practice, in three steps: first, collecting comprehensive information, ideas, and analyses to map out the decision space; second, making the necessary trade-off decisions; and third, communicating these decisions so people feel heard and remain engaged.

For example, the leaders of Stora Enso, a large European renewable materials company, engaged in "discovery expeditions" as part of their deliberate process to gain external perspectives. These included visits to innovative sites, such as their exploration of advanced wood construction methods in Seattle when considering an expansion in that sector. The experiences equipped them to better engage with stakeholders back home.

Internally, they also gathered diverse perspectives through a "shadow cabinet" – an advisory group of people spanning different silos and levels of seniority across the organization. People had to apply to the group, which ensured motivated participants, but the executives also selected members to ensure a diversity of perspectives. While sustainability was just one of several issues on the executives' radar, the advisory council significantly broadened their outlook on that critical area.

This approach differs significantly from a "pulse check" survey of employees. Leaders don't need to secure the agreement of the entire organization, but they do need to genuinely hear and consider varying perspectives. When people feel that their voices are ignored, they may disengage or silently resign from contributing altogether.

Likewise, to maintain engagement, executives must resist the urge to rush into implementation. It's far more effective to acknowledge stakeholder input by saying something like "We thoroughly discussed your idea and recognized its benefits, particularly in terms of important values. However, we also have other priorities, such as long-term impact, our reputation with environmental NGOs, and current cash flow pressures, which weighed heavily in our decision. So we chose a different path."

Leaders can benefit here from a comprehensive decision matrix that incorporates critical perspectives across the organization. While some leaders may naturally approach decisions this way, most executives, like children in a group, tend to jump to solutions prematurely. They latch onto one idea and focus on justifying it, often at the expense of exploring alternatives. Cultivating the patience and discipline to consider all options is crucial.

WHY THE OUTER JOURNEY ISN'T ENOUGH

While some leaders naturally excel at creating comprehensive decision matrices, making tough trade-offs decisively, or engaging humbly with stakeholders, many improve these skills through experience and challenges. Over time, they realize that focusing solely on external actions – the Outer Journey – is insufficient for effective leadership.

This realization arises partly because the outer journey contains inherent contradictions. Leaders are often expected to exhibit focus, confidence, and self-assurance while setting high standards and holding others accountable. However, these traits can inadvertently alienate colleagues, who may perceive such leaders as distant or unapproachable figures rather than relatable human beings with genuine emotions and vulnerabilities. The complexities and emotional weight of moving to sustainability makes connected, engaged colleagues critical.

The tension becomes most apparent when an organization commits to a specific initiative. Leaders must concentrate resources and attention on the chosen path while still motivating those who favored different approaches. Sustainability in a company likely involves a great many changes, many of which must be deferred, however inspiring. With a fair process that acknowledges and respects all voices, they can maintain engagement and foster inclusion.

Achieving this balance between decisive action and empathetic engagement requires patience and adaptability – qualities that rarely come naturally to leaders who advanced through environments promoting focus, confidence, and stringent accountability. This is where the Inner Journey becomes essential; leaders must cultivate equanimity along with achievement.

This Inner Journey also matters for the leaders' fulfillment and well-being. Even those who reach the pinnacle of corporate success often experience crises of confidence, feeling burned out and lacking meaning despite their professional achievements. They may struggle with private conflicts and strained relationships, leading to joyless striving that hampers their ability to inspire and lead effectively.

Colleagues and subordinates see both what leaders say and how they are. Authentic, balanced leadership emanates from inner stability and purpose, not just outward success.

THE INNER JOURNEY OF THE LEADER

Where the outer journey was about mobilizing and focusing the energy of others to drive the sustainability transformation, the inner journey is about mobilizing and focusing one's own energy on a sustainable basis, as illustrated in Figure 19.2.

Leaders must balance between two dimensions: Aspiration ("doing") and Equanimity ("being"). The vertical axis of aspiration captures the qualities of ambition, drive, and visionary thinking necessary for initiating and leading significant change. Leaders with high aspirations set challenging goals, push boundaries, and consistently strive for excellence. They are forward-thinking and proactive, always looking for innovative ways to make a meaningful impact.

The horizontal axis represents the degree of equanimity, which emphasizes the importance of being present, mindful, and balanced, with calm and centeredness even in the face of challenges or setbacks. It reflects a leader's ability to stay grounded, not overreacting to external pressures, and to approach situations with a clear, focused mind.

The framework highlights that true resilience and high performance in leadership come from integrating these two dimensions. Leaders who balance aspiration with equanimity are best equipped to lead sustainably. They can pursue ambitious goals while remaining grounded, thus avoiding the pitfalls of burnout, joyless striving, or aimless drifting that arise when one dimension is prioritized at the expense of the other. They sustain their energy, make better decisions, and inspire their teams over the long term to put the company on a sustainable path. Colleagues and employees don't just listen to what they say – they also observe how they are.

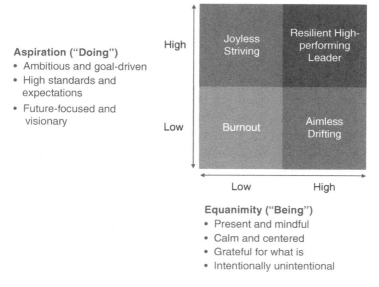

Figure 19.2   Doing and being.

ACCELERATING THE INNER JOURNEY

In many respects, the inner journey can be more challenging than the outer one. It demands that leaders remain grounded and open while driving progress with high standards and ambition. Research has identified three essential practices that can accelerate an inner journey: meditation, journaling, and plenty of restful sleep. When integrated into leaders' routine, these practices help them stay connected to their core values and priorities – so in turn they concentrate on what matters.

These practices create the inner space necessary for leaders to rise above the daily grind of putting out fires. With a broad perspective on overarching goals, leaders can better focus on long-term objectives, make difficult trade-offs, and engage with stakeholders intelligently and with humility.

By pursuing the Inner Journey, leaders fortify themselves, enabling them to navigate the outer journey confidently and effectively.

The two journeys are not just complementary, but dynamic and sometimes even contradictory. Sometimes leaders must act assertively and decisively, with little room for humility. At other times they must step back, reflect, and reassess the situation. The key lies in being engaged in the flow of business while remaining flexible in one's responses. If leaders are perpetually in action mode, relentlessly pushing forward, they risk alienating others and making avoidable mistakes. Conversely, if they stay in a reflective or humble state, they may struggle to act decisively when needed.

MEDITATION

Regular meditation boosts leaders' mindfulness, making them more aware of their emotions and impulses and better equipped to manage the intense pressures of the C-suite. A consistent meditation practice is likely to improve decisions, increase colleagues' perception that they are "present," boost emotional intelligence, and improve the handling of stress – all invaluable in steering an organization toward sustainability.

Mindfulness is a powerful skill in leading colleagues toward sustainability. With this self-awareness, leaders can navigate the conflicting, often emotional demands. Some stakeholders will argue passionately for a variety of measures that likely must be deferred, while some investors seek short-term returns that preclude investments in the future.

Maintaining a regular practice can be challenging, especially for executives constrained by demanding and unpredictable schedules. Micro-mindfulness techniques offer a practical alternative for those who struggle to find time, providing similar benefits in shorter intervals. Executives can practice these techniques whenever they feel stressed or have a few moments between meetings.

JOURNALING

Many leaders avoid reflection by diving into the next urgent task. This neglect can diminish their self-awareness and decision-making. Leadership, after all, is more about continuous improvement than relentless action, and it requires cultivating insight over time through reflection, not just reacting to daily demands.

Frequent journaling can encourage this reflection. Only a small fraction of people are naturally inclined toward self-reflection, and executives are no more likely than others to possess this trait. For the vast majority, a lack of regular introspection leads to myopia, like being caught in a whirlwind of activity without a clear sense of direction. Committed journaling can force leaders to reflect.

The optimal journaling times vary. Some leaders prefer morning reflections, while others go for the evening; both are fine. What matters is to align with one's style and prioritize the practice.

Deep reflection through journaling is crucial for navigating complex challenges and long-term planning, both essential for moving to sustainability. Leaders need a clear understanding of their motivations and biases and a nuanced view of their organization's culture. Those who neglect journaling may fall back on habitual thinking patterns, limiting their strategic vision and decisions.

Consistent journalers often excel at connecting disparate ideas and recognizing emerging patterns. They make more insightful decisions by regularly processing their experiences, learning, and intuitions. They show greater empathy and emotional intelligence, essential qualities for creating an environment where others feel empowered to contribute and innovate.

SLEEP

Most executives know that adequate sleep is essential for good health and longevity yet still believe they can "catch up on sleep later." They often sacrifice sleep to meet tight deadlines or excel in high-stakes projects, not realizing that inadequate sleep diminishes the quality of their work. Also, leadership is a marathon, not a sprint; it requires sustained performance over long periods, not just bursts of intense effort.

Only 2% of the population can function well on fewer than five hours of sleep, and executives are no more likely than anyone else to have this genetic advantage. For the vast majority, staying awake for more than 19 hours results in cognitive impairment equivalent to being legally intoxicated.

That said, as with journaling, people have different sleep timing – some are early risers, while others thrive as night owls. Both can achieve peak performance. Leaders can promote flexible work schedules that align with individual sleep patterns, benefiting not just themselves but the entire organization.

Being fully rested and alert is crucial for making complex, risky, and long-term decisions. Rested leaders can better maintain a broad and open-minded view of external signals, and hold a solid understanding of their company's true capabilities. They also excel at developing innovative solutions and addressing opportunities or threats. Additionally, they have the energy to create a supportive environment where others feel safe and encouraged to contribute ideas. In contrast, sleep-deprived leaders risk narrowing their focus to familiar variables and solutions, constricting their decision-making and strategic vision.

By integrating these three practices into their routines, leaders can cultivate the inner resilience, emotional intelligence, and clarity necessary to navigate the complexities of moving to sustainability. These tools empower leaders to maintain a balanced approach, leading with greater focus, better decisions, and inspired teams.

Leading a company toward sustainability, like any transformation, demands more than conventional skills and practices. Fortunately, most leaders can develop these abilities over time, through the intertwined Outer and Inner Journeys. Just as explorers in uncharted territories must monitor their stamina and morale to and succeed in their grueling and perilous adventures, leaders must attend to their inner state.

The transition to sustainability is not a sprint but a marathon. Leaders who balance these dual aspects – mobilizing and directing their teams while also nurturing their inner aspirations, resilience, and mindfulness – are more likely to succeed in creating lasting change. They make better decisions, maintain the engagement of their teams, and adapt to unforeseen challenges with grace and agility. In this way, they become not only effective leaders but also stewards of a better world.

TAKEAWAYS

1. Leading toward sustainability requires inner strengths as well as outer action, a process best seen as moving along Inner and Outer Journeys. Leaders especially need to thoughtfully manage the emotional aspects of sustainability.

2. The Outer Journey involves not just good decisions and sober trade-offs but also focusing and mobilizing the energies of others.

3. Leaders can accelerate their inner journey with meditation, journaling, and plenty of sleep.

FURTHER READING

Albrecht Enders et al., "A Good Night's Sleep Will Help You Make Better Decisions," *I by IMD*, March 17, 2022

Albrecht Enders and Arnaud Chevalier, *Solvable: A Simple Solution to Complex Problems*, FT Publishing, 2022.

Albrecht Enders and Lars Haggstrom, "How the World's Oldest Company Reinvented Itself," *Harvard Business Review*, January 30, 2018

Michael Watkins, "Seven Ways to Weave Mindfulness into Your Workday," *Harvard Business Review*, July 16, 2024

Chapter 20

The Courage of "Power With"

Susan Goldsworthy

Transitioning to true sustainability represents a profound shift in organizational operations, distinguishing it from other corporate initiatives. Many current business practices aren't sustainable, and the necessary transformation isn't merely about adopting new practices. It presents an opportunity to inspire deep levels of employee being and engagement.

To tap into this potential, leaders must embrace a new consciousness that promotes a different way of working – from a fear-based mindset of "power over" to a love-based mindshift of "power with." This approach fosters collaboration, mutual respect, and shared responsibility, crucial elements for building a sustainable future. Though challenging in a world accustomed to traditional hierarchies, this shift is essential for ensuring organizations are fully engaged and committed to the collective well-being of both people and the planet.

In recent years, the world has increasingly recognized the profound ecological challenges that threaten the stability of our planet. Climate change, biodiversity loss, and the degradation of natural resources are not just environmental issues; they are existential threats that demand urgent and comprehensive action. Addressing these challenges requires more than technological innovation or policy change. It necessitates a fundamental shift in consciousness – a transformation in the way we perceive our relationship with the Earth and each other.

This shift is essential not only for the survival of our species, but also for the well-being of individuals, including the leaders who are at the helm of our organizations. It offers a path toward collective empowerment and ecological responsibility.

FROM HIERARCHY TO COLLABORATION

In the past, leaders have advanced their careers within systems that emphasize hierarchical power – where authority concentrates at the top and decisions flow downward. In this "power over" model, the leader is the ultimate authority, dictating actions and decisions. This approach is becoming ineffective. Today's complex challenges require collective intelligence and co-creation, as no single individual has all the answers. To address the pressing ecological challenges we face, leaders must shift from controlling their teams to creating environments where collaboration and shared learning are the norm.

The traditional capitalist model has brought significant economic growth, yet it has also placed immense strain on our planet's resources. Earth Overshoot Day marks when humanity's demand for ecological resources and services in a given year exceeds what Earth can regenerate in that same year. Its significance lies in highlighting the unsustainable pace at which we consume natural resources, effectively living on ecological credit for the remainder of the year. This day serves as a stark reminder of the environmental consequences of overconsumption, including resource depletion, loss of biodiversity, and increased carbon emissions. For the past decade, Earth Overshoot Day has been calculated as between late July and early August.

The implications are profound, signaling an urgent need for transformative changes in how we manage resources, implement sustainable practices, and rethink economic growth to ensure the long-term health of future generations. Our current trajectory is unsustainable, with wealth concentrated in a way that fails to address societal needs.

Accordingly, in 2016, the United Nations established 17 SDGs to be achieved by 2030. Unfortunately, as of 2024, progress on these goals remains woefully insufficient. Continuing with business as usual will not meet these targets. Instead, organizations need a fresh approach that engages everyone in addressing these urgent challenges. In 2023, the Inner Development Goals (IDGs) were created to complement the SDGs, in recognition that these external challenges cannot be fully addressed without fostering the inner capacities of individuals and leaders.

While the SDGs outline critical global objectives for societal and environmental well-being, the IDGs represent a transformative approach to personal growth, emphasizing the critical role of inner development in achieving sustainable global progress. The purpose of the IDGs is to highlight and cultivate the necessary psychological, emotional, and cognitive skills that enable people to act with greater consciousness and responsibility in tackling the complex global issues outlined in the SDGs, thus bridging the gap between external actions and internal growth.

A big obstacle to this shift is not a lack of knowledge but a short-term focus driven by a reluctance to change and a hesitation to commit to the greater good. As environmental advocate Gus Speth remarked, the core environmental challenges we face – biodiversity loss, ecological collapse, and climate change – are rooted in deeper issues of selfishness, greed, and apathy. Addressing these requires a cultural and spiritual transformation that goes beyond mere technical solutions.

CULTIVATING A SUSTAINABLE FUTURE

The call for more inclusive and participatory leadership is not new, but it has gained renewed urgency in light of the sustainability imperative. To navigate this transition, organizations must encourage leaders to evolve in their roles, fostering environments where innovation and collaboration can thrive. Fortunately, even the most traditional leaders are capable of change.

Consider IG&H, a Dutch consultancy that faced a crisis in 2009. The founder, Jan van Hasenbroek, initially led with a controlling, perfectionist style that he felt was helpful but actually stifled his colleagues' growth. After several key consultants left, he had the courage to recognize the need for change. By adopting a more caring and daring approach and learning to delegate, he transformed the company's culture. This shift from "play to dominate" to "play to thrive" helped the company prosper, with leadership development as a core part of its strategy.

Companies need to move away from cultures that prioritize short-term gains and competition and toward those that value collaboration, long-term thinking, and ecological responsibility. This cultural shift is essential for creating an environment where sustainable practices can thrive.

Leaders play a crucial role in shaping organizational culture. ALPIQ, a Swiss energy company, has embraced secure base leadership principles. It has trained staff and created internal coaching ambassadors who support culture change alongside their "normal" jobs to practice a "power with" approach that promotes psychological safety, collaboration, and continuous learning. In the words of CEO Antje Kanngiesser, "We firmly believe that our company culture is our competitive advantage. We align all our actions with our company's purpose and values. In our complex environment, we consider value-based leadership essential. By both "caring" and "daring," we nurture an environment ripe for perpetual learning and growing and forge secure bases for constructive dialogue and daring decisions."

FROM SURVIVING TO THRIVING

As the world confronts severe ecological challenges, leaders must recognize that traditional methods focused on growth and control are no longer sustainable. We need a holistic approach that prioritizes the well-being of the planet and future generations – not just for sustainability, but also for the mental and emotional health of leaders. Many are operating in survival mode, leading to anxiety, stress, burnout and reduced performance. By adopting "power with" leadership, they can create supportive and sustainable work environments that benefit everyone.

While some argue that small organizations are better suited for this change, large companies can also embrace these principles. Leaders have more influence than they often realize and can drive significant change even within complex structures.

Resistance to this shift often stems from fear – fear of change, losing control, and the unknown.

Traditional systems reward maintaining the status quo, focusing on short-term results, making it hard for leaders to break free from entrenched behaviors. Clinging to old hierarchies can create toxic cultures, leading to higher absenteeism, lower productivity, and increased turnover. No leader intends to create a harmful workplace, but without conscious effort, they may inadvertently do so.

By embracing a "power with" mindset, leaders can create more inclusive and dynamic organizations. This approach also attracts diverse talent, fostering creativity and innovation. Leaders who are secure and open to new ideas are better equipped to unlock their teams' full potential.

A shift in perspective means moving away from seeing the planet as a resource to exploit and toward understanding it as a living system of which we are a part. This fosters a sense of stewardship and responsibility, encouraging leaders to consider the long-term impacts of their decisions on the environment, society, and future generations.

Conscious leaders create environments where psychological safety is paramount. They encourage open dialogue about the challenges facing the organization and the planet, reducing the stigma around discussing mental health and stress. This openness fosters supportive and resilient organizational cultures.

Companies need to move away from cultures that prioritize short-term gains and competition toward those that value collaboration, long-term thinking, and ecological responsibility. Leaders play a crucial role in this cultural shift by modeling "power with" leadership and prioritizing sustainability. This might involve redefining success to include environmental and social metrics, encouraging cross-functional collaboration on sustainability initiatives, and embedding environmental stewardship into the company's mission and values.

For example, companies can tie sustainability goals to performance evaluations and incentives, ensuring that sustainability becomes a core component of the organization's identity and not just a talking point. This alignment of values and actions sends a clear message that the company is committed to positively impacting the planet.

MOVING FROM A FEAR-BASED TO A LOVE-BASED APPROACH

Leaders can shift from a fear-based approach, with a fixed mindset and dualistic thinking, to a love-based approach that embraces a growth mindshift and non-duality. This transformation is not just about adopting new strategies; it is about fundamentally changing the way we perceive ourselves, others, and our relationship with the natural world. By moving away from fear and toward love, we can foster the healing and growth necessary to address the environmental crises we face.

A fixed mindset is a belief that abilities, intelligence, and talents are static traits that cannot be significantly developed. This mindset is closely tied to dualistic thinking, which categorizes experiences and individuals into rigid polarities: right/wrong, good/bad, success/failure. Leaders operating from this perspective tend to focus on control, predictability, and maintaining the status quo. They may be driven by a fear of failure, criticism, or losing their position of authority.

In the context of ecological challenges, a fear-based approach can lead to denial, paralysis, or, at best, incremental changes that do not address the root causes of environmental degradation. Leaders may be reluctant to take bold actions because they fear making mistakes or facing backlash from stakeholders. This mindset also fosters a short-term competitive rather than a long-term collaborative environment, where the focus is on winning rather than thriving through working together toward a common good.

The fear-based approach is also evident in how organizations often view sustainability. Many companies approach sustainability initiatives as a checkbox to be ticked – something that needs to be done to avoid criticism or regulatory penalties. This approach is transactional rather than transformational, focusing on short-term gains and risk mitigation rather than long-term systemic change.

In contrast, a love-based approach to leadership is grounded in a growth mindshift – the belief that abilities and intelligence can be developed through dedication, hard work, and learning. This mindshift is inherently humanistic, focusing on possibilities and potential rather than limitations. A love-based approach also embraces non-duality, which rejects the categorization of experiences into binary opposites. Instead, it recognizes the interconnectedness of all things and the complexity of the human experience.

A growth mindshift encourages leaders to view challenges as opportunities for learning and development. Rather than fearing failure, they see it as a natural part of the growth process. This perspective is particularly important when addressing ecological challenges, which often require innovative and unconventional solutions. Leaders with a growth mindshift are more likely to experiment, take risks, and adapt to changing circumstances – qualities that are essential for driving meaningful progress in sustainability.

Non-duality, as part of a love-based approach, means recognizing that environmental, social, and economic issues are deeply interconnected and cannot be addressed in isolation. It also means moving away from the notion of "us versus them" – whether in the context of business competition, political debates, or human-nature relationships – and toward a more inclusive and collaborative approach.

This shift toward non-duality also involves healing the divisions that exist within ourselves and our societies. A love-based approach encourages leaders to cultivate self-awareness, empathy, and compassion. It calls for an understanding that true leadership is not about exerting power over others but about empowering and uplifting those around us. By fostering environments where people feel truly seen, valued, and supported, leaders can create the conditions for collective healing and transformation.

Healing is a central component of a love-based approach to leadership, particularly in the context of the ecological crises we face. The environmental degradation we see today is not just a result of poor management or lack of foresight; it is a symptom of deep wounds in our relationship with the natural world. These wounds stem from centuries of exploitation, disconnection, and a mindset that views nature as something to be controlled and dominated rather than cherished and respected.

To move toward a sustainable future, we must heal both ourselves and our relationship with the earth. This healing involves acknowledging the harm that has been done, taking responsibility for our actions, and committing to a path of restoration and renewal. It requires leaders to model humility and vulnerability, admitting when they have made mistakes and showing a willingness to learn and grow from those experiences.

Healing also involves fostering a sense of belonging and connection. In a love-based leadership model, leaders strive to create spaces where individuals feel a deep connection to the earth and to each other. This sense of connection can inspire a greater commitment to environmental stewardship and motivate individuals to take action in their personal and professional lives. Leaders must look beyond the immediate impacts of their decisions and consider the long-term, cumulative effects on the environment, society, and future generations. It requires a shift from a narrow focus on financial profitability to a broad understanding of value that includes social and environmental well-being.

A holistic approach also emphasizes the importance of balance and harmony. In the natural world, ecosystems thrive when they are in balance – when there is a dynamic equilibrium between different species and elements. Similarly, organizations and societies thrive when there is a balance between various interests, needs, and perspectives. Leaders who embrace a love-based, holistic approach work to create this balance, ensure that their decisions contribute to the overall health and vitality of the system as a whole.

Ultimately, the shift from a fear-based to a love-based approach is about choosing to lead from a place of love rather than fear. Love, in this context, is not a sentimental emotion but a powerful force for positive change. It is a commitment to the well-being of others, the planet, and future generations. It is about recognizing our shared humanity and the interconnectedness of all life on earth.

NAVIGATING CHANGE WITH AWARENESS, ACCOUNTABILITY, AND ACTION

To successfully lead in this new era, leaders must awaken by following a three-step process: awareness, accountability, and action. The first step involves becoming aware of one's own biases and blind spots. Leaders must have the courage and self-awareness to reflect on their behaviors and the impact they have on others. This requires both personal reflection and insight as well as seeking feedback from others. The next step is accountability – taking responsibility for one's actions and resisting the urge to blame others when challenges arise. A sense of generational accountability can serve as a catalyst for the shift in consciousness needed to address ecological challenges. Finally, leaders must take action, gradually replacing old habits with new, more inclusive practices. Underlying these three steps is the concept of agency: that, as humans, we all have the opportunity to choose the way we respond. In the words of Victor Frankl, "Between stimulus and response there is a space. In that space is our power to choose our response. In our response lies our growth and our freedom."

Change can be inherently challenging, as it goes against established norms. But it can also be invigorating, sparking creativity and innovation. In a rapidly changing world, leaders must draw on ideas from across disciplines and work collaboratively to find solutions. This requires letting go of the illusion of control, a difficult but necessary step in building resilient and adaptable organizations.

An inspiring example is Satya Nadella, CEO of Microsoft, who moved the company from a "know-it-all" to a "learn it all" culture. Another is David Marquette, formerly a US Naval submarine captain, who transformed his leadership by empowering his crew to take ownership of their work. By fostering psychological safety and encouraging autonomy, he created a more effective and engaged team that resulted in outstanding high performance.

This transformation will not happen overnight, and it will require courage, commitment, and a willingness to embrace change. But by aligning actions with deep values and taking responsibility for impacts, leaders can create a legacy of stewardship and care that will benefit generations to come. As more leaders recognize the need for this shift, they can move from anxiety and stress to empowerment through hope and agency.

Ultimately, the path to sustainable leadership is about more than just business success; it is about creating a better world for all. Leaders must balance profitability with the well-being of their people and the planet. This requires courage, compassion, and a commitment to continuous learning and growth.

One way to inspire leaders to embrace this approach is to appeal to their sense of generational responsibility. Many executives are deeply influenced by their children and grandchildren, and framing sustainability as a legacy issue can be a powerful motivator.

At the same time, transparency and accountability are key components of "power with" leadership. Leaders must communicate openly about their goals and challenges, fostering a culture of trust and collaboration. By being honest about the difficulties they face, they can rally their teams around a shared vision and inspire collective action.

The transition to sustainable leadership is not just a necessity for business success – it is a moral imperative. By embracing a love-based "power with," "play-to-thrive" approach rather than the outdated fear-based "power over," "play-to-win" approach, leaders can create organizations that are robust, inclusive, and aligned with the ecological needs of our time. This shift benefits their companies and contributes to a healthier, more sustainable planet for future generations.

By awakening awareness, stepping into accountability and committing courageously to actions, they can create a much needed, more sustainable and equitable future.

TAKEAWAYS

1. To make their companies sustainable, leaders need to move from a fear-based to a love-based approach.

2. With a growth mindshift, leaders can give employees psychological safety and promote engagement and collaboration – essential for business success.

3. Inspired by generational responsibility, leaders can overcome anxiety and burnout and start thriving in their positions.

FURTHER READING

Susan Goldsworthy, "IG&H: Finding a New Way to Lead," *I by IMD*, February 17, 2023.

Susan Goldsworthy, *Care, Dare, Share: The Secure Base Coach*, IMD International, 2024.

Susan Goldsworthy and Sydney Goldsworthy, *Where the Wild Things Were*, IMD International, 2019.

Susan Goldsworthy and Walter McFarland, *Choosing Change: How Leaders and Organizations Drive Results One Person at a Time*, New York: McGraw Hill, 2014.

Chapter 21

Ecosystem Partnerships

Mark Greeven and Howard Yu

Making a company sustainable, as pointed out throughout this book, often requires going beyond company walls. The most important work here likely involves partnerships with the broad industry ecosystem, from direct rivals to suppliers, distributors, and customers. But this collaboration is much harder than working within a company's organization.

Paradoxically, companies that stay "future ready" in promoting sustainability are the ones that embrace ecosystems as the key arena to drive growth. This chapter delves into how to leverage ecosystems, what the pitfalls are, and how to use such an approach to drive the sustainability agenda.

OPEN ENTERPRISE

Executives and scholars have understood for a long time the importance of ecosystems or consortia. Companies don't behave as atomistic individual enterprises in the marketplace; they regularly collaborate and more with a variety of other firms or even nonprofit organizations and government agencies. In many industries, these exchanges are frequent and trusted enough that we can start to speak of networks, connections that open each enterprise to dynamic collaboration and even formal partnerships. Ecosystems are thus an interconnected group of interdependent businesses that combine their offerings in an orchestrated way to add value to customers.

In some cases, as Alibaba has found in China, partnering with companies in heavily regulated industries such as finance and healthcare can be challenging from a governmental perspective. Ping An, the world's largest insurer, has nevertheless succeeded in building a healthcare ecosystem around its core financial services, all to increase its reach and access to customers. In general, ecosystem partnerships are easier to pull off legally than direct ownership or control of the secondary activities.

Ecosystems can be vital for companies looking to expand their market share or volume. Take, for example, Mammut, a Swiss manufacturer of outdoor equipment and apparel. It worked with other firms and organizations to support the target audience of hikers and climbers. Mammut's partners provided maps, communication services, and other offerings outside of Mammut's capability but very much desired by customers. The company even helped to set up an Alpine school to train climbers. On Mammut Connect, the company included links to organizations so customers could donate to protect glaciers or to help refugees. Mammut has even collaborated with rivals such as Patagonia on various initiatives to minimize climate change. Much of this came from the special interest of Mammut employees, not from strategic dictates.

All of this work not only encouraged customers to go outside more and use Mammut's products, it also strengthened customers' (and employees') identification with the company. Mammut's ecosystem made a stronger community of, say, mountain climbers, which furthered the emotional connection. And these ecosystem ties in turn made Mammut more open, flexible, and digital than its rivals.

But Mammut is also a cautionary tale. While those investments may have helped establish the brand, they may not have kept adding value. A private equity firm recently bought the long-time family business and has cut back severely on the platform. Companies can get too comfortable with ecosystem partnerships as well and even risk their differentiation in the marketplace. As Haier's founder and chairman Zhang Ruimin emphasizes, an ecosystem is sustainable only if all of its stakeholders create, capture, and deliver value greater than the sum of the parts.

NOT ABOUT CORE COMPETENCE

This "open enterprise" concept is quite different from the move to "core competence," where a company spins off and outsources everything it does outside a main area where it has special skills or differentiation in the market. Ecosystems rarely start with companies outsourcing activities to adjacent firms.

Instead, companies support and collaborate with ecosystems in order to add value to their product or accomplish some other strategic goal, such as sustainability. Essential to ecosystems is complementarity. Companies collaborate only with firms that offer something they lack, whether it is resources, expertise, access to customers – anything vital to delivering value.

Often neglected is the shift in mindset that must take place to develop substantial partnerships. Executives quite rightly focus on what they control, and outside partners can't be controlled as internal resources can. Leaders who work with ecosystems need to drop their controlling tendencies and look for win-win arrangements that benefit all contributors over time, from informal ties to formal joint ventures. That shift can be particularly difficult with sustainability, when the payoffs are often only long term. The trust that ecosystems build up, more than from mere outsourcing, can help here.

As with outsourcing, ecosystems do promote interconnectedness with special implications for sustainability. That's true whether companies work with outsourced suppliers and distributors or with ecosystem partners. A key metric in sustainability is a company's end-to-end carbon "footprint." This footprint totals all the greenhouse gasses generated by the company's activities, including from scope three: suppliers generating the goods and services in the company's offering, customers making use of that offering, and finally in the disposing of that offering (such as with incineration). For many companies, scope three accounts for most of that footprint, yet they have minimal leverage over suppliers and customers as a single company acting alone in the market. When they collaborate with other firms and organizations, they have a stronger center of gravity.

In practice, it's hard for a single small firm to build an ecosystem; potential partners don't know it and don't want to make the effort to work with it. More often, a group of firms and organizations forms around a sizeable, successful company, such as Bayer in Germany and Alibaba in China. On the other hand, sometimes big companies can go too far and partner so broadly they lose the discipline necessary for success.

Ecosystems can also be opportunistic. A global company with divisions on multiple continents may form an intense ecosystem for a single market while engaging in only baseline cooperation elsewhere. A company's strategy may dictate ecosystem investments depending on local possibilities.

ECOSYSTEMS FOR SUSTAINABILITY

Ecosystems take time to develop. We don't have strong examples of these efforts specifically for sustainability, still a relatively new challenge for most companies. As described elsewhere in the book, sustainability is hard to accomplish when each company works alone. As executives realize the difficulties of moving toward sustainability, they'll pick their battles and be increasingly open to collaboration with outside firms.

That collaboration can work at multiple levels. In a simple way, it can bring scale in negotiations with suppliers or customers. With multiple firms, loosely coordinated, calling for sustainable practices, other links in an industry's value chain will take notice. Many sustainability investments require substantial investments to start out or involve multiple experiments with high uncertainty.

Collaboration also lowers the cost and risk of experimentation. Firms can learn from others' experiments and proceed with more confidence. They're not learning only from themselves but also from partners in the ecosystem.

Ecosystems also help to get reluctant organizations over the hump of resisting change. Absent strong pressure from end users, many value chains defer on sustainability and similar efforts. But when firms start to collaborate, they can generate the pressure needed for change.

A likely foundation in many industries will be digital platforms, which companies have set up for ecosystems in many areas. These platforms facilitate not just communication but also the sharing of resources. They can greatly reduce the transaction costs that discouraged many companies from pursuing ecosystems in the past.

A German chemical giant has promoted both environmental and social sustainability in building an ecosystem for farmers in developing countries. The company has provided seed, fertilizer, and pesticides, while a broad array of partners offered education, equipment, weather information, and even drone surveys from the sky. The division's digital platform helped make these offerings accessible. So far it's unclear how much these ecosystem partners can take credit for improvements in sustainability, but the direction of the work is promising.

PITFALLS FOR ECOSYSTEMS

While ecosystems bring several advantages, they're also fragile and can fall apart or limit their value for a variety of reasons. One of the biggest may be the mindset issue throughout the organization. If people on all levels of the company aren't aligned culturally with partners, at least on the goals of the collaboration, then trust dissolves and the partnerships can do little. A small group of people can get the collaboration going, but if they can't win over the rest of the organization, they can't by themselves maintain the effort and build the necessary trust.

Some organizations go in the opposite direction – people try to build an ecosystem for all aspects of the value chain. But the company needs to control some activities directly. So leaders should be selective. And there's no need for a big global launch.

Another problem is superficial interest. Some executives may see ecosystems as little more than loosely connected business networks and will resist serious collaboration. They may treat the ecosystem as just the first step in scouting new business partners, which is a valid pursuit but may turn off the rest of the ecosystem.

ANOTHER ORGANIZATIONAL TOOL

Ecosystem partnerships certainly aren't mandatory, even for sustainability. An ecosystem partnership is one more way to organize and mobilize resources and capabilities, especially for complex initiatives. Some companies may be large and well-resourced and already so connected to outside activities that they have little need for ecosystem ties. But most companies will need to work with others. And those outside ties can help companies work in far more ways than before. Companies can invest in a fund or rely on an NGO for part of the value chain.

Ecosystems typically offer a variety of potential partners in everything from technology to talent. For sustainability, they can bring unexpected capabilities and resources to the table but only if the company is willing to work at building the connection and trust. Ecosystems can be particularly helpful to address the concerns of a single customer that may not be worth a big investment by the company but is worth engaging a firm in the ecosystem to handle.

That's especially the case now that digital technology has greatly enabled ecosystem collaboration. Transaction costs have fallen dramatically, which is partly why the Alibabas and Amazons of the world have flourished. The many activities that startup companies would need to arrange on their own, they can get right off the web for an affordable price.

Take L'Oreal, the French cosmetic and personal giant. In 2018, it acquired Modiface, which became its digital platform. That platform worked so smoothly, thanks partly to 10 years' previous investment in digitizing, that it opened up the company up to numerous and profitable partnerships. It also facilitates collaborations to boost sustainability.

Going further, the Austrian energy company OMV has been adamant about employing its ecosystem in recyclability initiatives. Similarly, the American firm W.L. Gore, maker of waterproof Gore-Tex, has worked with partners to make its garments recyclable. Prior investments in digital technology, and especially an established platform, have helped enormously here – one more reason to invest in digitalization.

In the race toward a sustainable future, companies can either build bridges or burn alone. Embracing ecosystem partnerships isn't just smart business – it's the lifeline that will pull visionary companies across the sustainability finish line.

TAKEAWAYS

1. Companies need cross-sector collaboration. The complexity of sustainability challenges requires executives to go beyond their organizational boundaries, fostering collaborations across industries, governments, NGOs, and academia. These partnerships are essential to drive innovation, share risks, and scale sustainable solutions globally. Executives must prioritize building and maintaining these ecosystems to remain competitive and impactful.

2. They can innovate by engaging ecosystems. Working with diverse ecosystems can catalyze innovation in sustainability. Executives can strategically invest in and partner with startups, research institutions, and other entities within their ecosystems to co-create and deploy cutting-edge sustainable technologies. This approach not only accelerates progress but also positions companies as leaders in the sustainability space.

3. Ecosystems create long-term value. Sustainability increasingly promotes business viability. Executives must shift their focus from short-term profits to long-term value creation, where success is measured by environmental and social impact as much as financial performance. Ecosystem partnerships offer pathways to create shared value, boost the brand reputation, and ensure compliance with emerging regulations. This shift is critical for resilience in a future where sustainability is a key market driver.

FURTHER READING

Mark Greeven and Oliver Pabst, "How Using Digital Ecosystems Can Transform an Incumbent Business," in *The Power of Ecosystems*, curated by Stuart Crainer, *Thinkers* 50, 2023.

Mark Greeven and Wei Wei, *Business Ecosystems in China: Alibaba and Competing Baidu, Tencent, Xiaomi and LeCo*, Routledge, 2017.

Howard Yu et al., "What Makes a Company 'Future-Ready'?" *Harvard Business Review*, March 21, 2022.

Chapter 22

Changing Culture

Robert Hooijberg

Moving to sustainability isn't a matter of making a few top-down decisions. Companies need the entire organization engaged in seeking sustainable practices throughout the value chain and even in secondary activities. The only way to make that happen in the long run is to shift the company's culture toward sustainability. But how?

Culture is a notoriously difficult subject for leaders. But researchers have found several practical ways for nudging the culture in a different direction over time. The key is to avoid grand commitments to sustainability; instead, build up behaviors and a mindset conducive to this work. Over time, the culture will move and make sustainability self-supporting.

FORGET SLOGANS, FOCUS ON ORDINARY CONCERNS

A company's culture reveals its values, embedded in everything that the company does. But those values might not be what the leaders want; they're just the reality in that organization. Culture arises from the management systems, the performance systems, the rewards, structures, processes, and how leaders behave – but not just because of a few top-down decision from the leadership. A culture develops over time; it is most certainly not about putting fancy words on a screensaver or in your annual report. We should be able to derive the culture by just looking at what actually happens. My favorite definition: culture is what people do when they think nobody is watching.

That has big implications for sustainability because the culture comes from what ordinary people are concerned about. If you want people to care about, say, carbon neutrality, you can't start with the Paris Agreement on climate change; start with what matters to your employees and your clients.

For example, a Dutch company made high-performance electronics cables as part of their product portfolio. This was back in the early 2010s. The leaders announced that while they weren't going to focus on environmental concerns for its own sake, they did make a point of reading the sustainability reports of their customers. They paid attention to sustainability for competitive advantage. One of their main customers was Apple, which had just started making big promises on sustainability. The company figured out a way to cut the plastic in charging cables by half but at four times the price. It was still a difference of only a few pennies to Apple, which agreed to buy the cables because it helped them put real evidence behind their own statements on sustainability. The company resisted commodity pressures, maintained its margins, did good for the environment, and kept a big customer.

Not only did the move give the company a leg up in the marketplace, but it was a concrete step that made employees feel good about their work at no extra cost to the company. They connected sustainability not with cuts or deprivation but commercial success. Putting all of that together is what drives real cultural change. So leaders should focus the company's sustainability efforts on these win-win solutions. The achievement nudges everyone in the organization, in an emotional as well as rational way, toward developing an instinct for sustainable practice.

For changing the culture, the sustainability case isn't enough. To engage the full organization, companies need a solid business case too. If a move is purely about sustainability, it's unlikely to become an ingrained part of the culture. So leaders should pick their battles and focus on the commercial benefit. Even if that's not the main reason, there should still be some commercial opportunity.

START SMALL, FROM BEHAVIORS

Most companies start their sustainability journey with big, bold pronouncements that make no difference culturally. Say the company promises to be carbon neutral by 2030. Most employees don't care because they don't expect to stay at the company that long. And what does carbon neutral mean to them practically? Some employees may believe strongly in sustainability already. But most people have their heads elsewhere. Their mindset isn't ready. Too often with these grand pronouncements, little really changes, and the company's leaders, eager to report something, resort to greenwashing.

To get that mindset shift, especially if the company lacks immediate commercial opportunities, it can start nudging people in small ways. In many organizations, for example, each individual office has a garbage can with a small plastic bag. Most weekday evenings, a cleaning crew comes in and replaces each bag with a fresh one.

A Dutch dairy company named FrieslandCampina had an idea: What if the company simply took away most of those garbage cans and put one in the hallway for every 10 or 20 offices? People generally went along because most days people threw away just a coffee cup and napkins at most. The cost savings were minor, and mostly in labor, because the bags were cheap, but most people got behind the move. It was an easy change, with a direct impact, and a bit of savings, so there was a (small) business rationale. It nudged people into doing something small for the environment. There was also a small fitness and social benefit, as people had to get up and go into the hallway, where they might talk with colleagues. Or maybe they would switch to coffee mugs instead of disposables.

The garbage can idea might not work everywhere, but companies can gently impose, usually in a top-down way, other nudges. They might issue everyone reusable bottles or cups to minimize waste. They might hand out pens made from recycled plastic, especially if the pens look cool. These steps seem trivial, but they're likely to do far more to change the culture than fancy slogans or promises. They get people doing something different.

Indeed, leaders might look at the cost savings and say, "Why bother?" But the cultural gain might be significant and pay off in the long run financially. Too often, leaders start culture change on the wrong end. They try to change the mindset first and then hope for behavior change. But sometimes the process works in reverse: you need to change people's behavior to change the mindset. Fancy slide presentations appealing to emotions can help, but often it's better to change the behavior first. And after a few months, more ideas may bubble up. Starting small, with behaviors, can make people willing to consider big things.

Go back to the cable manufacturer focused on what its customers wanted. At first, some sales representatives pushed back, saying their customers didn't report on sustainability. Well, they had to ask anyway, and it turns out, many of their customers did have these reports. Behavior matters: if you try to change the mindset, people stick to their old habits, their old stereotypes, and resist. The leaders said nothing about sustainability, per se, as an emotional goal; it was all about the customers. "Let's give customers what they want." And all of a sudden, many of the salespeople started acting in more sustainable ways to support their accounts in delivering on their promises.

Too often, leaders hammer people over sustainability. They try to make people feel bad, what scoundrels we all are, not just polluting but also inattentive and inconsiderate. They try to shame people into behaving sustainably. That rarely works, especially for changing a culture. Better to just change some behaviors and the mindset will follow. That will lead to more culture change than anyone lecturing people (especially while flying around in a private jet).

THE CULTURAL BIAS AGAINST SUSTAINABILITY

Many companies, often for good reasons, have strong cultures that prompt short-term thinking. Those cultures often reject sustainability as a bad business decision because the payoffs are so long term. Leaders can't simply tell people to shift to long-term thinking. Often the only way to overcome that bias is to show some tangible immediate savings – with people changing their behaviors.

Eneva is a Brazilian company that explores for natural gas, especially in the Amazon. Most Brazilians from the eastern part of the country look down on the inhabitants, but the region does have one city with a university and an engineering program. Eneva was spending heaviliy to fly engineers over from Rio de Janeiro to work on projects. Finally the leaders said, "Let's hire some local engineers." Not only would the work help to build the local communities, but people could return to their families fairly quickly, whereas the Rio engineers were away for one or two weeks. The local engineers might not be as effective as their Rio counterparts, but they actually didn't require much more training than Rio engineers had. They were generally more eager to learn and prove themselves than the ones from Rio. In the end, the quality differences were minor, and the move succeeded.

Eneva was dealing with biases more than reality, and the behavior change – coupled with tangible savings – can lead to a changed mindset. Eneva's people will now be more open to sustainability ideas in the future. They might even think more medium or long term, so that sustainability becomes more rational, or defendable.

NARROW THE FRAME

Of course, some sustainability projects inevitably lack an immediate business rationale. But even for something as broad as culture, leaders don't need to talk about the organization as a whole. Some areas inevitably focus on exploring new possibilities; others exploit the current business with continuing investment and improvements. A long-term exploration of business models doesn't have to be done by the entire organization.

Regulators increasingly are paying attention to sustainability in companies, whether with formal structures or not. They don't really care whether leaders think climate change is real or dismiss environmentalists as tree huggers. They're going to restrict companies, so leaders pragmatically need to be prepared, regardless of personal feelings. Most companies have little choice but to explore new business models and new ways of doing things.

Eneva, the Brazilian energy company mentioned, also operates in the northwest of the country near Venezuela. For a long time, people there relied on diesel fuel from Venezuela for their electricity. But then Eneva did something bold and risky. When the Venezuelan government, desperate for fossil-fuel revenues, stopped sending diesel to the region, Eneva set up a plant to liquefy its abundant natural gas. It partnered with the Venezuelan government to build a 600-km railway to bring that liquefied natural gas (LNG) into that region. Concretely, this marked the company's expansion into the commercialization of small-scale LNG, which helps to deliver energy to regions not connected to the national grid.

Eneva used a crisis to create a business opportunity, which in turn provided cleaner energy to people in northwestern Brazil. It mattered that part of the company had started thinking about that possibility before the crisis hit, so they were ready. The rest of the organization knew nothing about that idea, but that was fine.

With that move, of course, everyone in the organization was aware. And the success helped with everyone's engagement on sustainability. It got creative juices flowing and made them more open to exploring other ideas, maybe even doing some longer-term projects.

CULTURE AS A TOOL

While culture often changes with behaviors, it is not a mere byproduct of what actually happens in a company. It's an essential tool for aligning strategy and engagement in the organization. We would even argue that sometimes the best way to change the culture is to never talk about culture change.

In the late 1990s, Domino's Pizza had an embarrassing problem. Its headquarters city of Ann Arbor, in the United States, was home to the main campus of the University of Michigan, and it had delivery restaurants all over town. Students were the main employees, mostly delivery drivers, and turnover was excessive, well over 100% per year, a headache for both HR and customer service. The restaurants also struggled with people driving while intoxicated. Many student employees, it seemed, wanted to earn spending money and, once they had some, didn't bother showing up for shifts.

Instead of trying to change the culture directly, the regional Domino's manager asked, "What do these kids really want?" Many of them wanted a job after graduation, for which a letter of recommendation would help. So the restaurants told its employees, "If you show up on time for every shift, deliver consistently and not intoxicated, for at least six months, we'll write you a recommendation." HR trained the supervisors, most of whom were just older kids, in writing the letters. Turnover fell by more than half, to 45%, and those requirements changed the culture – they became the informal work standard at the Domino's restaurants in Ann Arbor.

HR also installed in every restaurant a basic IT system to keep track of employees, which had the added advantage of notifying nearby restaurants when they fired someone – who then couldn't join another Domino's for a year. That was a stick that went with the carrot of the letter, but the stick by itself would have done little; the positive gain drove the main engagement. Throughout, the company never mentioned culture change, but they got it.

MEASURING CULTURE

That's how companies can alter their culture, but how can leaders know if they're making headway? While amorphous, culture can be measured, mostly with employee surveys, either big annual efforts or quick, short, monthly pulse checks. These instruments can't be entirely quantitative. More important, they need to be careful not to talk about culture change. A better approach may be just to see what people are saying. Suppose you do a version of the change with garbage cans in the hallway. If, in a few months, you hold a session on generating other ideas for savings, you can see if you had an impact. The garbage can switch might make people more open to further actions. They start internalizing sustainability, which is really what matters.

Outside developments also affect culture. Before 2020, at many companies, people might have thought nothing of client visits where the travel time far exceeded the meeting time. Now those company cultures are frowning on that calculus. Supervisors ask for strong justifications before approving that travel, especially if the person has already met the client once. They aren't really doing that for sustainability reasons, but people's awareness and imagination has changed. Most people don't really want to travel that much anyway, even on the company's expense. The client visits are shorter, but now people are communicating much more often with those clients. New technologies, hastened by the pandemic, changed people's instincts.

Company cultures get a lot more attention now than they did decades ago, which is a good thing. We all understand the power of those unwritten norms. But leaders must resist the temptation to try to rewrite those norms directly, especially around a concept as fraught as sustainability. Far better to move gradually, with small steps that build toward big projects. Small behavior changes will have a bigger payoff than big pronouncements or slogans. Culture is powerful, but it emerges on its own, from the real actions of everyone in the organization.

TAKEAWAYS

1. A company's culture comes more from ordinary behaviors than from ideology; intent and slogans matter less than day-to-day actions to attract and support customers.

2. Culture is a tool, so leaders can alter it to change behaviors, more with practical nudges than slogans or other overt messages.

3. Better to move gradually, with small steps that eventually yield changes.

FURTHER READING

Robert Hooijberg et al., *Leading Culture Change in Global Organizations: Aligning Culture and Strategy*, New York: Jossey Bass, 2012.

Chapter 23

Improving Governance

Natalia Olynec and Knut Haanaes

Sustainability practices require good governance. Unlike other corporate initiatives, these usually involve a change in the company's overall direction, including its strategy. That makes sustainability an issue of governance involving the entire executive team and the governing board. High-level commitment is essential to driving meaningful and lasting change, so companies need structures to integrate sustainability into the overall business strategy and their relationships with key stakeholders.

In previous decades, sustainability was often a sideline to the main work handled by people in communications or marketing. But now it's moved into the core of many companies. Getting there and staying there is not a choice but a strategic imperative in the company's actual context that requires governance.

FUTURE-READY GOVERNANCE

Indeed, sustainability is often a high-risk pursuit, but one reason we have companies is to manage and overcome risk. In some areas of the business, such as jet fuel, the fully sustainable option might not yet be profitable. If sustainability is not part of the strategy, a company will quite reasonably decline to invest in that area. But where the strategy does include sustainability, and the area matches well with the company's resources and ambitions, the company would respond quite differently. It would see the lack of a profitable option as a failure to innovate and an investment opportunity.

Doing so requires a long-term mindset in management, as well as supportive values. But most managements are consumed by short-term issues, leaving little time for long-term threats and opportunities. CEOs' tenures keep shrinking. Boards need to insist on making the firm future ready – not just exploiting current resources but also exploring new markets and technology. Directors can recognize macro trends and work with them. A food manufacturer might look at predictions of water scarcity and adjust the strategy toward precision farming, vertical integration, or regenerative agriculture so it still has a big business in 20 years. Board guidance is essential in getting management to think strategically. Indeed, the World Economic Forum's annual Risk Perception Survey includes many sustainability-related topics, both social and environmental.

Risk categories	2 years		10 years	
Economic	1st	Misinformation and disinformation	1st	Extreme weather events
Environmental	2nd	Extreme weather events	2nd	Critical change to Earth systems
Geopolitical	3rd	Societal polarization	3rd	Biodiversity loss and ecosystem collapse
Societal	4th	Cyber insecurity	4th	Natural resource shortages
Technological	5th	Interstate armed conflict	5th	Misinformation and disinformation
	6th	Lack of economic opportunity	6th	Adverse outcomes of AI technologies
	7th	Inflation	7th	Involuntary migration
	8th	Involuntary migration	8th	Cyber insecurity
	9th	Economic downturn	9th	Societal polarization
	10th	Pollution	10th	Pollution

Figure 23.1   Global risks ranked by severity over the short and long term.

Governance is especially important for handling trade-offs. Mining companies, for example, have been struggling with the need to shrink or shut down their coal sites. Those sites devastate a great deal of land, as well as bring out the dirtiest fossil fuel for carbon emissions. But they also employ a great many local laborers. Entire villages would suffer from shutting down the sites, worsening inequality and other social ills. How can sustainability-oriented companies handle this trade-off? A long-term-oriented management, spurred by its board, might explore new business models that could continue employing people while reducing coal production. Government action can help to make those business models easier (see Chapter 12 on nonmarket strategies).

Markets are good for short-term initiatives and not so good for the long term. We need companies to innovate in areas of market failure. Governance can also help with alliances with other companies to share best practices and set standards and common goals on sustainability. Their success requires voluntary disclosures that could help build trust and effectiveness. Yet companies lack ways to separate better alliances from the pack. With over 150 business sustainability coalitions identified through private research efforts, there is no global registry or any reporting requirements that could articulate their "theory of change" or identify potential conflicts of interest. But companies with strong internal governance on sustainability can help to develop these differentiators.

TOP-DOWN LEADERSHIP

For large-scale sustainability transformations, top-down leadership is crucial. While bottom-up initiatives are valuable and often spark innovation, a unified and consistent effort driven from the top is essential for ensuring strategic relevance, coherence, and effective resource allocation. When sustainability efforts are fragmented and poorly integrated into the overarching corporate strategy, they risk losing impact, becoming disconnected from the company's core objectives, and ultimately failing to deliver meaningful results.

Top-down leadership ensures that sustainability is not only prioritized but also deeply integrated into the company's overall strategy. This alignment is vital for setting clear objectives, coordinating efforts across different parts of the organization, and maintaining a consistent focus on long-term goals. When the board and executive management lead the charge, it sends a powerful message both internally and externally that sustainability is central to the company's mission and success. This strong alignment helps prevent efforts from dispersing into isolated projects that may not align with the company's strategic priorities.

Moreover, effective top-down leadership plays a key role in mobilizing both internal and external stakeholders around sustainability goals. Internally, clear direction from the top ensures that all levels of the organization are aligned, with employees understanding how their roles contribute to broad sustainability objectives. This unified approach fosters a culture of engagement, where everyone in the organization is motivated to contribute to the sustainability agenda. Externally, top-down leadership builds credibility and trust with stakeholders, including investors, customers, regulators, and the broader community. When executives clearly communicate sustainability commitments, they reinforce the company's dedication and help secure the buy-in of these critical groups.

This high-level commitment is particularly important when it comes to building alliances and advocating for sustainability-related policies. Executives and board members who lead by example can engage in high-level discussions with peers, government bodies, and international organizations to set industry standards, share best practices, and push for regulatory frameworks that support sustainable business practices. Such alliances are more effective when driven by a clear and consistent strategy articulated by the company's top leaders. Also, in the realm of public policy and lobbying, a unified, top-level voice is crucial when advocating for policies that support sustainability, such as carbon pricing, renewable energy incentives, or stricter environmental regulations. When the board and executive management are visibly leading these efforts, they boost the company's influence and ability to shape the regulatory environment in ways that align with its sustainability objectives.

As sustainability becomes a strategic priority, the role of the board and corporate governance structures must evolve. Top-down leadership necessitates that boards not only oversee sustainability initiatives but also become deeply involved in shaping the company's long-term vision and strategy. This shift requires governance frameworks that are flexible enough to incorporate sustainability considerations into decision-making processes at the highest level.

By driving the integration of sustainability into every facet of the business, top leadership ensures that the company is prepared to meet the demands of a rapidly changing business environment.

THE EVOLVING ROLE OF THE BOARD

Boards of directors play a crucial role in shaping companies' sustainability agendas. However, recent insights highlight significant gaps in their effectiveness. For instance, 70% of board members report being moderately or not at all effective in integrating ESG factors into company strategy and governance.

Moreover, 91% of board members believe that boards should prioritize strategic reflection over merely monitoring operations. This reflects a broader recognition that boards shift their focus toward long-term strategic thinking, particularly in areas such as sustainability that require a deep understanding of complex global trends and risks. The role of the board in sustainability is thus twofold: ensuring that these considerations are embedded into the core strategy of the company and fostering a forward-looking mindset that emphasizes strategic reflection and adaptability. This approach helps not only in mitigating risks but also in seizing opportunities that align with sustainable growth.

The board of directors plays three distinct and complementary roles in the management of sustainability within an organization: supervision, co-development, and support. Each of these roles is crucial for integrating sustainability into the company's strategy and operations.

1. *Supervision.* The board oversees the implementation of sustainability strategies and holds management

accountable for achieving goals. As part of supervision, the board ensures that sustainability risks are identified, assessed, and managed effectively. This includes overseeing the integration of risks into the company's broad risk management framework such that the board regularly reviews these risks.

2. *Co-development.* The board actively participates in shaping the company's sustainability strategy. It collaborates with management to set goals and priorities and determines how sustainability aligns with the overall business strategy. The board works alongside management to identify the most material sustainability issues for the company and its stakeholders.

3. *Support.* Here the board ensures that management has the necessary resources – such as budget, personnel, and technology – to implement the sustainability initiatives. The board plays a key role in supporting management's efforts to engage with stakeholders, including investors, employees, customers, and the broader community (Figure 23.2).

Key elements on Board agenda - Sustainability

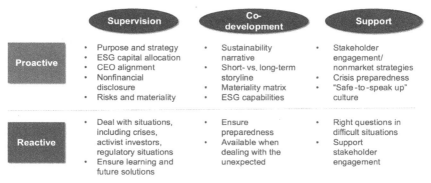

Figure 23.2 The roles of the board in sustainability strategy management.

How to get there? It's a bit of a chicken-and-egg situation as to who starts what: does management educate the board, or vice versa? Sometimes it takes a visionary CEO or board chair to drive this process.

Ownership plays a part. Directors in family-owned companies, for example, often start with a long-term, values-driven perspective: "We aren't going to wait for consumers to demand it." For example, J.M. Huber Corporation, one of the largest and oldest family-held companies headquartered in the United States, is a leading producer of hydrocolloids, specialty chemicals, minerals, agriculture solutions, and engineered wood products. Driven by family values, the firm set sustainability targets at the corporate board level and established strong governance of the impacts of new investments.

Since 2018, the investment review process includes formal expectations to quantify sustainability outcomes of all investments above $300 000 to include triple-bottom line (people, planet, profit) analysis. In one example, at the company's Danish plant, a project to reduce noise from cooling fans also made use of the surplus heat that was normally vented through cooling towers. The site installed a heat pump and heat exchangers to a local utility to supply heat to 2200 local households. The firm was the winner of the IMD Sustainability in Family Business Award for its focus on sustainable business transformation.

But sustainability governance at the board level can take many different forms. Stand-alone sustainability committees, unheard of a decade ago, are now common. Alternatively, responsibility for sustainability sometimes sits with existing committees, such as audit or finance or nomination and governance, as new regulations increase pressure on non-financial corporate performance.

Some firms appoint one board director with expertise as a lead. This can be helpful for small firms where impacts are felt in a narrow range of products or services. Finally, future-ready companies may have the full board manage sustainability to ensure a broad range of perspectives, experiences, and ideas – yet this approach risks inefficiencies, groupthink, or neglect if financial results dominate agendas. An informed and committed chair can ensure that sustainability risks and opportunities are featured as regular key agenda items.

Beyond the pioneers in business transformation, we need traditional companies with the strategic commitment to sustainability that enables them to push the envelope. Sustainability is no longer just a moral issue; it's increasingly a pragmatic issue. But companies still need leadership with values and the courage to balance long term and short term. Boards can balance executives' instinctive short-termism with long-term vision and determination.

INTEGRATING SUSTAINABILITY INTO GOVERNANCE STRUCTURES

The role of the chief sustainability officer (CSO) varies by authority and proximity to strategic decision making they have. Some organizations have C-level CSOs, while others constitute a one-person sustainability department. When Mattel released its "Chief Sustainability Officer" Barbie recycled plastic doll, the role of CSO had clearly gone mainstream. Growing global challenges, such as climate change, resource depletion, and social inequality, have forced businesses to reevaluate their risks, opportunities, and impact on the world. They also struggle to stay on top of changing regulations, investor demands for transparency, and employees seeking careers with "purpose." The CSO helps the firm manage these evolving dilemmas.

By integrating ESG data into strategy, operations, and disclosure, C-suite executives can improve their risk management and seize new business opportunities. That's why efforts on sustainability are also moving beyond the office of the CSO. As companies call for this work to reduce risk and create value, they are dispersing those responsibilities throughout the C-suite.

For example, CSOs now must work closely with chief finance officers (CFOs) as transparency and disclosure demands proliferate. CFOs are generally responsible for these kinds of issues, but many are finding themselves out of their depth in nonfinancial reporting. They have traditionally looked after the numbers while other departments dealt with what were once seen as reputational issues. However, those divisions are fading as evidence builds that sustainability directly influences financial performance. The CSO and CFO need to speak the same language and communicate nonfinancial performance and impact to investors, analysts, and rating companies.

Other functions are also actively involved. The chief operations officer might handle responsible procurement with the supply chain aspects. At the same time, the head of human resources promotes diversity, equity, and inclusion and fair labor standards. Some companies also have a separate sustainability steering committee involving executives in the divisions, though loosely coordinated by the CSO.

Before, CSOs moved from marketing, communications, or public affairs. Now, they come more often from operations or finance. Companies need CSOs with a deep knowledge of the supply chain or even the entire value chain – not just public relations, but also, for example, in helping to develop circular business models. CSOs must first get their hands dirty in the business to understand how sustainability can create value or manage risk.

CSOs thus don't work alone; they must be a bridge across the different functions. They explain or translate trends, context or science, to make sustainability relevant for specific functions or departments. They should also bring in a long-term perspective, and it's often other people who do the actual implementation.

A look at reporting lines can indicate the maturity of the firm and potential to succeed in transformation. According to a Gartner survey of 175 executives, 42% of CSOs now report to the CEO. Reporting to a general council or a communications lead can indicate more of a compliance- or reputation-focused orientation.

Eventually, as more executives accept the need for sustainability, the CSO role might even fade away. If sustainability is mainly a way to create value for the organization, it's part of the core strategy, little different from, say, AI: a new business opportunity to pursue. Similar to how the role of chief digital officer emerged a decade ago, the CSO is often tasked with transforming the business model. The main difference would be the need to pay attention to broader groups of stakeholders. For example, a mining company must balance relying on robots or machinery to increase safety and efficiency with the need for jobs in local communities.

CSOs can also ensure a place for values in this conversation; it's not just a profit-and-loss exercise. Values can drive engagement for these tough initiatives, and sustainability has a salience for personal or corporate purpose that AI and other corporate challenges lack. It can help to attract and retain talent, especially young people seeking purpose in work. Gen Zs and millennials are particularly concerned about sustainability and want employers to help with the transition to a low-carbon economy.

Indeed, according to a survey by Deloitte, many young people would switch jobs if their employer did not take action on climate change. Some firms, such as Nespresso, set up a shadow, or reversed, board of young, nonexecutive employees to work with the (typically middle-aged) executive board to provide perspectives and insights that can inform strategy and shift corporate culture toward more sustainable behaviors. Even executives in our programs at IMD say they are motivated to incorporate sustainability by the conversations they have at dinner with children or grandchildren.

Sustainability, more than other corporate initiatives, requires strong direction and oversight. Getting there is a long-term process with many pressures for delay and lost focus. Only with diligent governance can companies expect to achieve true sustainability.

TAKEAWAYS

1. Make sustainability a senior-level responsibility: It's not enough to appoint a director of sustainability, as companies need a strong voice at the senior level to integrate sustainability into C-suite decisions.

2. Focus on initiatives with impact: Prioritize scaling the most promising sustainability initiatives instead of spreading resources thinly across numerous small projects.

3. Collaborate broadly but with discipline: To avoid the compliance trap and promote innovation, promote work across silos and build alliances with outside companies and organizations.

FURTHER READING

Knut Haanaes et al., "Transparent Climate Alliances: Principles for Greater Effectiveness and Legitimacy," *Social Science Research Network*, 2023. http://doi.org/10.2139/ssrn.4513303.

Natalia Olynec, "Does Your Company Need a Chief Sustainability Officer?" *I by IMD*, 10 April 2022.

Natalia Olynec, "Leading Transformation Isn't Child's Play. Here are the skills your company needs," *I by IMD*, September–November 2023.

Natalia Olynec, "Sustainability Trends Shaping Corporate Priorities in 2024," *I by IMD*, 28 December 2023

Chapter 24

Family Business

Alfredo De Massis, Marleen Dieleman,
and Peter Vogel

Although little discussed, family-controlled enterprises make up most of the firms worldwide. Concentrated ownership enables families to decide quickly and to develop a long-term strategy with the proper degree of managerial discretion and political power that are needed to avoid the pressures that might delay or attenuate the efforts of other firms. They can thereby overcome some of the structural challenges – financial, strategic, and cultural – discussed elsewhere in the book. But does this ownership actually make these firms more likely to invest in sustainability? It depends, as these very advantages can also prevent them from aggressively promoting sustainability.

HOW FAMILIES WORK WITH COMPANIES

To start, we need to recognize that families affect companies in two ways. First is the usual path of a family-owned business, often one started by the first generation and continued, usually with decreasing involvement, into further generations. We call this the legacy company. We'll focus on that dynamic here, but a second common path is through investment. Families that build up wealth in the legacy business often buy into other companies, through private equity, venture capital, or angel investing, so they have a broad influence. Holding companies, family offices, family foundations, family museums, and portfolio investments are some of the mechanisms to spread the influence beyond an originally fully-owned business into a broad range of family-influenced activities. The impact of these "enterprising families" is complex and often hard to detect, but it's part of how families can promote sustainability.

Even limited to companies that families control directly, these still amount to two-thirds of all firms in the world. Most are small and privately held, but families control large private or publicly listed firms as well. In most emerging markets, over half of the publicly listed companies are family-controlled. If companies are to tackle the big environmental and social challenges of our day, family-controlled organizations could help lead the way.

After all, most families have strong noneconomic goals, such as involving younger generations in the business, instilling a spiritual sense (nurturing what's bigger and goes beyond individuals), promoting family cohesion and harmony, and benefitting the local community. Achieving these goals creates a kind of socio-emotional wealth, and sustainability fits well with these goals. So family-controlled companies are often inclined toward sustainability-related concerns.

Families also have a longer time horizon than companies with dispersed ownership whose CEOs have a tenure of only four to six years. The CEO of a small German manufacturer of writing instruments once said, "When I make investments, I need to think not just about my grandchildren, but also about their grandchildren." Those multigenerational considerations make it easier for family-controlled companies to invest into long-term projects common to sustainability.

If a family maintains control over multiple generations, that's because it has developed some discipline to prevent the nepotism and complacency that would otherwise make these firms uncompetitive. The family develops rules or principles that push relatives to add value rather than just take advantage of emotional ties for a luxurious life. No family is monolithic; its members vary in their competence, intelligence, and willingness to work hard. The trick is to put the relative in a position that fits well. Some might be managers, while others just own shares. Some might not be good at running a business but excel in investing money. Some might be too entrepreneurial, and others might care about different issues, including philanthropy; they can still serve as directors on the board.

Often these family businesses have executives that are younger than those in nonfamily corporations of a comparable size. These young leaders are often more committed to sustainability than their elders, especially as a moral imperative apart from commercial opportunities. Of course, in some family businesses, patriarchal CEOs hang on for longer than they would in a nonfamily business. Family businesses can be controlled by young leaders or by a persistent older generation.

Some family-controlled companies have made the cultural transition toward a professionally run organization. After that transition, they can gain the human-resource capability to carry out the organizational transformation that sustainability usually requires. Others rely on forward-looking family members to reorient the family business toward sustainability by using the speed and discretion that significant family ownership brings.

Whichever route they take to aim for sustainability, control is not as clear as it might seem. As families move into the third or fourth generation after the entrepreneurial founding, they develop complex systems of action. Cousins vary in how much they engage in the companies, how they direct their influence, and how much they unite.

Most families have substantial influence over the legacy company, either directly through stock ownership or indirectly through their credibility as representing the entrepreneurial heart of the firm. If not themselves the leaders, they might push the company's leaders to seek a social purpose beyond profit, to create value for stakeholders as well as shareholders, or to innovate in business models, supply chains, or sustainability reporting. They could act like any other controlling group over a company, often with an agility that broadly owned firms can't muster.

Families can also make a difference through financial control, where the family has a majority or large minority stake in a firm either acquired or heavily funded as a startup. With majority control, the family can transform a company through the board and leadership decisions. Even with just a minority stake, they can greatly affect operations. With a portfolio of investments, if they have a clear and strong ambition, they can allocate their resources and voices toward sustainability. Whether directly through invested companies, the family office, or a looser portfolio, they can make a difference in these family-influenced firms. Families can also promote sustainability through philanthropy, both from the companies they control and from their own private or family giving. Advocacy also matters; family members often have outsized credibility in their societies and can publicly argue for greater attention to sustainability. What we have increasingly witnessed over the past years is that enterprising families are starting to align their business, investment, philanthropic, and advocacy activities toward a greater and collective impact, seeking to maximize their impact by embracing a multistakeholder value creation mindset rather than a simple shareholder value creation mindset.

Here we focus on families' influence over the legacy company, not through their investment portfolio, philanthropy, or advocacy. It turns out they can support but also hinder executives' attempts to promote sustainability.

PIONEERS OR LAGGARDS?

In reality, some family-influenced companies are pioneers in sustainability, while others are laggards. To understand the difference, we need to delve into a theory of change. People and organizations, by nature or design, are generally reluctant to change. When they do change, it's usually for one of two reasons. One is through a strong intrinsic motivation, as we see in aspirational New Year's resolutions. Next year, say, a company's leaders might pledge to increase its sustainability reporting, revisit its supply chain, or broaden its energy supply. The second is through extrinsic motivation due to pressure from regulators, investors, or other outside groups. Wall Street analysts respond favorably or unfavorably to quarterly results. A big collection of funds such as Black Rock scrutinizes a company with public letters or even direct pressure. Or governments require heightened reporting on carbon emissions.

Families bring a third motivation to the table for companies, starting with that longer time horizon described above. Unlike most investors, looking ahead only a year for their return on investment, they often think in decades. A quarter for some investors is the same as 25 years for some families. But that vision works both ways: it can drive long-term investment, but it can also delay change. A family-controlled company should be able to transform quickly because concentrated ownership gives it agility. It can be quite entrepreneurial and pivot quickly. It can decide almost immediately to get out of a product category or market. But the current generation can also comfortably and confidently leave a big challenge to the next generation.

Also, those family systems aren't as unified as might appear. It's easy with one patriarch, or matriarch, calling the shots. But some families have hundreds of interested shareholders with wide-ranging opinions, and getting consent on a specific direction can actually be harder than in a broadly owned firm. After all, sustainability efforts often involve dividend cuts that cousins could well resist. On the other hand, family influence can be one more pressure point that tips the balance toward sustainability, along with the intrinsic and extrinsic motivation. So family influence can still be decisive, even if not unified.

Another challenge is that family-controlled companies typically protect their privacy and resist visibility. They might focus on doing good, but many are reluctant to be seen doing good. Especially in the early stages of the shift to sustainability, publicity is crucial to build a critical mass and reassurance about the transition. Many family-controlled firms have a more private profile and therefore also resist showing off the metrics to demonstrate their success, but that reluctance can lead to delays in doing good as well as being seen.

Finally, we need to distinguish between willingness and ability to change. Many family-controlled firms would like to do more for sustainability, but they move slowly because of these internal conflicts and tendencies to put off big decisions. Family-owned companies are also parsimonious about resources compared to nonfamily firms because these involve, in effect, family-owned resources. And that's on top of family-controlled firms, more than nonfamily firms, facing the great dilemma of tradition versus innovation. "What right do we have to change what our much-praised grandfather founded?" Publiclyheld companies can actually move faster in some cases.

We now have extensive evidence that family-controlled firms are no more inclined, and if anything actually slower, to promote sustainability due to these challenges. A recent example is in the United States, where both publiclyheld General Motors and family-influenced Ford invested in electric vehicles but are now pulling back after slow sales. The family influence made no apparent difference.

Still, when family-influenced firms do innovate, that longer horizon can still help in making longer commitments. These commitments have more credibility coming from them, compared to those from publiclyowned firms where leaders lose their job if they haven't met short-term goals within a few years. Family-controlled firms are also much more likely to compensate and evaluate leaders over a long time frame. They think and act long term. It's easy for the head of a publiclyowned company to promise carbon neutrality by 2050, and no one takes that seriously. But if it's the family business, and the leaders make such a commitment, their kids will be held responsible for it.

Families aren't as unitary as we often assume, but they do tend to have more patience. The CEO of Danone, the nonfamily food and beverage conglomerate, had committed the firm to sustainability in the late 2010s. But when the company fell short on financial returns, and a small group of investors gained some power in 2021, the company fired him. A family-controlled company would have had more patience.

FAMILY-CONTROLLED COMPANIES THAT MOVED QUICKLY

Perhaps the most likely family businesses to move aggressively are the medium-sized firms. They're big enough to enjoy considerable heft but still small enough to avoid the limelight and focus on one or two areas. Two of the past winners of the IMD Sustainability in Family Business Award, Velux and J.M. Huber, are leaders in their sustainability efforts and serve as role models to other family businesses around the world.

Velux is a Danish maker of roof windows and skylights. Founded in 1941 by Villum Kann Rasmussen, the company brought ventilation and light to attics and lofts for Europeans eager to use all their living spaces after World War II. After decades of success, in 1965, the company committed with its "Model Company Objective" to boost the environment and society. That commitment led over time to include sustainability in governance throughout the organization, culminating in a bold strategy for circularity by 2030. Remarkably, the company pledged to become carbon-neutral over the entire history of the company by that year. Rasmussen's descendants largely control the company through a foundation that owns a majority of the shares.

J.M. Huber is one of the largest privately held companies in the United States. Founded in 1883 as a dye maker by

German immigrant Joseph Maria Huber, the company now operates worldwide, producing specialty goods in personal care, food and beverage, agricultural nutrients, forestry services, and building materials. With a performance management system geared to sustainability, the company has innovated in both products and practices – it hasn't postponed this work to future generations. Director Molly Heany, a fifth-generation Huber, said, "As a family-owned business that thinks in terms of generations rather than years, sustainability is fundamental in supporting our long-term view. We feel a deep sense of responsibility to be a positive force in the world, caring for our people and our planet; mindful that our responsibility is not just to our stakeholders today but those who come after us."

ASIAN DYNAMICS

Family businesses, especially large corporations, are more common in Asia than in the West. There's greater trust within families and less trust in institutions. As is the case in most emerging markets around the world, successful families have built large, diversified business groups, some of which have a significant influence on a country's economy. An example is Samsung from Korea, which has a range of activities aside from the electronics products that most consumers are familiar with. Business groups such as Samsung have ample resources and more institutional momentum, enabling them to be forerunners in sustainability worldwide if their family owners choose to do so.

These companies can move quite quickly to address sustainability, and they bring many resources to bear. But these diversified business groups tend to respond to diverse commercial opportunities. Overall, business families across Asia have a great deal more authority over companies than elsewhere – the nonfamily directors and executives tend to go along with whatever the family decides.

Barito Pacific, an Indonesian group controlled by the Pangestu family, has invested impressively in geothermal and other forms of renewable energy. At the same time, the family is buying carbon-intensive stranded assets from Western companies trying to reduce emissions, such as a large oil refinery complex in Singapore previously owned by Shell. The two streams are going in parallel, united by commercial opportunities, and that's not necessarily a bad thing. India's Adani group, which is a key player in coal mining and trading, but also one of the world's largest investors in renewable energy, is similar here.

These family-controlled business groups, especially in emerging markets, start with what the market wants but also wish to do the right thing for the next generation and for society. A common tack is to give a new division to a young family member and see what happens. If the relative does a good job, then they might be brought in to have responsibility in the main business. The next generation gets its own corner, where they can learn and be away from their seniors who typically are involved in all details of the operations. Over time, these younger relatives, often highly educated, might push the entire business group toward sustainability, but the group structure enables the family to invest in quite different kinds of enterprises.

YTL is a Malaysian conglomerate that started with construction and over time moved into hotels, property management, power generation, cement, and utilities. The Yeoh family behind this group began emphasizing sustainability in the 1990s, in part because the granddaughter of the founder began articulating the sustainability concept in the group. Today, the YTL group is a sizeable player in sustainable investments, such as green data centers. In families, the next generation often finds and projects a new identity as engaged citizens of the world, attending the World Economic Forum, where they take leadership roles in moving businesses toward sustainability. They're transforming a traditional family business group into a purposeful global conglomerate.

Sometimes young family members move out of the traditional family business group to start new businesses. An example is Grab, a company similar to Uber operating across southeast Asia. The cofounder was a third-generation member of another Malaysian family that began as an importer of cars and that operates car manufacturing and car dealerships in the second generation. As emerging market families evolve, their business activities may not just grow internally by investing in future-ready new lines of business, but they may also spin off young and ambitious family members. These well-educated young entrepreneurs, with access to social and financial capital, may form their own modern businesses, such as by building digital platforms.

No matter whether within the traditional family business group or as a spun-off venture, the global status that comes from investing in sustainable businesses is attractive and allows Asian business families to play a role on the world stage. So those investments will continue. Whether sustainability becomes a guiding principle for the group as whole is unclear as most of these families also expand traditional legacy activities that may be carbon intensive.

The format of a sprawling business group with a multitude of businesses that may be separately listed on different stock exchanges makes it harder to assess what they're actually doing in the realm of sustainability. Some group firms may be more serious than others. Secrecy and related party transactions among group companies remain pervasive but are hard to understand for outsiders, who tend to evaluate the sustainability practices of just a single firm. Business families in Asia are also careful not to be seen to openly do many projects aiming for sustainable goals, lest they attract meddling political leaders seeking bribes or diverting these projects for political gain.

Over time, because of path dependence and capital accumulation, family-controlled business groups might still have power even if business trust increases and the conglomerate structure makes less economic sense. Family-owned business groups remain a powerful and fast-growing force in the private sector, at least in Asia outside of Japan and China. There, a family's commitment to sustainability matters enormously, at least for those economies. But rather than transforming or selling off existing businesses, they're more likely to start new businesses that make progress on sustainability. The existing legacy businesses follow regulations but are less likely to be pioneers. And that could be true for much of the world, not just Asia but also Africa and Latin America.

Family businesses are enormously diverse and powerful, especially outside the West. They are also increasingly concerned about sustainability. They bring extensive resources to bear, not just capital but also management and entrepreneurial talent. A long-term outlook also helps, though it can also delay action. Whether as a whole they tend to promote sustainability is unclear, but they will be major players on making economies sustainable over time.

TAKEAWAYS

1. Family businesses remain dominant in much of the world and are not limited to private or small firms.

2. The long-term view of family businesses can both promote sustainability because it makes leaders look ahead but also hinder it because leaders may cautiously prefer to pass the challenge to the next generation.

3. Family businesses, especially in emerging markets, often operate as business groups, where a sustainability shift may mean establishing new firms with a high sustainability profile while continuing legacy businesses that score low on sustainability practices. It is important to distinguish a family's willingness to embrace sustainability from its ability to do so.

FURTHER READING

Marleen Dieleman and Juliette Koning, "Articulating Values Through Identity Work: Advancing Family Business Ethics Research," *Journal of Business Ethics*, 2019, 163, 675–687.

Alfredo De Massis et al., "Family Firms and Environmental Performance: A Meta-Analytical View," *Family Business Review*, Spring 2022.

Alfredo De Massis and Emanuela Rondi, *The Family Business Book: A Roadmap for Entrepreneurial Families to Prosper Across Generations*, Harlow, UK: Pearson Financial Times, 2024.

Peter Vogel, *Family Philanthropy Navigator: The Inspirational Guide for Philanthropic Families on their Giving Journey*, IMD Publishing, 2020.

Peter Vogel, "How Private and Family-Owned Businesses Can Lead the Way in Building Stakeholder Value," *I by IMD*, May 6, 2024.

Chapter 25

Leading
for Inclusion

Josefine van Zanten

In today's rapidly evolving business landscape, fostering diversity, equity, and inclusion (DEI) is not just a moral obligation but a strategic imperative. As global markets expand and societies become more diverse, businesses that champion inclusivity are better positioned to attract top talent, tap into new customer bases, and navigate complex social dynamics. But achieving meaningful inclusion requires more than good intentions – it demands a robust, strategic approach that is integrated into the very fabric of the organization.

Inclusion goes beyond the superficial – it is about creating an environment where everyone, regardless of gender, race, disability, or background, feels valued, heard, and empowered to contribute. As a business leader, have you ever considered how your organization's approach to DEI could be the key to unlocking new opportunities and driving sustainable growth? This chapter explores how businesses can move beyond tokenism and compliance to truly embed DEI into their organizational DNA, driving both social impact and business success.

CONNECTING DEI TO BUSINESS GOALS

For DEI efforts to be effective, they must be directly connected to the company's overall business strategy. Inclusion cannot be an afterthought or a separate initiative – it must be integrated into every aspect of the organization's operations, from leadership and governance to talent management and customer engagement. Have you aligned your DEI strategy with your company's broader business goals, ensuring that it contributes to your competitive advantage?

The first step in this process is to ask strategic questions: Which aspects of diversity are most valuable to our business? How does inclusion align with our growth markets and customer base? What do we need to do to attract and retain diverse talent? For international companies, it's crucial to consider whether the leadership team reflects the diversity of the markets they operate in. If not, what steps can be taken to bridge that gap?

IMD offers a clear example of how to connect DEI to business strategy. In 2019, the school recognized that formalizing a DEI strategy was no longer optional but a necessity to stay competitive in the global education market. Feedback from clients and accreditation bodies made it clear that IMD needed to reflect the diversity of the world it operates in to attract and retain top talent and develop inclusive leaders. By embedding DEI into its core programs, including the MBA and EMBA, as well as in its interactions with staff, faculty, and participants, IMD positioned itself as a leader in inclusive education. This alignment with business goals ensured that DEI was not just a compliance exercise but a driver of the school's success.

Promoting inclusion is essentially a change management challenge – it requires altering the mindset and behaviors of employees across the organization. This change must be more than compliance or meeting a few targets; it needs to be tied to the company's overall strategy, with visible support from leadership. Have you considered how your organization can effectively manage this change to foster a more inclusive culture?

Inclusion involves addressing both visible and invisible aspects of diversity, such as gender, race, disability, religion, sexual orientation, socioeconomic background, and even personality traits like introversion or extroversion. These diverse characteristics bring valuable perspectives to the table, but they must be actively included to influence how companies operate. IMD's use of the "iceberg" model of diversity, highlighting both visible and invisible aspects, demonstrates how a deep understanding of diversity can enhance inclusion efforts.

When considering inclusion, it's important to recognize that different characteristics may be more salient in certain regions. For example, race is an enormously significant factor in the United States, Canada, South Africa, and the UK, shaping much of the discourse around inclusion. In contrast, in Europe, particularly in countries like France and

Germany, discussing race can be seen as inappropriate, a reflection of cultural differences in addressing identity. However, as these societies become more diverse, with increasing numbers of citizens from former colonies and other regions, these norms are beginning to visibly shift. Understanding these regional differences is crucial for multinational companies aiming to implement a cohesive, effective DEI strategy across their global operations.

For many organizations, the journey toward inclusion begins with gender diversity, often because it is the most easily measured and universally acknowledged. Gender is a clear and visible aspect of diversity that can act as a gateway to broader inclusion efforts, paving the way for addressing other forms of diversity within the company.

GENDER AS ONE STARTING POINT FOR INCLUSION

Gender diversity is often the most accessible starting point for companies looking to promote DEI, as gender is one of the most easily measured aspects of diversity across the globe. Moreover, achieving gender balance can pave the way for broader inclusion efforts. Despite the increasing number of women completing higher education, gender imbalances in leadership persist. Many companies are designed by men for men, with promotional ladders that favor those who can commit to extensive travel, long hours, and constant availability – criteria that can be particularly challenging for women who are still often expected to balance professional responsibilities with family care.

IMD recognized these challenges and took concrete steps to address them. The school's DEI strategy prioritized improving gender distribution among faculty, understanding that when women are represented in leadership, it becomes easier to include other underrepresented groups. By revising hiring practices to attract female faculty, adjusting meeting times to accommodate family responsibilities, and creating a more supportive campus environment, IMD made significant progress in gender inclusion in staff as well as faculty. Have you considered how your organization might need to adapt its structures to better support gender diversity and, by extension, other forms of inclusion?

One of the most pervasive challenges women face in the workplace is the double bind – being expected to be both warm and competent but penalized for being too much of either. Women are often expected to be participative but may be criticized for not being authoritative enough. These conflicting expectations create additional hurdles that men typically do not face. Addressing this double bind requires systemic change. Companies need to reevaluate their leadership criteria, ensure that women have equal opportunities for advancement, and create environments where diverse leadership styles are valued.

Consider DSM, a Dutch multinational, which recognized the importance of creating a more inclusive environment as part of its corporate responsibility. DSM's approach to gender diversity was comprehensive, encompassing both policy changes and cultural shifts within the organization. The company implemented flexible work arrangements, provided mentorship programs for women, and actively sought to increase female representation in leadership roles. These efforts not only improved gender diversity but also set the stage for other inclusion initiatives across the company.

Similarly, Shell, one of the world's largest energy companies, has made significant progress in promoting gender diversity and inclusion. Shell's approach included putting visible symbols of inclusion, such as the Pride flag, in its manufacturing plants, even in regions where LGBTQ+ rights were not yet widely recognized or protected. This bold move signaled the company's commitment to inclusion and set a precedent for other organizations to follow. By addressing gender diversity and inclusion head-on, Shell created a more inclusive culture that benefits all employees, regardless of their background.

Inclusion in the workplace also involves ensuring that women are not penalized for taking time off to manage family responsibilities. Many companies lose talented women in their early 30s when they have their first child, and again in their early 40s as their children grow older and need more attention. Recognizing these patterns, IMD took steps to retain talented women even when they were on leave, such as inviting them to important gatherings and accommodating their needs in ways that allowed them to stay connected and valued. These measures, while seemingly small, can have a profound impact on retaining female talent and ensuring that women have the opportunity to continue advancing in their careers.

Moreover, creating an inclusive environment for women in leadership positions can have a cascading effect, making it easier to include other underrepresented groups. Once an organization has made strides in gender inclusion, it is often more prepared to tackle other aspects of diversity, such as race, disability, or socioeconomic background.

Still, starting with gender might induce an organization to put other, equally important aspects of diversity on the backburner. Any of the other aspects of diversity could work as well, given the organization's context.

LEADERSHIP, METRICS, AND STRUCTURES

DEI initiatives require strong leadership and clear metrics. A dedicated DEI leader, with the gravitas and ability to engage at all levels of the organization, is essential. This leader must have regular access to the CEO and the board of directors and should be empowered to drive the DEI agenda forward. IMD's DEI Council, chaired by the chief DEI officer, and established shortly after the DEI strategy was formalized, played a crucial role in ensuring that DEI priorities were implemented effectively. The Council, which included representatives from the MBA and EMBA programs, executive committee members, staff, and faculty, acted as ambassadors for DEI, testing and challenging the strategy as needed.

Metrics are also crucial for tracking progress and ensuring accountability. Companies often measure a wide range of business activities, from sales to supply chains, and DEI should be no different. IMD used an Inclusion Index and other formal and informal measures to track its progress. These metrics helped the school identify areas for improvement and celebrate successes, such as the increase in female faculty and the growing diversity of the MBA and EMBA cohorts.

However, promoting inclusion is not just about people – it's also about the systems and structures within the organization. As companies increasingly rely on technology, such as AI, for hiring, assessment, and promotion, they must be vigilant about potential biases that these systems can introduce. AI systems, trained on vast datasets, often reflect the biases present in that data. This can lead to the perpetuation of stereotypes and the exclusion of diverse candidates. Have you considered how your organization's technological infrastructure might be affecting your DEI goals?

To overcome these latent structural barriers, companies can consider a variety of steps. These include providing bias training, revisiting faculty and staff recruitment processes, and making changes to accommodate diverse needs, such as providing free hygienic products in women's restrooms and accommodating various dietary needs in cafeterias.

DSM' embedded DEI into its organizational structures with comprehensive training programs aimed at raising awareness of unconscious bias and promoting inclusive behaviors. By making these programs mandatory for all employees, DSM ensured that DEI was not just a top-down initiative but a shared responsibility across the organization. The company also regularly audited its recruitment and promotion processes to identify and address any potential barriers to inclusion. These efforts, combined with DSM's focus on gender diversity, helped create a more inclusive and equitable workplace.

An emerging area of focus for DEI initiatives is the role of AI in perpetuating or mitigating bias. AI, when used for hiring or employee evaluation, can inadvertently reinforce existing stereotypes and biases present in the data on which it is trained. For example, if an AI system is trained on data that reflects a historical preference for male candidates, it may continue to favor men in hiring decisions. To counteract this, companies must take proactive steps to audit their AI systems regularly, ensuring that they are designed and operated in ways that promote rather than hinder inclusion.

Another critical structural element is the need to accommodate different work-life balance needs. Many traditional business practices, such as long hours and frequent travel, were designed without considering the needs of those who may have significant caregiving responsibilities, such as women or those from certain cultural backgrounds. Recognizing and adjusting these practices can make a significant difference in retaining a diverse workforce. For example, IMD's decision to schedule senior staff and faculty meetings at times that do not infringe on weekends or family time is a tangible step toward creating a more inclusive work environment.

SUSTAINING DEI EFFORTS

Promoting DEI is a continuing journey, not a one-time initiative. As the global landscape continues to evolve, so too must a company's DEI strategy. This requires ongoing commitment from leadership, continuous education, and the willingness to adapt to new challenges and opportunities. IMD's DEI journey, from the formalization of its strategy in 2019 to its recognition for successful DEI results in 2024, demonstrates the power of sustained effort and alignment with business goals. The school's experience shows that when DEI is embedded into the core of an organization, it can drive significant cultural change and lead to tangible business outcomes.

As businesses look to the future, they must remain committed to fostering environments that value diverse perspectives and inclusive behaviors. By doing so, they can build resilient organizations that are not only more equitable but also more successful in a diverse and rapidly changing world. Have you made DEI a long-term priority, ensuring that it evolves with your business and continues to drive positive outcomes?

The future of DEI will also be shaped by societal changes. For example, as immigration patterns shift and countries become more culturally diverse, businesses will need to consider how to include and support employees from different ethnic and national backgrounds. This might involve providing language support, cultural sensitivity training, or adapting workplace policies to accommodate different religious practices.

Furthermore, as the global focus on sustainability intensifies, DEI will increasingly intersect with environmental goals. Companies will need to consider how their DEI efforts contribute to broad sustainability objectives, such as reducing inequality and promoting social justice. This holistic approach to sustainability and inclusion can enhance a company's reputation, attract socially conscious consumers and investors, and ensure long-term business success.

DEI is not just a set of initiatives or policies – it is a strategic imperative that must be woven into the fabric of the organization. By aligning DEI with business goals, measuring progress, addressing structural barriers, and staying committed to the journey, companies can create inclusive environments that drive innovation, growth, and resilience. The challenge is great, but the rewards are greater. As a leader, are you ready to take the next step in your organization's DEI journey?

TAKEAWAYS

1. Align DEI with business strategy: Ensure that your DEI initiatives are directly connected to your company's overall business goals. This alignment will help integrate DEI into every aspect of your operations and make it a driver of your organization's success.

2. Focus on measurable outcomes: Implement clear metrics to track the progress of your DEI efforts. Use these metrics to identify areas for improvement, celebrate successes, and ensure accountability at all levels of the organization.

3. Embed DEI into organizational structures: Beyond people, focus on the systems and processes that can either
support or hinder DEI efforts. Be proactive in identifying
and mitigating biases in technology and other structural
elements to create a truly inclusive environment.

FURTHER READING

Josefine van Zanten, "Why DE&I Cannot Be Outsourced to AI,"
I by IMD, June 4, 2024.

Chapter 26

Talking the Walk

Heather Cairns-Lee

While leaders must focus on action, communication is equally crucial, both internally and externally, in promoting sustainability. Any significant shift, especially with a long-term vision, creates uncertainty that might distract employees from their main work or even induce resistance to the change. Effective communication is essential not only to gain internal alignment, but also to engage external stakeholders who are key to the success of sustainable business transformations.

Yet communicating about sustainability is fraught with challenges. Striking the balance is difficult, as leaders must navigate between the risks of greenwashing – where efforts are perceived as superficial or insincere – and greenhushing, where leaders refrain from discussing sustainability altogether out of fear of backlash. Many leaders today are opting for silence, avoiding the topic of sustainability lest they be accused of greenwashing. But silence is not a viable strategy because companies need action and messages. Communication, when done right, builds trust and advances genuine efforts.

ESTABLISHING INTENTION THROUGH LANGUAGE

The first task is to raise awareness of the sustainability challenge without resorting to alarmism. Narratives of doom and gloom might attract attention, but they rarely motivate people to take meaningful action. Human beings respond better to messages framed positively, even when urgent action is necessary. Leaders must communicate this urgency, particularly since the payoffs of sustainability efforts are often long-term, extending beyond the typical one-to-three-year horizon of business initiatives. The changes required are also likely to be profound, potentially transforming not only the company but also influencing change in the broader industry.

Here, leaders need to step back and focus on sense-making for the organization. Sense-making is essential when the current state of the world diverges from what was expected. It is an ongoing process in which people react to and shape the environments they are in, identifying cues from their environment to help decide what information is relevant and acceptable. It is fundamentally a social process based on communication, in which people assign meaning through sharing stories. These stories may be preserved, updated, or changed through an ongoing stream of individual and collective conversations to make sense of plausible futures.

Climate change, water scarcity, and social inequality are altering our experiences of the world, and people need to continually make sense of these shifts. Leaders can guide this process by shaping the narrative around sustainability, helping people confront the reality they face and challenging the status quo. This requires leaders to recognize that language can aggravate or resolve environmental challenges. As the linguist Michael Halliday has emphasized, "Language does not passively reflect reality; language actively creates reality." The intentional use of language to address sustainability challenges, known as ecolinguistics, is a powerful force for leaders to effect change by challenging the stories we live by to create more constructive narratives that support sustainable practices.

The first step is to establish a clear intention, which leaders must communicate not only within the organization but also to external stakeholders. Doing so sets the agenda for a broad understanding of the company's ambitions, both commercial and moral, within the external environment. Much of this early work in setting intention involves active listening to stakeholders to align goals with expectations. Leaders don't need to have all the answers right away, but they do need to outline direction and goals that encourage action.

Leadership, in this context, is about managing the evolving understanding of the world and the company's role within it. While executives might traditionally see their role as managing targets and people, they are fundamentally in the business of creating shared meaning through communicating a common vision, especially amid uncertainty. They bring this vision to life with metaphors, stories, and other communicative tools that resonate with people's experience, beliefs and emotions. Beliefs drive action, and are significantly shaped through communication.

PRESENTING AUTHENTICALLY

The challenge is avoiding the pitfalls of greenwashing while maintaining a positive and engaging narrative. Overusing certain terms can reduce them to buzzwords, stripping them of their meaning and impact especially when associated with superficial efforts. This can provoke cynicism and resistance to the very ideas these terms promote. Even foundational concepts such as "sustainability," "carbon footprint," and "recycling" can become buzzwords and be criticized for being vague or simplistic, despite their role in introducing and summarizing complex ideas.

To avoid the perception of greenwashing, where communication is dismissed as mere corporate jargon, leaders must ensure their messaging is both authentic and transparent. Authenticity in communication begins with a genuine commitment to sustainability, demonstrated through consistent actions and clear articulation of those actions. Leaders should focus on the broad, long-term sustainability goals of the organization and avoid hyping minor achievements. Sustainability is an ongoing journey that requires commitment to continuous improvement and transparent communication about both challenges and progress. Evidence-based data that substantiates claims boosts the credibility of messages.

Authenticity is crucial. Employees and stakeholders are more likely to respond positively when they perceive that the commitment to sustainability is sincere and aligned with the company's core values. By creating a shared vision, companies and their broader ecosystems create shared understanding and coordinated action toward achieving sustainability.

For example, when the American computer peripherals maker Logitech appointed Prakash Arunkundrum to lead global operations and sustainability, he communicated his urgency by expressing a personal commitment: "It's up to me to do something. I can't just kick the can down the line to my successor. That would be easy, but it would be irresponsible." This candid statement of personal responsibility resonated and enabled Arunkundrum and his team to focus on promoting a transparent approach to sustainability that gathered support with colleagues in Logitech and interest from external stakeholders.

LEVERAGING METAPHOR IN COMMUNICATION

After establishing a clear intent, Arunkundrum and his team sought to introduce carbon labeling to show the carbon footprint of Logitech products. They believed this level of transparency would empower consumers to make informed choices and that it could drive greater accountability about carbon use in the technology industry. However, carbon labeling is an abstract concept based on a complex methodology to calculate the footprint of products that is difficult for employees and consumers to grasp. Wondering how to make this abstract idea tangible, Arunkundrum was inspired while snacking on potato chips. He noticed the calorie label on the package and realized how a metaphor could simplify a complex idea: "carbon is the new calorie"! Just as calorie labels help people understand the health implications of their food choices, carbon labels could help consumers to understand the environmental impact of their purchasing decisions.

As in all communication, the metaphor is open to interpretation. Some interpreted it to suggest that a certain level of carbon emissions might be acceptable, just as some calories are necessary. Others interpreted it as a measurement of consumption, akin to the calories in food. The metaphor was effective in capturing attention and bringing awareness about carbon accountability in everyday purchasing decisions. This illustrates the power of leading with metaphor: to gain initial commitment with a vivid memorable message that resonates with the intended audience.

Metaphors are powerful framing devices because they use the familiar to explain the novel or abstract. As such, they are used frequently to frame the dialogue about sustainability, which is inherently complex, multifaceted and somewhat abstract. Examples of common metaphors include greenhouses, tipping points, atmospheric blankets, and time bombs. Table 26.1 outlines seven metaphors commonly used to frame sustainability, with the metaphors highlighted in italics. While these metaphors are prevalent in the discussion about sustainability, they are by no means exhaustive.

While metaphors can be powerful tools, they can also risk being misleading. For instance, the phrase "going green" has become synonymous with positive environmental actions. However, many organizations claim to be making progress on the environment without making the necessary commitments to support these claims. This discrepancy has given rise to two metaphors – "greenwashing" and "greenhushing" – that encapsulate the problematic ways that companies often communicate about sustainability.

"Greenwashing" refers to the overemphasis of minor actions as environmentally beneficial even if they do not truly advance sustainability; this can lead to cynicism and distrust among stakeholders. In contrast, "greenhushing" involves avoiding the topic of sustainability altogether, resulting in missed opportunities to engage and inspire stakeholders.

Table 26.1   Metaphors commonly used to frame sustainability.

Circular Economy	This compares the economy to a *circle*, where resources are reused, recycled, and regenerated, rather than following a linear path of production, use, and disposal. It emphasizes sustainability through continuous reuse.
Cradle to Grave	This encourages a holistic understanding of products throughout their entire *lifecycle* where each stage is scrutinized for potential improvements. As understanding of sustainability has evolved, so has the metaphor, which has sometimes been criticized for implying a linear process in which a product eventually reaches its grave. This can inadvertently reinforce a throwaway culture. Hence, this metaphor is evolving to *cradle to cradle* highlighting the need for continuous recycling.
Environmental Stewardship	This metaphor frames our relationship with the natural world as *caretakers* or guardians. Stewardship suggests a duty of care to manage and protect the environment for the benefit of current and future generations. For businesses, this implies balancing care for the planet with profit.
Environmental/ Carbon Footprint	This visualizes the impact of human activities on the environment as a *footprint*, suggesting that every action leaves a mark on the planet. It encourages businesses to reduce their footprint by minimizing emissions and waste.

(Continued)

Table 26.1 (*Continued*)

Green	This likens activities to nature by using the color *green* to symbolize health and vitality. Examples include green companies, green products, green energy. The term *green lung* compares forests and green spaces to the lungs of the Earth, emphasizing their role in absorbing carbon dioxide and producing oxygen, much as our lungs do for our bodies.
Sustainability as a Journey	This suggests that achieving sustainability is a continuous process, akin to a *journey* with milestones and progress along the way. It encourages businesses to engage with sustainability not as a destination but as a journey and to be transparent about the difficulties they encounter along the way.
The War on Climate Change	This metaphor of *war* instils a sense of urgency to act in defending the planet and uniting people against a common enemy. While the war metaphor can unite action, it can also divide opinions. It may also hide the fact that the actual enemy is the attitudes and behaviors of people who have created the environmental problems in the first place.

These risks highlight the importance of deliberate and intentional communication about sustainability efforts. Executives must ensure that their use of metaphors and other framing devices accurately reflects their genuine commitment to sustainability to foster trust and meaningful engagement.

Cynics and other critics may dismiss figurative language for obscuring clarity and precision, particularly when describing future-oriented goals. However, when used authentically, such language is often essential in fostering shared meaning and driving collective action for issues that might otherwise remain abstract.

FRAMING EFFECTIVE SUSTAINABILITY NARRATIVES

To communicate about sustainability, leaders need to understand the pivotal role of framing in shaping how people perceive reality. Framing involves presenting information to influence how it is perceived and interpreted. It includes the selection and emphasis of certain aspects and exclusion of others. Framing is a powerful communication tool because it shapes not just what people think about but also how they think by focusing attention on specific elements, thus influencing perception, behavior, emotional responses, and action.

Leaders can adopt different communication frames to enhance the effectiveness of their message relative to their audience and objectives with both individuals and groups.

Task Frame. Directs specific actions. Patagonia's "Don't Buy this Jacket" ad campaign urged consumers to consider the environmental impact of their purchases and to refrain from buying unnecessary clothes. This direct call to action emphasized reducing consumption for environmental benefits.

People Frame. Inspires people or groups through visionary messages. IKEA aims "to create a better everyday life for many people." This frame foregrounds IKEA's desire to have a positive impact on everyone, including people in the communities from which they source materials and their global customers, while encouraging all people to live more sustainable lives.

Structural Frame. Emphasizes organizational needs and the structural changes necessary to achieve sustainability goals. Microsoft pledged to be carbon neutral by 2030, which exemplifies this frame. The pledge highlighted their commitment to reducing emissions across global operations and also embracing environmental equity by procuring energy for under-resourced communities.

Political Frame. Engages and influences stakeholders by aligning sustainability goals with political strategies. Nestlé uses its influence as one of the world's largest food and beverage companies to engage with policymakers and stakeholders to influence policy and industry standards. It advocates for responsible water use and management to reduce the water footprint of agricultural practices.

Each frame emphasizes different objectives and requires tailored language and metaphors to resonate effectively with the intended audience. The ultimate goal of framing is to influence engagement of specific audiences by influencing the desired action.

BROADENING THE NARRATIVE

While internal communication is critical, leaders must also manage external messaging on sustainability. Broadening the conversation beyond the boundaries of specific companies or initiatives is vital because sustainability represents a fundamental shift toward new concepts and practices that affect society.

A compelling example of broadening the narrative comes from the LEGO Group, which committed to reducing its carbon footprint as part of a broad promise to benefit future generations. CEO Niels B. Christiansen emphasized the importance of this commitment by stating that they must "encourage future generations of LEGO employees, partners and suppliers to continue working with a sense of urgency to reduce the environmental impact of our business."

In 2021 LEGO announced plans to replace the plastic in its iconic bricks with materials made from non-fossil fuels. Their goal was to find an alternative to the plastic made from crude oil by using recycled PET bottles. Despite significant investment in research and development, the company acknowledged in 2023 that the initiative would result in higher carbon emissions.

While this was a setback for the company, LEGO's transparent communication about the challenges is an example that others can learn from. Their openness demonstrates the importance for global organizations of setting ambitious targets, researching science-based solutions, being willing to face setbacks, and changing course when necessary. Rather than abandon their sustainability efforts, LEGO redirected resources to other projects, reaffirming their long-term commitment by pledging to invest US$1.4 billion to reduce carbon emissions by 2025. This response underscores the importance of communicating resilience and adaptability in the face of challenges.

START WITH THE END IN MIND

Effective communication begins with a clear understanding of the desired outcomes and strategically uses language to align messages with the audience's values and concerns. Many employees are already predisposed to sustainability and prefer to work in organizations that actively make progress on the environment. It is therefore crucial for leaders to clearly communicate the company's commitments to tackling global challenges helping employees to see how their work contributes to addressing these challenging sustainability issues.

Sika, a Swiss construction materials manufacturer, has successfully integrated sustainability into its innovation strategy. The company has made substantial investments to reduce its freshwater consumption and carbon emissions. It stands out in the specialty chemicals industry as one of the first to develop and implement an externally validated Sustainable Portfolio Management system. This system evaluates, classifies, and markets products based on criteria for performance and sustainability. It uses 12 sustainability categories that support the UN SDGs. Starting with the end in mind to provide sustainable value for all stakeholders, Sika provides clarity, inspiration, and transparency in its communication with stakeholders.

Effective communication about sustainability requires a nuanced understanding of the social context in which messages are conveyed and received. The language that leaders choose helps to shape perceptions and motivate action. By thoughtfully selecting language that resonates and inspires, leaders can profoundly shape how individuals and communities make sense of and engage with sustainability.

This communication requires a delicate balance, avoiding the extremes of greenwashing and greenhushing. Leaders must craft authentic and transparent narratives that resonate with their audience and drive meaningful action. The use of appropriate frames and metaphors can be powerful tools in this process, transforming abstract concepts into relatable and compelling stories that drive change in habits, behavior, and decisions. By communicating with clarity, integrity, and a sincere commitment to sustainability, organizations can foster trust and galvanize collective effort to a more sustainable future that safeguards our planet.

TAKEAWAYS

1. Communicate with authenticity and transparency. Ensure that your sustainability messages are genuine and aligned with real progress to build trust and inspire action.

2. Avoid greenwashing and greenhushing. Engage in balanced communication that acknowledges challenges and progress, avoiding both exaggerating and under-communicating the impact of the company's efforts.

3. Start with the end in mind. Customize sustainability messages to align with the values and needs of different stakeholder groups, using language and metaphors that make the goals relatable and actionable.

FURTHER READING

Richard Benton, "How to Win Trust in Your ESG Communications and Marketing," *I By IMD*, March 10, 2022.

Heather Cairns-Lee and Julia Binder, "Carbon is the New Calorie: Logitech's Carbon Impact Label to Drive Transparency in Sustainability," IMD Case Study, 2023.

Arran Stibbe, *Ecolinguistics: Language, Ecology and the Stories We Live By*, Routledge, 2020.

Karl Weick, "Organizing and the Process of Sensemaking," Organization Science, 2005.

Conclusion

Julia Binder and Knut Haanaes

As you have explored throughout this book, the journey toward sustainability requires a delicate balance of strategy, leadership, and action – a synergy of the head, heart, and hands. The strategic vision, the emotional commitment to meaningful change, and the practical steps to implement that change are all essential to driving sustainable business transformation. This comprehensive approach is not just a roadmap for success; it's a blueprint for building resilient, forward-thinking organizations capable of thriving in an unpredictable world.

Yet as we look ahead, it's clear that individual efforts alone won't be enough. The challenges we face today demand a fundamental reimagining of our systems – how we produce and use energy, construct and deconstruct our buildings, grow and consume our food, and move from one place to another. The systems that have driven economic growth in the past are no longer sustainable in their current forms. Consider the energy sector: the transition from fossil fuels to renewable sources isn't just a technological upgrade; it's a complete overhaul of our energy infrastructure. Companies like Ørsted, once one of the most fossil fuel–intensive energy companies, have transformed themselves into global leaders in renewable energy by embracing wind power and committing to a sustainable future. This transformation requires not only the adoption of new technologies but also a shift in mindset – a commitment to reshaping the entire energy grid, integrating smart technologies, and adopting decentralized models of power generation.

The construction industry, too, must evolve from its traditional linear approach to embrace circularity. Imagine a world where buildings are designed not just for use but for eventual deconstruction, where materials are reused and recycled rather than discarded. Companies like Skanska and Holcim are leading the way by incorporating sustainable and circular practices into their projects, from using low-carbon concrete to designing buildings that can be easily deconstructed and repurposed. The challenge here is not just about reducing waste; it's about creating healthier, more resilient spaces that benefit both people and the planet.

Agriculture, the foundation of our food systems, also demands radical change. Companies such as Nestlé, Mars, Danone, and Unilever are facing similar challenges as they seek to feed a growing population more sustainably. Sustainable practices such as regenerative farming, agroforestry, and precision agriculture are essential to restoring ecosystems, improving soil health, and ensuring food security for future generations. These companies recognize that the health of the soil directly affects the quality of their products and the sustainability of their business. But it's not just about farming techniques – it's also about rethinking our diets, reducing food waste, and ensuring that our food systems are equitable.

Transportation, responsible for a significant share of global emissions, requires a fundamental rethink. The shift is already underway, as companies explore biofuels, hydrogen, and other renewable fuels to reduce their carbon footprints. For example, airlines are beginning to adopt sustainable aviation fuels that can significantly lower emissions, while the shipping industry is experimenting with ammonia and methanol as cleaner alternatives to conventional fuels. Despite these advancements, the reality is that new technologies and fuels alone may not be enough – we will also need to engage in difficult but necessary discussions about reducing overall emissions from global aviation and shipping.

The future of mobility must also move beyond the traditional model of individual car ownership to embrace Mobility as a Service solutions. This shift involves reimagining how we design our cities and infrastructure, prioritizing public transit, shared mobility, and active transportation options like cycling and walking. Companies such as Uber and local initiatives worldwide are beginning to offer integrated mobility solutions that reduce reliance on personal vehicles, thereby lowering emissions and improving urban living conditions. How can your organization contribute to this transformation? Are you ready to rethink not just your products but the entire ecosystem in which they operate?

The good news is that the technology to support these new systems is already available. We have the tools to transition to renewable energy, build circular economies, and create sustainable food and transportation systems. But technology alone is not enough. The real challenge lies in how we, as people – as consumers, politicians, shareholders, and business leaders – choose to adopt and implement these technologies. This isn't just about making incremental improvements but embracing a new paradigm that prioritizes sustainability at every level.

Entrepreneurs play a crucial role in envisioning these new systems and challenging the status quo, often pioneering innovative solutions that push industries forward. Small- and medium-sized enterprises, the backbone of many economies, are instrumental in implementing these solutions on a local level, driving change from the ground up. Local communities, with their deep understanding of regional needs and challenges, are best equipped to find practical solutions to local problems. However, to scale these innovative approaches and achieve global impact, multinationals – many of which we've mentioned earlier – will be essential. They have the resources, networks, and influence to bring these solutions to the wider world. This isn't just about making incremental improvements, but embracing a new paradigm that prioritizes sustainability at every level.

This transformation requires a level of collaboration that has rarely been seen before. It demands that we come together across countries, industries, sectors, and functions to forge a new path forward. This isn't just an operational challenge; it's a social one. How do we mobilize diverse groups with different interests, agendas, and values toward a common goal? How do we break down silos and build bridges that enable collective action on a global scale?

At a time when many societies are experiencing fragmentation and polarization, sustainability offers a unifying vision. It's a vision that transcends borders and differences, providing a shared goal that can bring people together. Imagine a world where sustainability is the common thread that unites governments, businesses, and communities in a collective effort to create a better future. This is more than just a vision; it's a necessity if we are to address the global challenges we face. Can we change the narrative of sustainability to make it the driving force that unites us in purpose and action? How can you, as a leader, contribute to this vision?

To realize this vision, we must begin by accounting for nature and society in company balance sheets. We need to internalize social and environmental costs, recognizing that our current economic models often overlook the true value of natural resources and societal well-being. André Hoffmann, vice chairman of Roche, is a leading voice in this area. He advocates for a fundamental shift away from the narrow focus on short-term profits, urging businesses to quantify social and environmental impacts on their balance sheets. Hoffmann eloquently states, "We need to be able to talk about nature in the way that we talk about time and about talent. Nature matters." This approach is gaining traction, particularly in Europe, where regulatory changes like the CSRD are beginning to push companies toward more comprehensive reporting.

Recognizing the critical role of leadership in driving these transformations, we've dedicated half of this book to exploring it's importance in achieving sustainability. Leaders today need to evolve to effectively transform their organizations and contribute positively to society. Systems leadership is about understanding the interconnectedness of our global challenges, and recognizing that no single entity can solve them alone. It's about creating frameworks that encourage collaboration, innovation, and shared responsibility. Leaders such as Paul Polman, former CEO of Unilever, exemplify this approach and challenge other leaders to critically ask themselves, "Is the world better off because your company is in it?" What would be your response to this question?

These systems leaders challenge the status quo, convene diverse groups, and build consensus around a common purpose. They understand that the complexity of the challenges we face requires a collaborative approach, where different perspectives are valued and integrated into the decision-making process. They are the bridge builders, ensuring that efforts are aligned and mutually reinforcing across public, private, and civil society sectors.

Systems leaders also play a critical role in inspiring collective action. They articulate a compelling vision for the future and mobilize people to work toward it. They are skilled communicators who can convey the urgency of the challenges we face while also offering hope and direction. These leaders don't just talk about sustainability; they live it, leading by example and embodying the values they advocate for. Their ability to inspire trust, foster collaboration, and drive innovation is what makes them effective agents of change.

To effectively drive sustainable change, leaders must cultivate unique skills, mindsets, and approaches that go beyond conventional "business-as-usual" thinking. They need to craft a compelling vision that resonates with their teams and stakeholders, inspiring collective commitment to long-term sustainability goals. This requires more than just strategic acumen; it demands emotional intelligence, the ability to listen actively, and the skill to communicate through powerful storytelling. Leaders must navigate pressing environmental and social challenges by engaging diverse stakeholders and articulating a clear, persuasive narrative.

Moreover, these leaders must lead by example. Embodying their values is crucial to establishing credibility and inspiring others. In an era where trust and authenticity are paramount, the most impactful leaders are those who walk the talk — who advocate for sustainability and live it in their daily actions. How can you ensure that your actions align with the values you promote? What steps can you take to lead by example and inspire others to follow?

However, leading in this way has its challenges. The pressures are immense, and the pace of change is relentless. This is why it's also vital for leaders to find a sustainable way to lead on a personal level. Burnout and fatigue are real risks, and the ability to maintain energy, focus, and well-being is essential for long-term effectiveness. Personal sustainability means developing the resilience to face ongoing challenges, the mindfulness to stay grounded, and the balance to maintain well-being. Leaders must take care of themselves if they are to take care of their organizations and the broader society. What are you doing to ensure your own sustainability as a leader?

As we move forward, the conversation around sustainability will continue to evolve, shaped by new technologies, shifting geopolitical landscapes, and the ongoing demands of our planet and its people. But one thing remains clear: the path to a sustainable future is one that must be led with intention, courage, and a deep commitment to making a positive impact. The leaders who embrace this challenge – who integrate the head, heart, and hands – will drive their businesses to success and contribute to a more sustainable, inclusive, and prosperous world.

At IMD, challenging what is and inspiring what could be is at the core of what we do. We develop leaders and organizations that contribute to a more prosperous, sustainable, and inclusive world. As an independent academic institute with close ties to business and a focus on impact, we are uniquely positioned to support the transition to a new model that balances prosperity and growth with ecological sustainability and social inclusion. Our commitment is deeply rooted in the belief that transformative leadership is essential to driving meaningful change. We focus on developing leaders who can not only transform their organizations but also profoundly impact society.

As we conclude this exploration, we want to thank you for embarking on this journey with us. The road to a sustainable future is challenging but filled with opportunities to make a real difference. We hope that the ideas and insights in this book have sparked new perspectives and equipped you with the tools to lead with purpose and impact. Now, more than ever, the world needs leaders who are ready to challenge the status quo and drive the kind of change that not only transforms organizations but also benefits society as a whole.

The future is yours to shape. Are you ready to lead the way?

Contributors

Julia Binder, co-editor

She is professor of sustainable innovation and business transformation. She is a renowned thought leader recognized on the 2022 Thinkers50 Radar list for her work at the intersection of sustainability and innovation. As director of IMD's Center for Sustainable and Inclusive Business, Binder is dedicated to leveraging IMD's diverse expertise on sustainability topics to guide business leaders in discovering innovative solutions to contemporary challenges. She serves as program director for Creating Value in the Circular Economy and teaches on the school's key open programs. She is involved in the school's EMBA and MBA programs and contributes to IMD's custom programs, crafting transformative learning journeys for clients globally.

Knut Haanaes, co-editor

He is professor of strategy and Lundin Chair Professor of Sustainability. He teaches on many key programs, including the MBA, and is co-director of the Leading Sustainable Business Transformation program and the Driving Sustainability from the Boardroom program. His research interests are related to strategy, sustainability, strategic renewal, and business models. He was previously dean of the Global Leadership Institute at the World Economic Forum and a senior partner at the Boston Consulting Group, where he founded their first sustainability practice.

David Bach, Foreword and Chapter 12

He is the president of IMD, a position he has held since September 2024. He is focused on broadening and deepening IMD's global impact through learning innovation, program excellence, and applied thought leadership. As Nestlé Professor of Strategy and Political Economy, he helps leaders navigate the myriad political challenges facing business today. Recognized globally as an innovator in management education, Bach previously served as IMD's dean of Innovation and Programs. Under his leadership, the school won multiple awards for groundbreaking pedagogy and executive programs.

Richard Baldwin, Chapter 4

He is professor of international economics and editor-in-chief of VoxEU.org, which he founded in June 2007. He was president/director of CEPR (2014–2018), a visiting professor at many universities, including MIT, Oxford, and EPFL, and a long-time professor of international economics at the Graduate Institute in Geneva. He is an expert in global economic policy and theory, specializing in international trade.

Simon J. Evenett, Chapter 4

He is professor of geopolitics and strategy and a leading expert on trade, investment, and global business dynamics. With nearly 30 years of experience, he has advised executives and guided students in navigating significant shifts in the global economy. In 2023, he was appointed co-chair of the World Economic Forum's Global Future Council on Trade and Investment. He founded the St. Gallen Endowment for Prosperity Through Trade, which oversees key initiatives like the Global Trade Alert and Digital Policy Alert. His research focuses on trade policy, geopolitical rivalry, and industrial policy, with over 250 publications. He has held academic positions at the University of St. Gallen, Oxford University, and Johns Hopkins University.

Sophie Bacq, Chapter 8

She is professor of social entrepreneurship and Coca-Cola Foundation Chair in Sustainable Development. As a globally recognized thought leader in social entrepreneurship and change, she investigates and theorizes about entrepreneurial action to solve intractable social and environmental problems at the individual, organizational, and civic levels of analysis. She leads the Social Entrepreneurship Initiative, which aims to inspire entrepreneurs, leaders, scholars, and organizations to change the system and to create and share new solutions for positive societal change.

Vanina Farber, Chapter 8

She is an economist and political scientist specializing in social innovation, sustainability, impact investment, and sustainable finance. She has two decades of teaching, researching and consultancy experience, working with academic institutions, multinational corporations, and international organizations. She is the Elea Professor of Social Innovation and dean of the EMBA program. In 2022, she launched the Driving Innovative Finance for Impact program.

Patrick Reichert, Chapter 8

He is a term research professor at the Center for Social Innovation. He conducts research at the intersection of entrepreneurship, finance, and social impact, with a particular focus on the mechanisms and logics that investors use to seed investment in social organizations. His research has been published in internationally recognized academic journals including the *Journal of Business Ethics, Journal of Business Venturing Insights*, and *Oxford Development Studies*.

Carlos Cordon, Chapter 9

He is professor of strategy and supply chain management. His areas of interest are digital value chains, supply and demand chain management, digital lean, and process management. His research and teaching focus on supply chains in the face of persistent disruptions and how they are driving revenue, reshoring and onshoring, and digital strategies. His programs include Leading the Future Supply Chain.

Frédéric Dalsace, Chapter 10

He is professor of marketing and strategy. He focuses on two distinct areas: B2B issues such as customer centricity, buyer–seller relationships, and value management, and sustainability, inclusive business models, and alleviating poverty. Prior to IMD, he spent 16 years as a professor at HEC Paris where he held the Social Business/Enterprise and Poverty Chair presided by Nobel Laureate Professor Muhammad Yunus. Prior to his academic life, Frédéric accumulated more than 10 years of experience in the business world, both with industrial companies (Michelin and CarnaudMetalbox) and as a strategy consultant with McKinsey & Company. He directs the Integrating Sustainability into Strategy program.

Goutam Challagalla, Chapter 10

He is professor of strategy and marketing and Dentsu Group Chair in Sustainable Strategy and Marketing. His teaching, consulting, and research addresses digital transformation, B2B commercial management, value-based pricing, sales management, distribution channels, and customer and service excellence. He directs the Advanced Management Program, Digital Marketing Strategies, and Strategy Governance for Boards.

Salvatore Cantale, Chapter 11

He is professor of finance. His major research and consulting interests are in value creation, valuation, and the way in which corporations structure liabilities and choose financing options. Additionally, he is interested in the relation between finance and leadership and in the leadership role of the finance function. He directs the Finance for Boards, Business Finance, and Finance programs, as well as the Driving Sustainability from the Boardroom and Bank Governance programs.

Karl Schmedders, Chapter 11

He is Professor of Finance at IMD. His research and teaching focuses on sustainability and the economics of climate change. He is therefore able to provide key insights on the transition risk arising from the shift to a greener economy and help companies face up to the challenges of potential asset degradation and increasing carbon prices. Schmedders is passionate about the importance of a "just transition" in which no one loses out as a result of action to tackle climate change. He believes that more attention needs to be paid to the S and G elements of the ESG (environmental, social and governance) equation to ensure that action on the environmental component does not adversely affect people with low incomes and those living in developing countries. In his view, humanity will fail in its fight against climate change and global warming if it does not also address inequality and ensure a just transition.

Before joining IMD in 2019, Schmedders was Professor of Quantitative Business Administration at the University in Zurich and Associate Professor of Managerial Economics and Decision Sciences at the Kellogg School of Management at Northwestern University in Evanston, Illinois. He received his PhD from Stanford University and received several teaching awards from both Stanford and Kellogg.

Michael Yaziji, Chapter 12

He is professor of strategy and leadership. He is an award-winning author whose work spans leadership and strategy. In the area of sustainability, he is recognized as a world-leading expert on nonmarket strategy and NGO–corporate relations. His research includes the world's largest survey on psychological drivers, psychological safety, and organizational performance and explores how human biases and self-deception can impact decision-making and how they can be mitigated.

Florian Hoos, Chapter 13

He is professor of sustainability and ESG accounting. He directs the Measuring and Managing Sustainability Impact program and is managing director of the Enterprise for Society Centre. He is an award-winning teacher, innovator, and writer who was named by Poets&Quants as one of the world's 40 best business school professors under 40 in 2014. His work in academia and practice focuses on helping organizations from startups to multinationals to execute strategies with measurable economic, social, and ecological impact.

Didier Bonnet, Chapter 14

He is professor of strategy and digital transformation and program co-director for Digital Transformation in Practice and Leading Customer Centric Strategies. He also teaches strategy and digital transformation in several open programs, such as Leading Digital Business Transformation, Digital Execution, and Digital Transformation for Boards. He has more than 30 years' experience in strategy development and business transformation with a range of global clients.

Michael Wade, Chapter 14

He is TONOMUS Professor of Strategy and Digital and directs the TONOMUS Global Centre for Digital and AI Transformation. He also directs a number of open programs including Leading Digital and AI Transformation, Digital Transformation for Boards, Leading Digital Execution, and the Digital Transformation Sprint. He has written 10 books, hundreds of articles, and hosted popular management podcasts, including *Mike & Amit Talk Tech*. In 2021, he was inducted into the Swiss Digital Shapers Hall of Fame.

Öykü Işık, Chapter 15

She is professor of digital strategy and cybersecurity and directs the Cybersecurity Risk and Strategy program. She is an expert on digital resilience and the ways in which disruptive technologies challenge our society and organizations. Named on the Thinkers50 Radar 2022 list of up-and-coming global thought leaders, she helps businesses to tackle cybersecurity, data privacy, and digital ethics challenges and enables CEOs and other executives to understand these issues.

José Parra Moyano, Chapter 15

He is professor of digital strategy. He focuses on the management and economics of data and privacy and how firms can create sustainable value in the digital economy. An award-winning teacher, he also founded his own successful startup, was appointed to the World Economic Forum's Global Shapers Community of young people driving change, and was named on the Forbes "30 under 30" list of outstanding young entrepreneurs in Switzerland. He teaches in the MBA and Strategic Finance programs, among others, on the topics of AI, strategy, and innovation.

Jean-François Manzoni, Chapter 16

He is professor of leadership and organizational development and was IMD President and Nestlé Professor from
2017 to 2024. His research, teaching, and consulting activities focus on leadership and the development of high-
performance organizations and corporate governance. In
recent years he has also been increasingly focused on finding ways to ensure leadership programs have lasting impact,
particularly through the use of technology-mediated
approaches, and on closing the growing "knowing-doing
gap" between what managers know they should be doing
and how they behave in practice.

Anand Narasimhan, Chapter 17

He serves as Shell Professor of Global Leadership and dean
of research. He directs the Team Dynamics Training for
Boards program. He is an expert in leadership development
for senior executive teams and boards, and his research
focuses on institutional change, organization design, social
networks, and emotions in the workplace.

Jean-Louis Barsoux, Chapter 17

He is a term research professor, where he helps organizations,
teams, and individuals change and reinvent themselves.
He was educated in France and the UK and holds a PhD in
comparative management from Loughborough University in
England. His doctorate provided the foundation for the book
French Management: Elitism in Action (with Peter Lawrence)
and a Harvard Business Review article, "The Making of French
Managers."

Richard Roi, Chapter 18

He is an affiliate professor of leadership and organization.
He is a senior business psychologist who advises boards
and CEOs on matters related to board renewal, CEO

succession, top team effectiveness, and leadership transitions. His primary research focus is leadership ambidexterity – the need for leaders to simultaneously optimize their existing business operations and create future sources of revenue and profit by developing new business models or exploring opportunities. His assessment tools and talent development solutions are designed to improve leadership ambidexterity and strengthen executive performance.

Mikołaj Jan Piskorski, Chapter 18

Also known as Misiek, he is professor of digital strategy, analytics, and innovation. He is also dean of executive education, responsible for custom, open, advisory, talent, online, and coaching programs, impact measurement, publishing and marketing. He is an expert on digital strategy, platform strategy, and the process of digital business transformation. He co-directs the AI Strategy and Implementation program.

Albrecht Enders, Chapter 19

He is professor of strategy and innovation and co-director of the Business Leadership Training program. His major research, teaching, and consulting interests are around managing discontinuous change and top-team strategy development processes. Before joining IMD, he spent three years as a consultant with Boston Consulting Group in Cologne, where he worked on projects in the areas of financial services, energy, and industrial goods.

Michael Watkins, Chapter 19

He is professor of leadership and organizational change. He has authored 12 books, including *The First 90 Days, Master Your Next Move*, and *Predictable Surprises. The Six Disciplines of Strategic Thinking* explores how executives can lead their organizations into the future. A Thinkers 50-ranked management influencer and recognized expert in his field, his work features in *HBR Guides* and *HBR's 10 Must Reads*. Over the past 20 years, he has used his First 90 Days® methodology to help leaders make successful transitions, both in his teaching and through his private consultancy practice Genesis Advisers. He directs the First 90 Days program and co-directs the Transition to Business Leadership program.

Susan Goldsworthy OLY, Chapter 20

She is an affiliate professor of leadership, communications, and organizational change. Co-author of three award-winning books, she is also an Olympic swimmer. She is a highly qualified executive coach and is trained in numerous psychometric assessments. She co-directs the Executive Coaching Certificate and is director of the Leading Sustainable Change program.

Mark Greeven, Chapter 21

He is professor of innovation and strategy, and dean of Asia. He co-directs the Building Digital Ecosystems and the Strategy for Future Readiness programs. Drawing on two decades of experience in research, teaching, and consulting in China, he explores how to organize innovation in a turbulent world. He is ranked on the 2023 Thinkers50 list of global management thinkers. He has written three books: *Business Ecosystems in China: Alibaba and Competing Baidu, Tencent, Xiaomi and LeEco; Pioneers, Hidden Champions, Change Makers and Underdogs: Lessons from China's Innovators*, and *The Future of Global Retail*.

Howard Yu, Chapter 21

Hailing from Hong Kong, he is LEGO Professor of Management and Innovation. He leads the Centre for Future Readiness, founded in 2020 with support from the LEGO Brand Group, to guide companies through strategic transformation. Recognized globally for his expertise, he was honored in 2023 with the Thinkers50 Strategy Award, recognizing his substantial contributions to management strategy and future readiness. He directs the Strategy for Future Readiness and Business Growth Strategies programs.

Robert Hooijberg, Chapter 22

He is professor of organizational behavior. His areas of special interest are leadership, negotiations, team building, digital transformation, and organizational culture. Before joining IMD in 2000, he taught at Rutgers University in the MBA and EMBA programs in New Jersey, Singapore, and Beijing. He directs the Breakthrough Program for Senior Executives and the Negotiating for Value Creation course.

Natalia Olynec, Chapter 23

She is the chief sustainability officer. She designs and implements sustainability strategy, develops executive education programs and advisory, publishes research, builds cross-sector partnerships, and communicates IMD's ambitions and progress. The Centre for Sustainable and Inclusive Business, co-led by Olynec, aims to support leaders and companies to take steps toward a more sustainable and inclusive business world by harnessing IMD's knowledge and expertise in the area and offering tools to help them deliver systemic, innovative, and impactful responses.

Alfredo de Massis, Chapter 24

He is professor of entrepreneurship and family business and holds the Wild Group Chair in Family Business. Named on Family Capital's 2022 100 Family Business Influencers list, his research has advanced understanding of how family business leaders balance economic and noneconomic goals in strategic decision-making to manage the paradox of tradition and innovation. He was recently ranked as the most influential and productive author in the family business research field in the last decade. Prior to his academic career, he was a manager for SCS Consulting, a strategy consultant at Accenture, and a financial analyst at the Italian Stock Exchange.

Marleen Dieleman, Chapter 24

She holds the Peter Lorange Chair in Family Business. She is an expert on the challenges faced by emerging market enterprises in their strategic trajectories. Her research focuses on the governance, strategy, internationalization, innovation, and transformation of business families in emerging markets and also on emerging market state-owned enterprises and the interaction between these companies and their governments. She directs the Future-Proofing Your Business Family program.

Peter Vogel, Chapter 24

He is professor of family business and entrepreneurship, directs the Global Family Business Centre, and is Debiopharm Chair for Family Philanthropy. He is also director of the Leading the Family Business, Leading the Family Office, and Lean Entrepreneurship programs. Named in the Poets&Quants 2022 list of the best 40 MBA professors under the age of 40, Peter has published in peer-reviewed academic journals and has written a number of books, book chapters, and scientific and practitioner-oriented reports.

Josefine van Zanten, Chapter 25

She is the chief diversity, equity, and inclusion officer, and she works as a senior advisor on DEI with global organizations. She has been active as an HR executive most of her global career, working in Fortune 500 organizations. As a senior vice president, she was in charge of DEI, Culture Change, and Leadership and Organizational Development departments. Her experience spans across various industries, at HP (IT), Royal Dutch Shell (oil and gas), Royal DSM (life sciences and chemicals), and Holcim (construction).

Heather Cairns-Lee, Chapter 26

She is an affiliate professor of leadership and communication, a member of the DEI Council, and an experienced executive coach. She works to develop reflective and responsible leaders and caring inclusive cultures in organizations and society. Her research focuses on learning and leadership, including the development of self-awareness, authenticity, and sensemaking. She has particular interests in inclusive language, the pivotal role of questions, and the importance of metaphor in breakthrough thinking and creativity.

Index